'This is a must read for those interested in learning more about responsible fashion business in practice. The authors have created a valuable tool, named The Responsible 9 Framework and this is introduced and explained throughout the book. Insightful contemporary case studies and industry insights excellently serve to justify and clarify each of the 9 elements of the framework'

Paolo Taticchi, *Professor in Strategy and Sustainability, UCL School of Management*

'This book offers an insightful take on how to re-think sustainability within the fashion industry, in all organisational areas, and at all stages of the product lifecycle. Definitely a must read for all fashion business leaders, students in the field and fashion consumers who want to make more informed purchase decisions'

Eva Baquedano, *Chief Omnichannel & Client Officer, LOEWE*

'An essential and accurate guide for every responsible business leader and consumer who is seriously committed to embracing the transition to a more sustainable future. A better future starts by asking ourselves the right questions, as this book brilliantly does.'

Francesca Ragazzi, *Head of Editorial Content,* Vogue Italia

RESPONSIBLE FASHION BUSINESS IN PRACTICE

This unique text offers a holistic, insightful and timely exploration of sustainable practices across the fashion industry.

The book takes the reader logically through each part of the authors' new **Responsible 9 Framework™**, providing a clear perspective and examples for each component. The framework thoroughly explains the move away from a singular product commercial focus to a **Conscious Item** approach and **Circular Services** business mindset. An organisation's people are at the heart of the new framework and have therefore been rebranded as **Community**. Next addressed is the **Perceived Value** of an item or brand, and how sustainable pricing initiatives actively influence consumer purchase. Insights into **Accountable Systems** are reviewed to examine the importance of responsible processes when considering and integrating a successful, sustainable supply chain into a fashion business. The section on **Governance** looks at the different global organisations available to fashion brands and customers alike, which support their transition into a responsible and sustainable future existence. The last two sections of the framework are labelled **Storytelling Platforms** and **Honest Communication**, where transparent and honest strategies are highlighted and discussed from a viewpoint of how modern brands are engaging and connecting to the new conscious consumer. For each of the nine aspects, contemporary case studies from global brands such as Stella McCartney, Zalando and Arc'teryx, alongside insights from current, leading experts within the fashion world, bring the theory to life.

Showing how sustainability has been integrated throughout the entirety of the fashion business, this textbook is perfect for advanced undergraduate and postgraduate students Fashion Management, Fashion Brand Management and Fashion Marketing, as well as reflective leaders and practitioners within the industry.

Sennait Ghebreab is Programme Leader, Fashion Business, at the Istituto Marangoni School of Fashion, UK.

Sally Heale is Senior Lecturer, Fashion Business, at University of Westminster, UK and a Senior Tutor, Fashion Business, at the Istituto Marangoni School of Fashion, UK.

MASTERING FASHION MANAGEMENT

The fashion industry is dynamic, constantly evolving and worth billions worldwide: it's no wonder that Fashion Business Management has come to occupy a central position within the Business School globally. This series meets the need for rigorous yet practical and accessible textbooks that cover the full spectrum of the fashion industry and its management.

Collectively, *Mastering Fashion Management* is a valuable resource for advanced undergraduate and postgraduate students of Fashion Management, helping them gain an in-depth understanding of contemporary concepts and the realities of practice across the entire fashion chain - from design development and product sourcing, to buying and merchandising, sustainability, and sales and marketing. Individually, each text provides essential reading for a core topic. A range of consistent pedagogical features are used throughout the texts, including international case studies, highlighting the practical importance of theoretical concepts.

Postgraduate students studying for a Masters in Fashion Management in particular will find each text invaluable reading, providing the knowledge and tools to approach a future career in fashion with confidence.

Fashion Marketing and Communication
Theory and Practice Across the Fashion Industry
Olga Mitterfellner

Fashion Buying and Merchandising
The Fashion Buyer in a Digital Society
Rosy Boardman, Rachel Parker-Strak and Claudia E. Henninger

Sustainable Fashion Management
Claudia E. Henninger, Kirsi Niinimäki, Marta Blazquez Cano and Celina Jones

Fashion Supply Chain Management
Virginia Grose and Nicola Mansfield

Celebrity Fashion Marketing
Developing a Human Fashion Brand
Fykaa Caan and Angela Lee

For more information about the series, please visit https://www.routledge.com/Mastering-Fashion-Management/book-series/FM

Responsible Fashion Business in Practice

Sustainable Concepts and Cases Across the Fashion Industry

Sennait Ghebreab

Sally Heale

Routledge
Taylor & Francis Group

LONDON AND NEW YORK

Cover image: 'The Responsible 9 Framework™' © Ghebreab and Heale, 2023

First published 2023
by Routledge
4 Park Square, Milton Park, Abingdon, Oxon OX14 4RN

and by Routledge
605 Third Avenue, New York, NY 10158

Routledge is an imprint of the Taylor & Francis Group, an informa business

British Library Cataloguing-in-Publication Data
A catalogue record for this book is available from the British Library

ISBN: 978-1-032-25970-3 (hbk)
ISBN: 978-1-032-25917-8 (pbk)
ISBN: 978-1-003-28591-5 (ebk)

DOI: 10.4324/9781003285915

Typeset in Palatino
by Apex CoVantage, LLC

Access the Support Material: www.Routledge.com/9781032259178

CONTENTS

CONTRIBUTORS

FOREWORD

Andrea De Santis, part of the Global McKinsey AF&L team. De Santis specialises in the retail sector, currently leading the AF&L practice in the Italian office

INTRODUCTION

Disha Daswaney, Fashion Consultant, specialising in consumer behaviour and trend forecasting and Lecturer at the London College of Fashion and Regents University, London

CHAPTER 1 – CONSCIOUS ITEM

Charlotte Turner, Sustainable Fashion and Textiles Consultant and Lecturer

Massimo Casagrande, MA Programme Leader, Fashion Design Istituto Marangoni, Paris

Karen Spurgin, Textiles Consultant and Senior Lecturer at Istituto Marangoni, London

Jeffrey Heiligers, Design Consultant with a background in mechanical engineering and product design, from The Future Prospects Lab

CHAPTER 2 – CIRCULAR SERVICES

Professor Andrew Groves, Director Westminster Menswear Archive, University of Westminster

Felix Kruger, Partner and Associate Director, Fashion & Luxury at Boston Consulting Group

Gemma A. Williams, Editorial Director, *Jing Daily*

Laura Coppen, Head of Circularity at Zalando and **Daniel Newton** Senior Expert Circularity at Zalando

CHAPTER 3 – COMMUNITY

Craig Crawford, Tabbie award winning author and founderprenuer of Crawford IT, specialising in the digital transformation of brands

Lisa Nan, Researcher and Journalist at *Jing Daily*

Mathew Dixon, Director Fashion and Luxury Practice at The MBS Group

Liliana Sanguino Ramirez, Associate Professor, Parsons School of Design, New York

CHAPTER 4 – PERCEIVED VALUE

Mytro Angelidou, co-founder of Sinister Sisters, a Brand Development, Sales & PR agency and incubator representing emerging designers. Lecturer at Istituto Marangoni, London

Lucy Litwack, CEO of Coco de Mer a female owned, run, and focused lingerie and pleasure business

Erica Charles, Program Leader, Glasgow Caledonian University, London. Brand Ambassador for Save the Children from 2010–2016

CHAPTER 5 – ACCOUNTABLE SYSTEMS

Archana Chandrasekar, Senior Lecturer, at Istituto Marangoni, London, and the University of Westminster. Design Consultant for small and upcoming brands

James Clark, Senior Postgraduate Lecturer, London College of Fashion, UAL. Author of *Fashion Merchandising: Principles and Practice* and is a chapter contributor to *Fashion Management, a Strategic Approach*

Joanne Yulan Jong, London based ESG sustainability and brand consultant and author of *The Fashion Switch*

Amy Lee, Senior Manager, Trends and Insights Apparel at Avery Dennison

CHAPTER 6 – GREEN ENVIRONMENT

Patsy Perry, Reader in Fashion Marketing, Manchester Fashion Institute, Manchester Metropolitan University

Juliet Russell, Head of Sustainability at Stella McCartney and **Philip Mak**, Global Head of Content and Editorial at Stella McCartney

CHAPTER 7 – GOVERNANCE

M. Fernanda Hernandez Franco, Head of Sustainability for a leading Italian multi-brand retailer

CHAPTER 8 – HONEST COMMUNICATION

Peter Rees, former VP of Marketing in the media industry. Senior Lecturer, London College of Fashion

Martin Deal, Digital Strategist and visiting Senior Lecturer at City University London

Veronica Bates Kassatly, independent analyst, writer, and speaker in the Sustainable Apparel Industry

Darren Black, fashion photographer and Senior Lecturer at Istituto Marangoni, London and London College of Fashion

Giorgia Pagliuca, green influencer. Author of *Let's fix the world: Diary of an environmentalist in the climate crisis*

Sarah Vaughan, Global Chief Purpose and Sustainability Advisor at Marie Claire and Advisory Board Member for The World Humanitarian Forum

CHAPTER 9 – STORYTELLING PLATFORMS

Nick Pye, Co-founder and Managing Partner of Mangrove Consulting

Vittorio Cosma, Marketing and Startup Mentor at aaa/unbranded® and **Mario Innocente** Founder at aaa/unbranded®

Rae Sims, Co-owner. WerkHaus Margate, UK and Lecturer at the University of Westminster

Samara Croci, media expert, and leading podcaster on sustainability

FOREWORD

The foreword is kindly provided by Andrea De Santis; who is part of the Global McKinsey AF&L team. He specialises in the retail sector, currently leading the AF&L practice in the Italian office.

De Santis is passionate about;

- Serving Italian and global luxury maisons and visionary entrepreneurs.
- Supporting the cultural shift to become data/digital driven in order to exploit the full customer centric potential.
- Building contemporary lifestyle brands and ecosystems oriented beyond luxury.
- Supporting brands transitioning from a product-oriented business to a human centric organisation.
- Defining strategy to balance purpose with profit, while respecting the planet.

De Santis also supports Altagamma and the Italiana Fashion Luxury Chamber on the development of the fashion industry and talents.

A FRAMEWORK FOR RESPONSIBLE FUTURE BUSINESS LEADERS

The issues of purpose and environmental, social, and governance (ESG) are critical challenges for both boards and executive teams in the fashion industry.

They are especially relevant in the aftermath of the COVID-19 pandemic, which has compelled corporations to reconsider their responsibilities and role in society.

According to *Fashion on Climate*, the fashion industry emits approximately 2.1 billion tonnes of greenhouse gases in a single year, accounting for 4% of total global emissions. This astounding figure is comparable to the combined annual GHG emissions of France, Germany, and the United Kingdom. Between 2018 and 2030, if the sector continues to decarbonize at its present rate, it will be able to remove emissions attributable to incremental growth, linked to global warming. However, this is 50% more than the 1.5°C pathway abatement objective necessary by 2030.

The 17 Sustainable Development Goals (SDGs), adopted by the UN in 2015 are aimed at reducing global poverty, inequality, environmental degradation, and promoting peace and justice. The fashion industry can become a place that promotes global equality, biodiversity, and overall well-being if fashion brands and companies work together to adopt the SDGs.

The UN is increasingly interested in incorporating new and dynamic sectors into the Sustainable Development Goals in the future. Changing the production and consumption patterns of the fashion industry would have a domino effect on many aspects of development and would make a visible and meaningful contribution to the achievement of the 2030 Agenda for

Sustainable Development. In this current scenario, the fashion industry, in particular, offers two entry points for action:

- Top down (due to the power of governments and business corporations to influence change).
- Bottom up (because we as consumers have a choice when purchasing a garment and can thus influence production and marketing).

Both approaches must be combined; currently, government- and business-led initiatives to make the sector more sustainable are dispersed, uncoordinated, and frequently address only one side of the problem. Similarly, the sustainable fashion market is limited to small businesses.

The framework of this book, **The Responsible 9 Framework**, provides a rare opportunity to bring sustainable fashion to the forefront of international debate demonstrating how it can help to achieve many of the SDGs.

This book sets the right business scenario for fashion businesses. This is a framework for assisting organisations in developing a set of guiding value-centred principles concerning the environment, social relationships and structures, people, fixed assets, and financial performance. As fashion brands strive to connect with the eco-conscious consumer, they are on a journey to becoming more environmentally and socially responsible through honest and transparent business practices. The framework looks at all the main key critical factors that can really bring an effective change to their chain of value, as it transitions from a linear business model to a circular one. In the fashion industry, across all the market levels, supply chains have traditionally been designed for cost and time efficiency, but as stakeholder expectations and legislation shift, a redesign is required.

Fashion businesses must support the transition to a more sustainable future in order to maintain competitive business advantages.

The Responsible 9 Framework can provide critical enablers for building a long-term supply chain. There are numerous factors to consider, some of which are industry-specific, but there are certainly two key aspects that all companies should consider when embarking on a journey toward a more sustainable supply chain. These are linked to the new framework:

- Insight and traceability for a more conscious customer.
- Industry collaboration for operational excellence.

Using six major trends, the fashion luxury industry has a unique opportunity to position itself at the forefront of this sustainability transformation.

1. Greater implementation – there are real warning signs all over the world, but the implementation of more "traditional" solutions has been limited thus far. This could change; chemical recycling of cellulosic and polyester materials has a scaling potential of 5–40%.
2. Environmental regulation that is more aggressive – Regulation is driving scale up and cost reduction, fostering adoption.
3. Increasing investor sustainability requirements – ESG investors manage $12 trillion in assets, with a 21% annual growth rate.

4. Shifting customer expectations – For consumers, sustainability is an important consideration when purchasing clothing; more than two-thirds of customers would accept a price premium for sustainable products. Whilst more than 80% of Generation Z and Millennials are enthusiastic about sustainability.
5. Talent is migrating to more sustainable companies – a purpose-driven organisation fosters loyalty and reduces turnover by 25–50%.
6. First movers have already captured value – In terms of pricing increase and distribution penetration, sustainable brands are growing faster than competitors.

Currently more fashion companies are putting in place innovative solutions; such as redesigning (designing out waste and using new sustainable materials), upcycling (repurposing upcycled materials from vintage clothing and deadstock fabric), and partnering with innovative tech start-ups.

Stakeholders are becoming increasingly concerned about carbon emissions, water usage, deforestation and reforestation, and how a company's operations affect people and the environment. Small changes in the supply chain are no longer sufficient in the twenty-first century.

As the late economist Milton Friedman put it, "the business of business is business."

Consumers, regulators, and stakeholders are concerned about sustainability because it affects their lives.

The impact on our environment and marginalised communities is undeniable.

Companies are facing increasing pressure to become more sustainable. The call for action is the way forward for businesses now and for future generations.

Alea iacta est ("The die is cast")

ACKNOWLEDGEMENTS

Firstly, we would like to thank Andrew Piller for his unwavering support and valuable insights. You have been instrumental in the development of **The Responsible 9 Framework** and the writing of this book. You have been incredibly generous with your time; we are forever grateful.

Next comes Emma Cheevers, Rebecca Leary, Doug McCarthy, Disha Daswaney, Karen Spurgin, Katya Ionova, Giulia Cosso, and Archana Chandrasekar. Each of you, thank you! Your expert editing skills, research, and knowledge has been indispensable.

A special note of gratitude goes to ECO AGE Ltd, and in particular Nicola Giuggioli, for continuing to inspire us, and our students, about all things sustainable. You have been a trusted long-term supporter and furthermore you kindly introduced us to some key industry thought leaders and now chapter contributors.

Introduction

Responsible fashion business practice and The Responsible 9 Framework

This book examines the fashion industry in order to highlight the opportunity for responsible, sustainable, and honest fashion business approaches. Environmental concerns have placed the fashion industry at the centre of conversations all over the world for all of the wrong reasons. It is now seen to be a major contributor to air, water, and soil pollution, as well as a facilitator of exploitative sweatshop conditions for garment workers in production facilities all over the world.

The fashion industry needs to evolve to become more accountable, the content inside this book explores the need for responsible practices throughout the fashion industry. The conscious consumer has emerged; this important customer group is now paying close attention to the term sustainability and have a far greater interest in it.

WHAT DOES SUSTAINABILITY MEAN IN THE FASHION BUSINESS NOW?

The term sustainably is ultimately the proactive use of methods that do not harm the environment or its people. However, the word has become somewhat overused and confused in the fashion sector, and often associated specifically with sustainable product ranges. This book's aim will be to examine every element of the fashion business, to show that sustainability doesn't need to, and shouldn't sit in product creation and development alone.

Fashion is, by nature, constantly evolving, it is often defined as a succession of trends influenced by sociological and cultural changes. Sustainability grew out of this, however, an important evolution has occurred and the sustainable movement now sits above all trends, as a wider arching theme that encompasses the whole business. Sustainability is not seen as

DOI: 10.4324/9781003285915-1

an additional attribute but an essential one. Mindful consumers are starting to demand their products be made ethically, using materials that do less damage to the environment and the people that make them. Awareness on post-purchase opportunities is also apparent: consumers are starting to think more about the vital importance of the circular economy and caring for their fashion items for longer.

Some fashion brands and retailers are pivoting their practice in order to become more transparent and sustainable throughout their whole business, including changing how they communicate with the customer. These companies have become a benchmark for others, and their practices will continue to influence the industry to create a viable fashion future in line with the consumer mindset and emerging government guidelines and regulations.

THE EMERGENCE OF THE MINDFUL "ECO-CONSCIOUS CONSUMER"

The customer is at the heart of any successful industry. They touch all aspects of the businesses' marketing mix and they are catalysts for key business decisions.

If a business has an engaged consumer base and an open dialogue with their customers, more often than not, that business will see sales grow and brand affinity increase. Conversely, if a brand fails to take their customers' views and values into account, the most likely outcome is that its promotional campaigns and product offers will struggle, sales short- and long-term will not be maximised, whilst brand equity and affinity will deteriorate over time.

Younger generations are perceived to have more interest in sustainability and actively seek out sustainable brands. However, as society moves to a post-pandemic era, there is immense scrutiny around ethics and the environmental impact, and all generations now understand the importance of buying more mindfully. Today's fashion consumer has changed. They are more complex, demanding, and, through mass and immediate exposure from all forms of media, they have a greater understanding of the impact that human activity and fashion brands are having on the environment. Consumers are more mindful of their purchase decisions, and they are beginning to decisively reward those fashion brands that are actively pursuing an environmentally responsible approach to business activity. And, perhaps more importantly, they are now holding to account the fashion brands that don't pursue a responsible approach.

The purchase decisions of the fashion consumer of the past were often driven by:

- Lowest price is the best
- Waiting for solutions
- Always asking "what's in it for me?"
- Seeking more "stuff"

- Trusting marketing messages
- Passive recipient of communications.

Today's consumer is much more complex:

- Wanting total value on many different levels, not just on price
- Demanding credible solutions that are always clearly and honestly communicated
- Asking "what's in this for all of us?"
- Seeking meaningful experiences that are community building, educational, and informative
- Looking at ingredients/information to justify sustainability claims
- Active co-creators of brand content, working alongside the brand.

This important pivot in mind-set cannot be ignored by fashion brands. The consumer now expects all fashion brands that they interact with to be fully accountable; and they are actively seeking answers from fashions brands on:

- Where is production taking place?
- What is the company doing to reduce impact?
- What is the company doing to drive down emissions?
- What is the company doing to use less water?
- What is the company doing to produce less waste?
- What is happening to this waste?
- How is the company supporting the livelihood of its people?
- How does the company promote responsible consumption?

FIGURE 0.1   All you need is less. Image from shutterstock / Netrun78

FIGURE 0.2   Apparel and footwear brand Allbirds sourcing merino wool. Credit Allbirds

As the expert insight piece by Disha Daswaney outlines, responsible business practices have become one the most important factors in driving purchase decisions across all demographics, and its importance will only continue to grow.

Expert insight from Disha Daswaney

Disha Daswaney is a Fashion Consultant (specialising in consumer behaviour and trend forecasting) and Lecturer in Fashion Communication & Business.

Consumers of all ages are more concerned about sustainability than ever before, in fact 75% of the global population would like to see single-use plastics banned (Reuters, 2022). In a world where carbon offsetting has been deemed greenwashing and 130 companies pledged to halve their greenhouse gas emissions by 2030, all eyes are on sustainability.

But this is not the only call to action that has recently surfaced, namely COP26 highlighted the need for manufacturers in the fashion industry to shift their strategies. This gained immense attention for global consumers, especially since fashion has long been in the spotlight for its negative impact on the environment. For many years, fast fashion has led to a rise in consumerism and a 'throw away' culture, which is still prevalent in society.

However, there are many global conscious consumers and people have become very granular in their understanding of sustainability. Thus, examining how their behaviours affect the planet in every sense, we are at a stage where our relationship with the planet is at a critical point especially with vulnerable ecosystems and at-climate risk communities. We are revaluing the connection we have with the planet and nature, which is a significant move, but this was only realised once the pandemic hit.

Specifically, our tangibility of environmental disasters became a pivotal point of focus. This drove a mindset shift in terms of the power we possess as individuals towards a collective mentality. It is no longer just Gen Z who possesses their views towards climate activism, but older generations are recognising its impact too. A survey by cosmetics brand Garnier found that 81% of global respondents want to be more sustainable in 2021, ranging from 94% of Indonesians to 65% of Germans. In Latin America, Ecuador has seen a phenomenal rise of 120% in online searches for sustainable goods in the past five years.

Younger consumers have been the most impacted by sustainability, due to their lives being shaped by a combination of social, political, and environmental upheaval. This is why it's imperative that marketers play into value-based messaging, in which the brand connects to consumer desires for a meaningful sense of existence. This comes as no surprise, since 72% of Gen Z claim they would not work for a company that does not have a good record on sustainability (McKinsey, 2022). They are a generation, who will call-out brands when they aren't doing enough and making these "fake" claims. Hence, leading the change for companies to shift their corporate practices to reflect their progressive values.

To attract eco-shoppers, overhyped, sustainable buzzwords are not going to cut it anymore. Now there needs to be legitimate evidence to the claims brands are making across fashion and beauty.

But attention to sustainability is clear across all levels of the market. True, luxury consumers expect brands to approach sourcing, production, and sales in an ethical manner – globally, 56% claim they investigate a brand's social responsibility (BCG, 2020). As the climate emergency deepens, luxury consumers will expect brands to provide easy-to-access sustainability information. Luxury brands will be required to go the extra mile to ensure they keep these consumers, as sustainability becomes synonymous with premium-level spending.

References

Online: BCG, Luxury Daily (2022). Past year in luxury was more evolution than revolution.

Online: Beauty Matter (2022). What Gen Z and Millennials think about natural skincare.

Online: Cosmetics Design Europe (2022). 2020 was a wakeup call to protect our planet.

Online: Cosmetics Design Europe (2021). Garnier Green Beauty Initiative aligns with consumers sustainability goals for 2021.

Online: McKinsey (2022). The State of Fashion 2021, Business of Fashion.

Online: Reuters Business (2022). 75% of consumers want single use plastics banned.

Online: *The Guardian* (2022). Out of style: Will Gen Z ever give up its dangerous love of fast fashion?

FROM PLANNED OBSOLESCENCE TO CIRCULAR SYSTEMS

Shoppers actively seeking out sustainable fashion items cannot be ignored. They are a rapidly growing consumer group and many can now be labelled as eco-conscious consumers who are willing to invest more on a product if it comes from a brand with transparent and credible sustainable credentials. This growing consumer group is on a mission to live in a plastic-free, less-polluted world, consuming more mindfully and consciously in order to make a positive difference to the planet.

Many fashion brands have recognised the changing behaviour of this mindful consumer, and now understand that in order to connect with this consumer they need to be wholly honest and clear in their marketing approach. Significantly, brands understand they will need to adapt or change their commercial model to the changing demands of their consumer in order to future-proof their business.

Planned obsolescence is a commercial strategy of ensuring that a product will go out of date within a time period, which then forces consumers to seek replacements or alternatives in the future. This has historically been common practice within the industry and has underpinned most of the industry's commercial models.

Typically the fashion industry revolves around seasonality and fast trends – the industry makes products for consumers depending on the season, ergo they are planning obsolescence. This planned obsolescence is now being heavily criticised especially in today's environment where sustainability and circularity have become the new key words. The traditional practice of marketing and advertising has been widely criticised for pushing consumers to buy products they don't need or didn't even know they wanted to buy.

In the push-commercial model, fashion brands create products based on projected demand. These fashion brands then push these products into the market. For years businesses have encouraged marketers to develop campaigns to push products on the consumer in a way to make the consumer feel like they need them, often feeding insecurities. However, we are

FIGURE 0.3   image of planned obsolescence / seasonality - Shutterstock/Sundry Photography

in an era now where this is being labelled as damaging and unnecessary. Traditional fashion marketing practices need to be held accountable and its processes and value needs to be rethought entirely.

As the fashion industry strives to be more responsible, the production of an item and the end of its life have become equally important. Increasingly, how the materials can be used at the end of the product life are key components of the design process. Longevity is one of the key considerations of the circulatory system, which is the complete opposite of the fast fashion model, which is focused on inexpensive, trend-led products produced rapidly by mass-market retailers.

If the fashion industry could adopt a closed-loop system, materials could be endlessly reused and recycled, and therefore waste and pollution minimised by limiting the production of virgin raw materials and decreasing textile waste.

Some fashion brands and retailers have created short-term, bolt-on schemes to attract the sustainable shopper in an attempt to convince those consumers that they are dealing with their environmental impact. However, many of these brands have been exposed as simply claiming to be engaged in sustainable commitments, and not committed to implementing honest and responsible practices throughout the whole of their business.

It is quickly becoming clear that if a fashion brand has an honest, authentic, and transparent in-built proposition the customer is more likely to want to engage with the brand in a more committed way. Moreover, if a brand doesn't clearly communicate a responsible business proposition it is less likely to connect with this new, more complex and demanding customer.

DISSECTING AND UNDERSTANDING THE 7P'S

In 1960, Jerome McCarthy developed the 4P framework, which is still used widely in classrooms and businesses all over the world these 4P's are: Product, Price, Promotion and Place. In 1981, Booms and Bitner added an additional three elements to the 4P's, these are: People, Process, and Physical Evidence. Essentially the 7P framework is a proposal of marketing tools also known as a Marketing Mix, which provides companies with a marketing framework with which to review issues that can affect the success of the products or services they offer.

THE 7P'S ARE

1. **Product** refers to the products, services, or a combination of both, which a company produces, and is developed to meet the core needs of its consumers.
2. **Price** relates specifically to the price that the customer must pay for the product or service. All companies should have a clear pricing strategy, which is developed by understanding the cost to the business of creating the product, what price a customer will pay for the product, the consumer demand for that product, and competitor pricing.
3. **Promotion** refers to the way in which a customer finds out what is for sale, and the benefits should they purchase that item. Businesses need to develop marketing messages that are suitable and appealing to the customer in order to create a desire to purchase the product.
4. **Place** relates to the space where people will buy a product or service; this could be a physical store or through an app or via a website. Larger companies will have multiple distribution channels where they sell to their consumers.
5. **People** refers to the people that work inside a company; this will include people on the shop floor, but also the people in the warehouses and head offices. People are critical in the marketing mix and are key to a business's success, given the potential for the company's employees to interact with the customer. They can be an advocate for the brand throughout the customer journey, from initial interaction through to taking and processing enquiries, orders, and dealing with complaints.
6. **Process** relates to the systems or tools a business runs/puts in place in order to get the product or service to and from the consumer, and it encompasses everything from enquiry, checkout, shipping, transportation packaging, delivery, and reviews.
7. **Physical Evidence** relates to the environment (be it physical or digital) in which the customer interacts with one's product/brand. It is about ensuring a positive buying experience for the customer and encompasses everything from the look and feel of the website, store decor, social media, logo, branding, product packaging and even the post-purchase confirmation "thank you."

FIGURE 0.4   7P's Marketing Mix diagram. Authors own. Original McCarthy 1960, Booms and Bitner, 1981

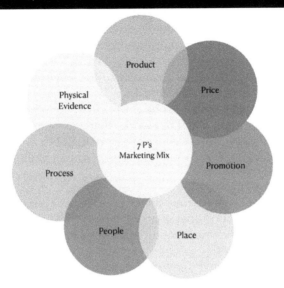

Product	It refers to the products, services, or a combination of both that a firm generates in order to fulfil the fundamental demands of its customers.
Price	It explicitly refers to the amount the client must pay for the goods or service. All businesses should have a clear pricing plan, which is formed by knowing the business cost of generating the product, the price a customer would pay for the product, consumer demand for that product, and competitive pricing.
Promotion	It relates to how a consumer learns about what is for sale and the benefits of purchasing that thing. Promotion is concerned with how a company conveys its marketing messages to its customers in order to increase product awareness, interest, desire, or purchase.
Place	It refers to the location where consumers will buy a product or service; this might be a real store, an app, or a website. Larger corporations will have many distribution channels via which they sell to their customers. The essential considerations to make in this marketing mix are to ensure that one sells in areas that are both acceptable for one's brand and accessible to one's intended client, while also taking into account the practicalities of delivering things to the end consumer, such as storage and shipping.
People	It refers to the employees of a corporation, including those on the shop floor as well as those in warehouses and corporate headquarters. People are essential components of the marketing mix and are vital to a company's success, given the possibility for workers to connect with customers and advocate for the brand throughout the customer journey, from initial contact through taking and processing inquiries, orders, and complaints.
Process	It refers to the processes or instruments that a company uses to provide a product or service to and from the consumer, and it includes everything from checkout, inquiry, transportation, shipping, delivery, packaging, and reviews.
Physical Evidence	It is about the environment (physical or digital) in which the client interacts with one's product/brand. It is about providing a great shopping experience for consumers and includes everything from the style and design of the website, store design, social networks, logo, branding, packaging design, and even the post-purchase confirmation 'thank you.'

INTRODUCING THE RESPONSIBLE 9 FRAMEWORK™

Every part of a fashion brand's marketing mix now needs to be environmentally and socially responsible with honest and transparent business practices apparent, in order to connect with the eco-conscious consumer. This journey is often further complicated by a customer expectation that businesses should overnight become "sustainable". This unrealistic expectation is further exacerbated, as businesses often solve individual problems without taking a larger holistic and broader approach to their business. Moreover, as soon as they solve one problem, yet another problem arises. There is a need for tools and frameworks that enable businesses and their employees to critically analyse every aspect of their business practice.

If you look at the 7Ps through the lens of sustainability, key questions are raised:

1. **Product:** how can the products or services that a company offers to its consumers be (more) sustainable?, how can the services be circular?
2. **Price:** how can the price that the customers pay for the product or service be transparent?
3. **Promotion:** how can the communications tools and platforms communicate sustainable practice developments and tell the customer about the brand values authentically and transparently?
4. **Place:** how can the location of the business be used to connect to the sustainable customer?
5. **People:** how can a brand ensure that the people within the organisation are all treated fairly and equally?
6. **Process:** how can the products get to and from the customer without additional environmental damage and waste?
7. **Physical Evidence:** how can the brand spaces be used to engage, educate, and support the consumer?

This book will explore sustainable business practices within the marketing mix, and will adapt the current 7Ps to develop **The Responsible 9 Framework**.

- Product becomes **Conscious Item**; and also
- Product sits in **Circular Services**.
- Price becomes **Perceived Value**.
- Promotion becomes **Honest Communication** (but needs to be towards the end of the new framework as you should not promote anything before you have full visibility).
- Place becomes **Green Environment**.
- People becomes **Community** (is a vital component and comes 3rd in the new framework as it affects every part of it).
- Process becomes **Accountable Systems**.
- Physical Evidence becomes **Storytelling Platforms** (but needs to be at the end in the new framework as you should not promote anything before you have full viability).
- New addition **Governance** (the support network).

THE RESPONSIBLE 9 FRAMEWORK

1. **CONSCIOUS ITEM** *(was product)*
2. **CIRCULAR SERVICES** *(was product)*
3. **COMMUNITY** *(was people)*
4. **PERCEIVED VALUE** *(was price)*
5. **ACCOUNTABLE SYSTEMS** *(was process)*
6. **GREEN ENVIRONMENT** *(was place)*
7. **GOVERNANCE** *(new addition)*
8. **HONEST COMMUNICATION** *(was promotion)*
9. **STORYTELLING PLATFORMS** *(was physical evidence)*

Ghebreab and Heale 2023.

OBJECTIVE OF THE BOOK AND HOW THE BOOK IS STRUCTURED

The book will examine different aspects of the fashion business through the lens of **The Responsible 9 Framework**. Key content has been provided by a number of credible global innovators, fashion brands and organisations. Academic and industry experts have added important opinions, which will be featured throughout each chapter. The book will provide evidence of fashion brands engaged in responsible practice and communicating with their consumer in a clear, honest, and transparent manner.

RESPONSIBLE 9 FRAMEWORK. Credit Ghebreab and Heale 2023

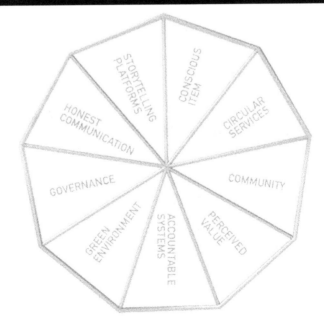

Chapter 1 – Product to CONSCIOUS ITEM. The first chapter focuses on the P of Product and examines how the value and importance of products are changing. It highlights how many brands are now attempting to develop items more consciously, ones that are respectful to the environment.

The expert insights are provided by: Massimo Casagrande, Jeffrey Heiligers, Karen Spurgin, and Charlotte Turner.

Chapter 2 – Product to CIRCULAR SERVICES. The second chapter examines the value of the conscious item post purchase, introducing resale, rental, repair, and other key services gaining popularity with fashion brands and their consumers.

Fashion brand examples include: Ahluwalia, APC, Arc'teryx, Depop, H&M, Ebay, Mulberry, Monki, Napapijri, Nike, Nona Source, Patagonia, People Tree, Stella McCartney, The Restory, Uniqlo, RAEBURN DESIGN, Rent the Runway, The Littleloop, The Real Real, Vestiaire Collective, and Zalando.

The expert insights are provided by: Laura Coppen and Daniel Newton, Professor Andrew Groves, Felix Kruger, and Gemma A. Williams.

Chapter 3 – People to COMMUNITY. This chapter focuses on the vital importance of equal representation. It discusses diversity and inclusion and examines what brands are doing to address misrepresentation. The chapter also examines the value of diversity of voice.

Fashion brand examples include: Burberry, Gap, Gucci, Ikea, Lululemon, Marks & Spencer, Nike, Patagonia, Procter & Gamble, Reformation, Tiffany, Timberland, and Stella McCartney.

The expert insights are provided by: Craig Crawford, Mathew Dixon, Lisa Nan, and Liliana Sanguino Ramirez.

Chapter 4 – Price to PERCEIVED VALUE. This chapter explores key considerations around pricing and how fashion brands are beginning to understand the importance of transparent pricing strategies to connect with the more aware shopper. The chapter also discusses how important it is for fashion brands to show empathy and support to credible causes and charities in line with their customers' values.

Fashion brand examples include: Bottletop, Coco de Mer, Kenzo, Michael Kors, Pangaia, Patagonia, Ralph Lauren, Stella McCartney, and The Reformation.

The expert insights are provided by: Myrto Angelidou, Erica Charles, and Lucy Litwack.

Chapter 5 – Process to ACCOUNTABLE SYSTEMS. This chapter examines a number of processes used by the fashion industry, including the supply chain and the packaging used by fashion brands. The chapter explores some of the key issues with traditional processes and the changes that are occurring in the attempt to make the whole of the fashion business system more circular.

Fashion brand examples include: Reformation, Pangaia, Amazon, Alibaba, H&M, Marni, Nike, Notpla, Boox, Nordstrom, Selfridges, Ren, Avery Dennison.

The expert insights are provided by: Archana Chandrasekar, James Clark, Amy Lee, and Joanne Yulan Jong.

Chapter 6 – Place to GREEN ENVIRONMENT. This chapter provides information on the evolution of the store, an element of the original P of Place. The chapter explains how this important part of the brand experience is also changing in order to incorporate sustainable values.

Fashion brand examples include: Brainform, Cortec, Pasqual Arnella, Ralph Lauren, PVH, Stella McCartney, and Timberland.

The expert insights are provided by: Patsy Perry, Juliet Russell, and Philip Mak.

Chapter 7 – GOVERNANCE. This chapter introduces the organisations that exist and support and educate both consumers and brands on more responsible practices.

Organisation examples include: United Nations, Global Fashion Agenda, Fashion Taskforce, The Ellen MacArthur Foundation, Fashion Roundtable, The Sustainable Fashion Forum, The Fashion Pact, The Sustainable Angle, The World Wildlife Fund, The Environmental Justice Foundation, Sourcemap, The British Fashion Council, The Institute of Positive Fashion, The Fifteen Percent Pledge, Good On You, Fashion for Good, B Corp Certification, The Textile Exchange, The Fairtrade Foundation, The Forest Stewardship Council, The Butterfly Mark, Positive Luxury Sustainability Council, Fashion Revolution, Extinction Rebellion, Greenpeace, Fashion Takes Action (FTA), The Clean Clothes Campaign, The Slow Fashion Movement, The Slow Factory, The Ethical Trading Initiative (ETI).

The expert insight is provided by M. Fernanda Hernandez Franco.

Chapter 8 – Promotion to HONEST COMMUNICATION. This chapter identifies the fundamental challenge with traditional promotional tactics historically employed by brands. The chapter also introduces the term greenwashing and examines the shift towards honest marketing. The chapter outlines several simple marketing academic concepts in order to further examine modern practice.

Fashion brand examples include: Lush Cosmetics, Patagonia, Adidas, The North Face, Savage X Fenty, Tory Burch, Allbirds, and REI.

The expert insights are provided by: Veronica Bates Kassatly, Darren Black, Martin Deal, Peter Rees, Sarah Vaughan, and Giorgia Pagliuca.

Chapter 9 – Physical Evidence to STORYTELLING PLATFORMS. This chapter explores the importance of relevant and authentic in-store activations in order to engage with the connected customer. It builds on the importance of creating a relevant community in order to showcase the fashion brands' credentials.

Fashion brand examples include: Lululemon, Public Lands, United by Blue, Levi's, H&M, RAEBURN DESIGN, Veja, Nike, aaa/unbranded, WerkHaus, Glossier, Gap, Macy's, Sephora, Stella McCartney, Mulberry, The Reformation, and Patagonia.

The expert insights are provided by: Vittorio Cosma and Mario Innocente, Samara Croci, Nick Pye, and Rae Sims.

Conclusion – This chapter focuses on insights from Eco Age, who are an end-to-end agency for sustainable business strategy. Eco Age explain how the industry is evolving and what developments we are likely to see over the next decade.

The rationale for each component of **The Responsible 9 Framework** is further supported, highlighting why each element has been brought together and ordered systematically to wholly consider responsible fashion business practice.

THE RESPONSIBLE 9 FRAMEWORK

1. **CONSCIOUS ITEM**
2. **CIRCULAR SERVICES**
3. **COMMUNITY**
4. **PERCEIVED VALUE**
5. **ACCOUNTABLE SYSTEMS**
6. **GREEN ENVIRONMENT**
7. **GOVERNANCE**
8. **HONEST COMMUNICATION**
9. **STORYTELLING PLATFORMS**

Ghebreab and Heale 2023

RESPONSIBLE 9 FRAMEWORK. Credit Ghebreab and Heale 2023

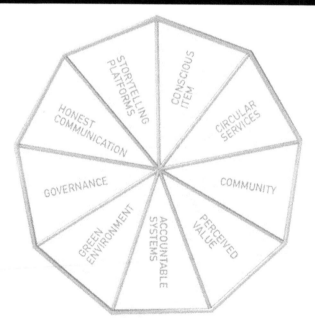

REFERENCE

Booms, B.H. and Bitner, M.J. (1981) Marketing Strategies and Organisation Structures for Service Firms. In: *Marketing of Services*, American Marketing Association, Chicago.

FURTHER READING

Blanchard, T. (2007). *Green is the New Black: How to Change the World with Style*, London: Hodder and Stoughton Ltd.

Bonacich, E. and Appelbaum, P.P. (2000). *Behind the Label: Inequality in the Los Angeles Apparel Industry*, Berkeley, CA: University of California Press.

Ellen MacArthur Foundation (2021). *Circular Design for Fashion*, Ellen MacArthur Foundation.

Fung, A., O'Rourke, D., and Sabel, C.F. (2001). *Can We Put an End to Sweatshops?: A New Democracy Form on Raising Global Labour Standards*, Boston: Beacon Press.

Gwilt, A. (2014). *Practical Guide to Sustainable Fashion*, Bloomsbury.

Ottman, J. (2012). The New Rules of Green Marketing, Berrett-Koehler.

Perrault, W. and McCarthy, J. (2000). *Applications in Basic Marketing*, Irwin McGraw Hill: Boston.

Posner H. (2015). *Marketing Fashion*, London, Laurence King Publishing.

Ross, R.J.S. (2004). *Slaves to Fashion: Poverty and Abuse in the New Sweatshops*, The University of Michigan Press.

Thomas, D. (2019). *Fashionopolis: The Price of Fast Fashion and the Future of Clothes*, Apollo.

West, D., Ford, J., and Essam, I. (2010). *Strategic Marketing: Creating Competitive Advantage*, Second Ed., Oxford: Oxford University Press.

WEB MATERIAL

Baalbaki Y. (2015). History of Marketing Mix from 4Ps to 7Ps. Retrieved from: www.linkedin.com/pulse/history-marketing-mix-from-4ps-7ps-yousef-baalbaki.

BCG Global (2022). From Compliance to Courage in ESG. Retrieved from: www.bcg.com/publications/2022/compliance-to-courage-in-esg.

BCG Global (2022). The Five Digital Building Blocks of a Corporate Sustainability Agenda. Retrieved from: https://web-assets.bcg.com/be/28/2262959d4ff8ba21ade6f9f4a151/bcg-the-five-digital-building-blocks-of-a-corporate-sustainability-mar-2022.pdf.

Bailey, E.G. et al. (2022). Sustainability Bulletin: January 2022. WGSN. Retrieved from: https://tbaileyam.co.uk/blog/january-2022-mid-monthly-update/.

Ellen Macarthur Foundation (No Date). Redesigning the Future of Fashion. Retrieved from: https://ellenmacarthurfoundation.org/a-new-textiles-economy.

Farra, E. (2020). Activewear is Booming, But Only a Few Labels Are Making it Consciously. Vogue. Retrieved from: https://bayouwithlove.com/blogs/press/activewear-is-booming-but-only-a-few-labels-are-making-it-consciously-by-vogue.

Kent, S. (2021). Measuring Fashion's Sustainability Gap. The Business of Fashion. Retrieved from: www.businessoffashion.com/reports/sustainability/measuring-fashions-sustainability-gap-download-the-report-now/.

McKinsey (2022). State of Fashion 2021. Business of Fashion. Retrieved from: www.mckinsey.com/~/media/mckinsey/industries/retail/our%20insights/state%20of%20fashion/2022/the-state-of-fashion-2022.pdf.

Ward, C. (2019). Communicating with Conscious Consumers. Stylus. Retrieved from: https://stylus.com/communicating-with-conscious-consumers.

(Please note all Stylus content is subscription only).

CHAPTER 1

The Responsible 9 Framework
#1 = Conscious Item

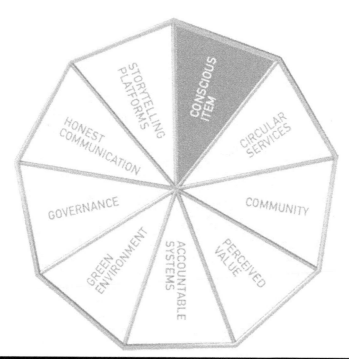

THE RESPONSIBLE 9 FRAMEWORK: #1 = CONSCIOUS ITEM

DOI: 10.4324/9781003285915-2

INTRODUCTION TO THE CHAPTER

Fashion brands attempt to develop products suitable for their target customers and are now realising the importance of sustainability. Many companies are now actively working towards developing better and less environmentally impactful items, on this journey many are identifying alternative materials and altering manufacturing processes (which will be discussed in Chapter 5, and number 5 in **The Responsible 9 Framework – ACCOUNTABLE SYSTEMS**). However, there is still a long way to go before the term "100% sustainable" should be applied to a fashion item, as further discussed by industry expert and Educator, Charlotte Turner.

Expert insight from Charlotte Turner

Charlotte Turner is a Sustainable Fashion and Textiles Consultant and Educator.

The myriad inputs, processes and outputs involved in making, using, and ultimately disposing of materials and consumer products in our current linear system means that there are inherent environmental and social impacts at all stages of the product lifecycle, and therefore it is difficult, if not impossible, to describe any product or material as fully "sustainable." However, we are increasingly seeking ways to minimise, neutralise, and even reverse these impacts in a bid to reach global targets from net zero emissions to the eradication of poverty and inequality – though there is much more progress to be made if there is to be any hope of achieving any of these goals.

There are several approaches we can take that address both environmental and socio-economic issues when considering how we can create, use, maintain, reprocess, and ultimately, when all other options are exhausted, dispose of products in more responsible, positive, and "sustainable" ways.

Among these, materials are often one of the first elements we consider as they have such a visible role in the design and function of a product, and their full life cycle impacts – from cradle to cradle, encompassing cultivation or extraction, processing, production, care, disposal, and end of life behaviours – can make up a significant proportion of the products' overall environmental footprint.

There are some tools in place to try to aid better choices, including global certifications that apply to different issues and stages of the supply chain (for example use of chemicals in agriculture, wet processing, pollution mitigation, or labour standards). Whilst these can be good indicators of the practices in a textiles supply chain, it is important to note that they are not all equal or in fact foolproof, and therefore cannot offer a standardised guarantee of "sustainability."

Therefore, when we do want to make responsible materials choices, there has developed a tendency to oversimplify matters by trying to numerically "compare apples and oranges" using inconsistent methodologies and parameters, often through the use of scoring indices and matrices that have been built using out-of-date and inconsistent life cycle assessment data. These tools are in fact so inconsistent, that we have been falsely led to believe that synthetics could offer a lower impact materials solution, when in fact the opposite is true – we should be prioritising natural and renewable fibres.

We therefore need to go far beyond these incomplete methodologies and consider the socio-economic impacts of materials (such as the significant role agriculture plays to certain economies and developing nations), as well as the full cradle to cradle environmental lifecycle impacts of each individual material, understanding that fibres come from all around the world and can be created in different environments and climates using varied processes and inputs – and therefore trying to give all fibres (for example cotton, silk, or wool) the same environmental impact score is unrealistic – there are too many variables at play.

We need to ask a multitude of questions, not just look for a number. For example, has the material been derived from non-renewable resources such as oil, or can it be cultivated within a regenerative farming system that actually helps to restore soil health and sequester atmospheric carbon? Will it release harmful microplastics during its lifetime and beyond, or when the product reaches the end of its useful life can it biodegrade or compost back into the natural environment, with the ultimate goal of breaking down and returning nutrients rather than toxins into the soil?

If we reframe our thinking in this way, then only after we have taken steps to use what we already have (for example through repair, upcycling, rental, or resale), should we lean towards more renewable natural fibres and move away from oil-based synthetics which are polluting the earth's land, air, and water. Some of the many options include wool which can come from regenerative farming systems and which has inherent performance properties such as temperature and odour control. Or cotton grown in suitable climates across the globe without the use of synthetic pesticides, herbicides, fertilisers, or genetic modification, which can all have detrimental effects on soil health, biodiversity, and the financial and physical well-being of farmers. Bast fibres such as flax for linen can grow with minimal to no chemical or water intervention, resulting in a low impact and durable natural fibre, and every part of the plant can be utilised to create food, fibres, and even building materials.

Whilst many nascent technologies and systems are not yet commercially available, recent years have also shown a growth in innovation and new systems thinking. We are seeing some producers of natural fibres begin to go back to basics by utilising regenerative agriculture methods that work in harmony with the planet's natural systems to restore soil health and help sequester carbon back into the soil, and technology companies develop processes that could enable us to create renewable bio-based alternatives to oil-based synthetics, materials, and dyes made from carbon dioxide taken from the atmosphere, or even materials that can themselves help to draw carbon dioxide from the air. There has also been extensive investment into recycling technologies with the aim of enabling the creation of new materials from used garments in a bid to achieve a circular economy, although as less than 1% of textile waste is currently reported to be recycled into new materials, these technologies require accompanying investment into logistics systems that will allow us to efficiently collect, sort, and reprocess end of life products and materials without resorting to destroying or shipping unwanted and often low quality or damaged goods abroad as is often the case at the moment.

In order to sufficiently address socio-economic risks, we must also strive for more transparent and traceable supply chains which can enable us to properly monitor social and environmental conditions at all supply chain stages, safeguarding against forced labour and modern slavery, and protecting the health of global communities.

However, any materials and production innovations must be accompanied by an overall reduction in consumption and disposal in order for the positive impacts to register. There is no benefit in creating new products with less harmful materials or processes if we continue to significantly increase our rates of production, consumption and disposal, contributing to the devaluation and vast underutilisation of products, alongside exponential pollution of our environment. In fact, the best way to reduce the overall lifecycle impact of a product is simply to use it more – decreasing its "impact per wear" score.

This means that we should be prioritising degrowth, where we decouple economic success from the depletion of the earth's resources and the creation of new products, and instead prioritise building relationships, socio-economic well-being, and offering services which allow us to connect with each other and the items we own or have "guardianship" over.

An influential group of consumers are actively seeking out new and existing fashion brands that make items that do not unduly harm the environment. Many of these customers are also considering not purchasing at all if the brand is not perceived to be working towards cleaner and more responsible practices. While, at the moment, there is no such thing as a completely sustainable product, as highlighted by Charlotte Turner, there are some, that when they are created are much better in terms of the environmental impact than others. This chapter covers the first key component in the transformation of the word **Product to a CONSCIOUS ITEM**, it is also number 1 in **The Responsible 9 Framework**.

RESPONSIBLE FASHION DESIGN

Fashion designers are in charge of the design and development of clothing and other fashion products. It is important that responsible design practice is followed by these key people, they are the gatekeepers and have the power to continue to improve the industry. The importance of responsible fashion design is further discussed in Massimo Casagrade's expert insights below.

Expert insight from Massimo Casagrande
MA Programme Leader, Fashion Design Marangoni, Paris.

"With great power, comes great responsibility." – Voltaire.

I repeat this phrase often to my students, although they tend to associate it more with Spider-man than Voltaire. Either way, the message is the same: they are the generation who have the power to change the industry, rewrite the rules and set new solid foundations for a more responsible and eco-conscious industry.

Responsible design isn't only about the making of the product but is something that continues beyond the product's purchase. During the conceptual stage process of the project, designers need to ask themselves: What impact will the product have on the environment? What can be done to lessen that impact? What is the responsible way of creating the product?

A successful result of an eco-conscious design is one where the designer completely understands a product's entire journey: from seeing where the textiles come from, their surrounding ecologies, seeing how their products are made and disposed of and truly understanding what is possible for a product's second and sometimes third life.

Addressing overproduction and consumption is one of the first steps towards being eco-conscious and understanding the consumer is essential. The more we know about how they live, their needs and habits, the more we can design products which are inclusive, sustainable, and ethical. Once we know the needs of the market, we design accordingly, thereby helping to reduce the number of products that end up unsold or discounted, which ultimately end up in landfills.

Designing smaller adaptable, interchangeable, and consumer focused collections is, I believe, a possible solution to the overproduction issue. An example I always like to highlight would be Donna Karan's 1985 "Seven Easy Pieces." This was revolutionary in that it allowed women to rework the basics into different styles and a concept, which is still relevant today. This concept of adaptable, interchangeable pieces is aligned with the lifestyle of today's contemporary consumer.

For the past four years, I have been working with the Latin American Fashion Summit (LAFS) and mentoring LatinX designers, and it has been fascinating to see that a majority of them are making garments from deadstock materials, working with and supporting local communities and artisans. This approach is creating business models that empower communities. Annais Yucra, a womenswear designer from Peru and recipient of the Pitch to LAFS prize, uses recycled and regenerated materials to produce her collections. These attitudes are becoming more relevant within business models, as can be seen by designers such as Mara Hoffman, Ganni and Gabriela Hearst – 25% of her collections are made from deadstock materials. When my students are creating their toiles, we use old bedsheets donated to us by Soho Beach House, this avoids the sheets having to go to landfills and students save money as they don't have to go out and buy white cotton for prototyping.

Repair, resale, and recycle are becoming an important approach to responsible design. Brands such as Patagonia and Levi's are the forerunners in this; both offer repair services, Patagonia even having DIY repair tutorial videos. Levi's has teamed up with Renewcell's pioneering Circulose fiber to create a fully circular denim, which can be recycled and reused more than once, thereby allowing their new 501's to have a second (and third, and fourth) life. This is a huge achievement for a polluting industry such as the denim industry.

I have regular design discussions with students getting them to think "out of the box," consider solutions and understand consumer pain points. UX design, I believe, is not to be limited only to a digital experience, but one related to physical products as well. I encourage students to think of solutions, what if, instead of just having the spare button on the shirt/dress/trouser we include a repair kit? This will allow consumers to repair their garments. What if we take IKEA's example and have flat-pack garments? The consumer becomes emotionally attached, as they have to sew the garment and are less inclined to throw the garment away, or can work with a local seamstress and support a small business. Again, this concept was explored by Miyake's A-POC (A piece of cloth) where the consumer interacts with the garment.

Responsible design also challenges designers to consider inclusivity and adaptability in their products, by considering all body shapes, sizes and focusing on people with disabilities. Victoria Jenkins with her brand Unhidden Clothing is creating sustainable adaptive and inclusive garments for people with disabilities, as well as being co-founder of No Comment Required, an ethical slogan clothing range focusing on positive representation for people with mental health issues and disabilities as well as all marginalised groups. Becca McCharen-Tran, with her brand Chromat, is creating a world that empowers women, femmes, and non-binary people in fashion.

As future industry players, graduates today have the responsibility to educate and instruct the consumers about the benefits of eco-conscious and responsible design, as this will make them demand environmental standards from other brands and, above all, lead to them respecting and valuing the product more, but also ensure a longer life for the product.

TEXTILES AND FIBRES

Introducing textiles and natural and man-made fibres

The term fibre describes the raw material that is used to manufacture textiles. Yarn is produced by spinning fibres into long and twisted lengths, which can then be either woven or knitted to create a material or fabric. Fibres can be broken down into two main categories, either natural or man-made.

Natural fibres are grown and can either be plant based, as in the case of cotton, or an animal product such as wool. Only natural fibres can be labelled organic and must comply with specific criteria and are certified as such.

Man-made fibres are described in terms of generations, the first being fibre such as viscose which is derived from plant or cellulosic material. Fibres like nylon and polyester are part of the second generation and utilise petroleum as the raw material. Man-made fibres are never labelled as organic.

Organic clothing is clothing made from materials raised in, or grown in, compliance with certified organic agricultural standards.

Natural plant fibres are identified simply by the type of the plant that produces the fibres. Where the fibre is grown, the way it is harvested and processed can affect the quality. Each natural fibre is unique; each one will have their own distinguishing set of characteristics. Traditionally, fabric is engineered to make best use of the particular properties of a fibre. For example, cotton is the usual choice for T-shirts as it has the qualities needed for that particular garment.

COTTON

FIGURE 1.1   photo of cotton plant. Shutterstock/Muratart

Currently around half of all textiles are made from cotton. The production of this natural fibre provides income for over 200 million people worldwide. However, there are huge environmental and social concerns connected to the cotton industry. The cultivation of cotton, if produced without sensitivity, can cause soil degradation, impact water resources and biodiversity causing long-lasting consequences for the environment. In some countries the use of child labour and slavery has been connected to this vast industry.

Organic cotton

Some fashion brands are beginning to introduce cotton fabrics whose fibres are produced organically. Organic cotton is grown using methods and materials with low environmental impact. A strict set of rules and regulations ensures that organic production maintains and even replenishes soil fertility. Additionally, it can also contribute to reducing the use of toxic chemicals, such as harmful pesticides, fertilisers, and defoliants.

Cotton sold as organic must meet strict regulations regarding how it is produced. Independent organisations oversee the certification ensuring that organic growers use only approved methods and materials. (Certification companies will be discussed in Chapter 7 in **The Responsible 9 Framework – GOVERNANCE.**)

Recycled cotton

Waste is now considered a resource on many levels (also see "the waste opportunity" in **CIRCULAR SERVICES,** Chapter 2). Recycled cotton is viewed as a more environmentally friendly method of utilising cotton waste. Millions of unwanted cotton fabrics can now be recycled into a new material. The production of recycled cotton at a satisfactory standard can contribute to reducing landfill waste from pre- and post-consumer textiles. In addition, recycled cotton uses less water and energy than virgin cotton.

Global fashion brands are now committing to using fabrics with greater eco-credentials. As an example, H&M has set a deadline of 2030 for when they will only use recycled materials such as cotton or virgin materials that are sustainably sourced.

Regenerative cotton

Regenerative agriculture refers to holistic practices that promote soil health and restore the soil's organic carbon. Farming methods such as no-till and low-till, the use of cover crops, rotating livestock with crops, alongside avoiding or reducing synthetic fertilisers and pesticides all play a part. In addition to reducing greenhouse gas emissions, these practices can be more effective at trapping carbon than conventional agriculture with the resulting soil becoming a net carbon sink. Cotton grown in this way meets regenerative organic standards, the highest possible organic certification. (Certification companies will be discussed in Chapter 7 in **The Responsible**

9 Framework – GOVERNANCE). Examples of regenerative agriculture are replacing the destructive techniques used by the conventional cotton industry with brands such as Patagonia, Eileen Fisher, and Stella McCartney moving in this direction.

Linch

Linen

FIGURE 1.2   photo of linen. Credit Shutterstock / Auhustsinovich

The flax plant is harvested and used to make the textile linen. Linen, both as a fibre and fabric, has been in existence for thousands of years and is classed as a natural fibre. Unlike cotton, the flax plant does not require much maintenance and is able to grow in poor soils. Compared to cotton it also requires very little water. Linen fibres are absorbent, strong, and antibacterial. Flax plants are extremely versatile and the entire plant can be utilised, so none of it is wasted making it a very eco-friendly choice.

Hemp

Hemp is a natural bast fibre and has been used to create textiles for centuries. The hemp plant is found all over the world and is attracting a lot of attention in terms of sustainability due to its many desirable characteristics. For example, hemp grows quickly, it preserves and replenishes soil fertility and requires little water to flourish. Hemp can be turned into a variety of durable materials such as denim. Alongside antibacterial properties, it even has the ability to help regulate a wearer's body temperature.

FIGURE 1.3   photo of Hemp. Credit Shutterstock/ Natalia Golubnycha

NATURAL ANIMAL FIBRES

Wool

Wool is a natural protein fibre derived from sheep's fleece that can be used to create textiles. Additionally, the hair of other animals such as goats, alpacas, camels, and llamas can also be utilised to make fabric. As with other forms of animal husbandry, raising animals for fibre can have an impact on the environment. However, when sourced organically, it has some very important sustainable attributes; it is renewable, biodegradable, and recyclable. Wool is thermo-regulating and needs washing less frequently than many other fibres. When disposed of in the soil wool can act as a fertiliser releasing nutrients into the soil. As fashion labels seek to develop garments that can be branded as circular, wool fibre has been identified as a possible contributor.

The Woolmark Company is a global authority that offers extensive information on the benefits of wool. It is constantly exploring ways that the wool industry can improve its practices and reduce its carbon footprint (Certification companies will be discussed in Chapter 7 in **The Responsible 9 Framework – GOVERNANCE**).

Leather

Leather is a natural material made from the skin of an animal. While there are multiple animals that provide leather, most are sourced from cows. Some believe that leather is unethical and environmentally unsustainable, however, others argue that the production of ethical leather is far better for the environment than other materials and new alternatives that are being developed to replace leather. Like all materials, it therefore becomes critically important for brands and suppliers sourcing leather to better understand where their leather comes from and the responsible practises that went into its manufacture.

Alongside intensive use of both energy and water, cattle farming (dairy and meat) is known to contribute to deforestation, loss of biodiversity, and extensive greenhouse gas emissions. On the leather manufacturing side, there is also evidence that in less developed countries, with less regulation, toxic chemicals associated with tanning, such as formaldehyde, cyanide, lead, and chromium can be disposed of in unresponsible environmental ways.

Responsibly sourced and manufactured leather can have a positive effect. The future vision for the leather industry will include a new, more environmentally sustainable model that addresses many of the outstanding issues that have negatively affected its reputation, such as ethical treatment of animals and unsafe tanning and finishing practices. Links with sustainable pasture management, that includes cattle, is at the heart of regenerative farming and can help build up and store carbon in the soil, reducing the negative effects of climate change. Well-maintained leather can last a lifetime and longer when compared to some plastic and bio-based alternatives. Good quality leather products can also be repaired, refurbished, or repurposed to extend their lives even further.

Silk

Silk production is called sericulture. The Bombyx Mori silkworms used for conventional silk are fed exclusively on mulberry leaves. The silkworms spin cocoons creating a silk filament fibre. Cocoons are boiled to loosen their long fibres so they can be reeled ready for processing. Silk, like wool, is a protein fibre. This lustrous material is associated with luxury. Sericulture is often a part of traditional systems that have existed for millennia and benefit some of the poorest in the global south. In terms of sustainability the production of silk, up to the finishing and dyeing stages, is relatively benign. In contrast to other synthetic fibres including polyester and viscose, silk has a very low environmental impact, requiring little or no synthetic pesticides, insecticides, or fertilisers and is biodegradable.

Preconceptions associated with silk are based on the fact that the silk worms are boiled to obtain the filament fibre, yet these preconceptions can be challenged as this occurs as they prepare to metamorphose and are considered insentient as a result. This is often cited as a reason not to use silk; however, perhaps forgetting the hidden cost of other fibres such as polyester (micro fibres) and viscose (deforestation and loss of biodiversity) to the environment.

Regenerated man-made fibres

Of the two types of man-made fibres, artificial or synthetic, artificial fibres are made from regenerated cellulose, usually sourced from wood pulp. There are various artificial fibres including rayon, viscose, acetate, modal, and lyocell.

Tencel

Austrian company, Lenzing AG, produces **Tencel**, a semi-synthetic lyocell fibre. Tencel is considered a high-quality fibre that is strong, soft to the touch, absorbent and breathable. This innovative, environmentally friendly fibre can be combined with other fibres to make fabric that is lighter and stronger. Tencel's regenerated cellulose fibres are completely compostable and biodegradable.

Modal

Lenzing AG produces another viscose fibre, **Modal**. Modal is a brand name like Tencel. Modal uses beech wood pulp sourced from sustainably managed forests. This fibre is manufactured slightly differently than Tencel, incorporating additional steps to make it lighter, flexible, and soft.

Bamboo

A sustainable viscose fibre can also be produced from bamboo, a plant considered ideal as a raw material. Unlike many other plants, it grows fast and

FIGURE 1.4   Bamboo plant. Credit Pixabay

FIGURE 1.5   Bamboo made into a fibre. Credit Pixabay

FIGURE 1.6   PANGAIA product advertising made from Bamboo. Credit PANGAIA

requires minimal resources and pesticides. Despite some claims that it leads to habitat destruction, it is still a far less intensive and destructive process than processing either crude oil or growing conventional cotton.

SYNTHETIC MAN-MADE FIBRES

Synthetic fibres are chemically synthesised polymers derived from coal, oil, or natural gas derivatives. While these fibres are widely used and extremely useful in the fashion industry, their production is associated with environmental concerns. In addition to utilising a finite resource as a raw material, they do not break down readily, often taking hundreds of years to degrade. Man-made fibres include polyamides (nylon), polyesters, acrylics, polyolefins, vinyl, and elastomeric fibres. The properties of synthetic materials vary and many are engineered to mimic and replace natural materials. Synthetic fibres can be engineered to incorporate specific properties such as high absorbency or the ability to hold pleats.

Nylon

Nylon was the first synthetic man-made fibre created in 1938 as an alternative to silk. Derived from petrochemicals, it is used extensively throughout the fashion industry but its use as a material is now questioned in terms of sustainability, due its reliance on crude oil as its raw material. However, it is possible to recycle nylon which introduces the idea of developing nylon as a circular fibre.

Polyester

The fashion industry relies heavily on polyester, one of the world's most popular fibres. Typically, polyester fibres are made from petroleum and are a type of plastic. Polyester contributes to pollution around the world as clothing made from this fibre often ends up in landfill and is not biodegradable. Material scientists have developed various alternatives to polyester derived from oil, including those made from recycled plastic, agricultural crops, and even waste but these are only just becoming mainstream. Polyester is often blended with cotton or other natural fibres; this is then called a poly-blend. Creating a poly-blend, as in the case of poly-cotton, introduces yet another environmental problem. Combining natural and man-made fibres makes recycling more challenging since natural and synthetic fibres are each processed in a different system.

Microfibres

Synthetic materials such as polyester and acrylic are often manufactured using microfibres. When the garments are laundered microplastic fibres are released in the wastewater. The wastewater treatment facilities cannot filter these microscopic fibres, which end up in our waterways. Approximately half-a-million tonnes of microfibre pollution enters the sea yearly, and microfibres are now found in the human food chain.

FUTURE ALTERNATIVES

There are a number of companies that are developing fibres for fabrics that fashion brands are beginning to use when sourcing products for the conscious consumer.

These new materials, while not 100% sustainable, can be less impactful than conventional fibres. By investing in materials developed using new more environmentally friendly fibres, the fashion industry can potentially lower its waste, water, and energy consumption, something it desperately needs to do.

Pinatex

Popular with brands and customers seeking out vegan alternatives to animal leather, Pinatex is a versatile material that can be used for both large or small items. Manufactured by the company Ananas, Pinatex is made of pineapple leaf fibre. The leaves are a by-product of pineapple farming. As the plant only produces fruit once, its stem and leaves would otherwise be considered waste. The concept of recognising waste as a resource is evident in the use of this raw material, which benefits both farmers and the environment. However, Pinatex is not wholly sustainable, as currently the processes used in manufacturing can impact the environment. It takes around 16 pineapples to create one square metre of Pinatex.

Orange Fiber

Italian company Orange Fiber has been making fibre from orange peel waste since 2014. Citrus juice by-products are provided free by the juice industry

FIGURE 1.7   Orange Fiber. Credit Shutterstock / Tshakopy

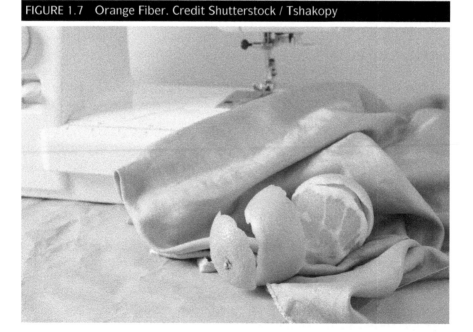

as an alternative to sending them to landfill. The 100% citrus cellulose textile has a lightweight, soft, and silky handle. Often labelled as an artificial silk, it can be engineered to be either matt or shiny in finish. Despite being produced in a closed loop system, the fibre cannot be considered 100% sustainable due to some of the manufacturing processes involved. Salvatore Ferragamo supported this innovative company by purchasing the initial production run, debuting the first-ever collection made of this fibre, the Ferragamo Orange Fiber Collection.

Mylo

Developed by Bolt Threads, Mylo is a leather-like and partly sustainable material made from mycelium, the underground root structure of fungi. It takes just days to produce by growing mycelium in beds of corn stalks. Some of the processes employed in creating this leather alternative are not yet eco-friendly, so consequently at present it cannot be labelled as 100% sustainable. The material is hardwearing, supple and breathable making a useful material for various items of clothing, footwear, and handbags.

A growing number of fashion brands are now employing Mylo for some of their products, Adidas has redesigned its classic Stan Smith sneakers, Lululemon uses it for yoga mats and accessories and Stella McCartney as an alternative to animal leather.

Aquafil

ECONYL is a regenerated nylon produced by a company called Aquafil. ECONYL uses recycled materials to create nylon from post-consumer plastic and textile waste. ECONYL employs a closed loop system to regenerate plastic already in circulation meaning no new resources and no waste.

Maria Giovanna Sandrini, Group Chief Communication Officer at AQUAFIL further explains ECONYL

The Four Rs at ECONYL are as follows;

REIMAGINE – The ECONYL® Regeneration System starts with collecting waste from fishing nets, fabric scraps, carpet flooring, and industrial plastic. This waste is then sorted and cleaned in order to recover as much nylon as possible.

REGENERATE – Through a radical regeneration and purification process, the nylon waste is recycled right back to its original's purity.

REMAKE – This means that ECONYL® regenerated nylon is exactly the same as fossil-based nylon. Regenerated nylon ECONYL® is processed into yarns and polymers for the fashion and interior design industries.

REIMAGINE – The core mission at ECONYL is to create and acquire new products in a limitless time frame. Fashion designers and carpet manufacturers use ECONYL® regenerated nylon to create innovative new products. Nylon has the ability to be recycled indefinitely without losing its quality. The goal is for all products containing ECONYL® to return to step one of the Regeneration System once they are no longer useful to customers.

FIGURE 1.8   Mixed nylon waste - credit Aquafil/Econyl

FIGURE 1.9   Polymer Econyl - credit Aquafil/Econyl

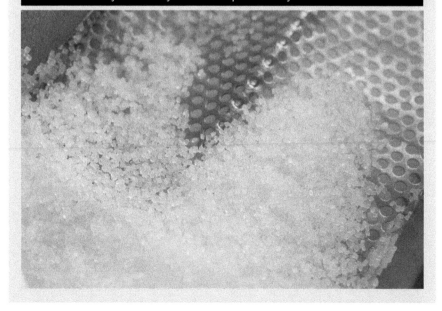

FIGURE 1.10   Econyl yarn - credit Aquafil/Econyl

DYES

Along with materials, textile dyes should also be considered in the journey to become more sustainable. This topic is discussed in detail by Karen Spurgin in the expert insight below.

Expert insight from Karen Spurgin

Textiles Consultant and Senior Lecturer Karen Spurgin provides information on textile dyes and their impact on the environment. She also highlights some more environmentally conscious alternatives.

Most textile dyes used today are synthetic, petroleum-based ones, creating problems in terms of sustainability. Dyeing with synthetic colour is one of the most polluting parts of textile production, posing numerous problems for people and the planet. The environmental impact of colouring textiles is significant, traditionally synthetic colour requires high temperatures and the use of large amounts of water in its process.

Alongside the volume of water needed, conventional dyeing chemicals and heavy salts can contaminate rivers and seas. The introduction of effluent results in the reduction of photosynthesis and oxygenation in waterways. Around 15–50% of azo dyes do not adhere to fibres, and their presence can inhibit microbial colonies in the soil, limiting plant growth. Toxic dye residues can negatively impact organisms throughout the food chain and have been found to be carcinogenic. When dyed with synthetic petroleum-based colour even natural fibres cannot easily biodegrade, exhibiting similar issues to microfibres associated with nylon and polyester.

However dyeing processes are beginning to improve with a more scientific approach, awareness of environmental issues and legislation. There are many examples of good practice that are being adopted by dyeing companies. With exhaust dyeing, for instance, it is possible to calculate the exact dye to fibre ratio, meaning all the dyestuff is absorbed during the dyeing process, reducing effluent.

As companies become more conscious of their water use, they are recycling and reusing dye baths rather than dumping into the waterways. Increasing understanding of the impact of colour for textiles has led to the development of innovative new technologies. In the future, the possibility of an environmentally friendly process of biodegradation of synthetic dyes by microbes is in the pipeline but in the meantime companies such as ColorZen, DyeCoo, and AirDye amongst others offer solutions to limiting water, energy, and chemical use in creating colour for textiles.

ColorZen® technology revolutionises cotton dyeing, making it more efficient and sustainable. Cotton is the most widely used natural fibre for textiles, with ColorZen® pre-treatment, it can be dyed with less water, reducing water use by as much as 90%. Additionally, energy use is reduced by 75%, dye and toxic chemicals by 95% with no toxic discharge.

DyeCoo uses a closed loop dyeing system which replaces water with supercritical CO_2 (an intermediate phase between a liquid and a gas), saving up to 60% of the energy needed for conventional dyeing. When in this state CO_2 becomes a very strong solvent allowing dyes to dissolve easily and deeply penetrate fibres. With the **AirDye** system, the dye is transferred from paper to polyester fabric with the aid of printing machines. Compared to conventional print and dye methods, this method uses up to 95% less water, 86% less energy, and 84% less greenhouse gases. On a single garment, water savings can be as high as 45 gallons. The paper used in the process is recycled, and, as the dyes are inert, they can return to their original state and be reused.

Both the DyeCoo and AirDye method is restricted to polyester. ColorZen technology can only be used for cotton fibres. Currently, all these innovative dyeing technologies are not widely available due to high equipment costs, the switch from conventional dyeing is a long way off with consumers not necessarily willing to absorb the additional costs. Both Nike and Adidas employ DyeCoo and AirDye for some of their synthetic textiles.

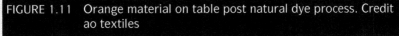
FIGURE 1.11   Orange material on table post natural dye process. Credit
ao textiles

Alternative plant-based dyes

Synthetic dyeing at industry scale began in the late 1800's proving compatible with the linear model adopted by textile manufacturers during the industrial revolution. At this time and throughout the decades that followed, natural colour sourced mainly from plants, was not seen as a viable, commercially sound alternative. The false perception, which continues to this day, is that plant-based dyes are neither scalable, repeatable, nor colourfast. Natural dyeing was classified as niche, very much a craft-based artisan practice, not suitable for industry. However, natural dye did not always equate with good environmentally friendly practice, many of the mordants and assistants used in the past were toxic.

Modern natural dye colourists, such as **ao textiles**, have reworked historic recipes to eliminate toxic chemicals. Realisation that dyeing with synthetic petroleum-based colour is one of the most polluting has led to a re-examination of plant-based colour. Ongoing research has identified key directions colour could develop in the future including natural colour derived from plant-based waste, bacteria, incorporating natural colour in dope dyeing regenerated cellulosic fibres **(Lenzing AG)** and the realisation dye plants could contribute to our health alongside playing a part in a regenerative agricultural system. While we are far away from making a change from colour created from petrochemicals to plant-based colour there are various emerging examples of companies attempting to make this shift. Pangaia, Chloe, and Dior are among several fashion brands that have incorporated plant-based colour into their collections enhancing their environmental credentials.

ao textiles

Colour for the 21st century, ao textiles specialises in developing vibrant natural dye colours for textiles in commercial production. Pioneers in the field, ao textiles combine historic dye recipes alongside investigations associating dye plants with health and well-being as found in both Chinese and Indian traditional medicine. They are the only UK-based company offering bespoke naturally dyed jacquard fabric using GOT certified plant-based colour (further information on GOT certified is covered in Chapter 7 – GOVERNANCE).

Lenzing

TENCEL branded modal fibre with indigo colour technology uses a one-step spun-dyeing process to deliver indigo colour whilst using substantially fewer resources.

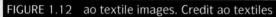
FIGURE 1.12   ao textile images. Credit ao textiles

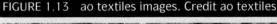

FIGURE 1.13   ao textiles images. Credit ao textiles

Archroma

Supporting a transition to a circular economy, EarthColors by Archroma create colour from renewable non-edible waste products from food and herbal industries (nut shells and leaves).

Colorifix

Colorifix identifies and replicates pigments found in nature and engineers bacteria in a lab converting them into dyes for textiles. The company uses renewable raw materials such as sugar, yeast, and plant by-products. Their manufacturing process ensures no harmful chemicals, less energy wasted, and less water is used.

Post Carbon Lab

This biotech start-up is researching and developing microbial textile finishing technologies, such as microbial colouration and Photosynthetic Coating®.

Their system uses microorganisms, such as bacteria, fungus, and algae, to colour, process, and treat existing fabrics. With Photosynthetic Coating®, the photosynthetic microbes not only colour the textiles but absorb CO_2 while generating fresh oxygen, giving the treated textiles a possibility to become climate-positive.

SLOW FASHION

The term slow fashion is gaining momentum, this is the opposite of fast fashion and connects well with the conscious and environmentally aware consumer, who is starting to question seasonality and planned obsolescence (as discussed in the Introduction of the book). High-quality materials are used in the creation of slow fashion garments; fabrics are designed to last longer, appealing to a more minimalist approach to consumption. With slow fashion there should be no toxic chemicals used in dyes, removing concerns about water pollution from manufacturing processes and water disposal. Ethics are also a key component with slow fashion, while reducing impact when creating garments; it also includes the supply chain and the lives of workers on the farms and in the factories (which will be discussed in Chapter 5 in **The Responsible 9 Framework – ACCOUNTABLE SYSTEMS**).

This process of slowing down is further highlighted below, with insight provided by mechanical engineering and product design expert, Jeffrey Heiligers.

Expert insight from Jeffrey Heiligers

Jeffrey Heiligers is a design consultant with a background in mechanical engineering and product design, from The Future Prospects Lab.

The first and maybe most important factor I would like to address is that we need to stop blaming the consumer for the issues brands, designers and various industries create with the products and/or services they offer. We should stop designing trends and focus on long-term solutions that last a lifetime. We, brands and designers have the power to change consumer, production, and post-purchase consumer behaviour and convince others with new services, designs, or different supply chains. We need to step away from current mass production practices and slow down processes, make them more insightful and transparent and find new ways of designing for actual consumer needs. As a design consultant I take a more individual, slow, and mindful approach and design with the product's end of life in mind.

Within all my projects I collaborate – during the entire process from beginning to end – with experts to ensure the integrity of my work. It is not easy and sometimes can be a slow process, but it does validate the outcomes I design. I use my projects as a communication tool to lower barriers and open the conversation with multiple stakeholders about all different kinds of urgent topics. I strongly believe that overwhelming people with negative information is never the solution, I actively look for, design, and provide solutions or strategies for future consumer needs. For example, with my project, Posture, I worked with several physiotherapists and a tailor to create a custom designed shirt to support your back muscles whilst working behind your desk.

In another one of my projects, I played with the idea of making the consumer part of the design process to address the issues around fast fashion items being created in faraway countries under very poor conditions. Most of these garments lack in quality (poor material choices) and are designed to become obsolete as trends change. Flat-pack Couture is a mailbox package containing high quality GOTS-certified materials and an instruction manual instructing how to construct the garment you bought. You can either do this yourself or bring it to a local tailor. By cutting out the manufacturing process I wanted to showcase that you can buy a high-quality garment for fast fashion competitive prices, but without all the nasties. Sewing the pieces together yourself not only builds an emotional connection between the customer and the garment, but also gives them the knowledge of how to repair the garment if it ever breaks. Another advantage is that it can be altered to your body. I'm not saying this is THE solution to fast fashion. The downside of only using this method would be factory workers being displaced from their jobs, causing a humanitarian disaster.

My process consists of a lot of different steps, starting with fully researching and understanding the context of the product or service I'm going to design. I reach out to experts, who sometimes are not the ones you think they are. They can vary between D&I specialists, marketers, manufacturers, and directors and not to forget factory workers who sometimes have more knowledge about a product than CEOs. They are easily forgotten as a resource while knowing the products they make every day inside out. When I feel confident with the gained knowledge, I start creating my vision, run tests, and begin to prototype. I then follow up with experts again and take their advice to alter my design, repeating this process until the outcome is representative of the vision. I'm always questioning every step I take. It's a constant debate to validate each step along the way to make the right impact with my design.

This chapter has provided insight into how important it is for fashion brands to develop CONSCIOUS ITEMS. Key takeaways include:

- The importance of understanding and developing responsible fashion items begins at school.
- Having an advanced understanding of where materials come from and the impact they have on the environment should be a key consideration for any fashion brand.
- Certifications are important and help give visibility on many things including the origins of the materials used to create the product.
- As fashion businesses use new materials in the production of their item they should proactively research the most responsible options.

- The impact of dyes should not be overlooked by fashion brands, research and development into alternative and less environmentally damaging options needs to continue.
- Brands adopting a slow fashion philosophy will resonate well with the consumer.

FURTHER READING

Ali, H. (2010). Biodegradation of Synthetic Dyes—A Review. Water Air Soil Pollution.

Baker, S. (2006). *Sustainable Development*, London: Routledge.

Burroughs, W.J. (2007). *Climate Change: A Multidisciplinary Approach*, Cambridge: Cambridge University Press.

Bulkeley, H. and Newell, P. (2010). *Governing Climate Change* (Global Institutions), London: Routledge.

Ellen MacArthur Foundation (2021). Circular Design for Fashion, Ellen MacArthur Foundation.

Jackson, T. (2011). *Prosperity without Growth: Economics for a Finite Planet*, Routledge.

Thomas, D. (2019). *Fashionopolis: The Price of Fast Fashion and the Future of Clothes*, Apollo.

WEB MATERIAL

Bates Kassatly, V. and Baumann-Pauly, D. (2022). The Great Greenwashing Machine Part 2: The Use and Misuse of Sustainability Metrics In Fashion. Geneva Center for Business and Human Rights, Geneva School of Economics and Management. Retrieved from: www.veronicabateskassatly.com/read/the-great-green-washing-machine-part-2-the-use-and-misuse-of-sustainability-metrics-in-fashion.

Bayon, R. Hawn, A., and Hamilton, K. (eds) (2007). Voluntary Carbon Markets: An International Business Guide to What They Are and How They Work. London: Earthscan. Retrieved from: www.routledge.com/Voluntary-Carbon-Markets-An-International-Business-Guide-to-What-They-Are/Bayon-Hawn-Hamilton/p/book/9780415851985.

Berkhout, F., Leach, M., and Scoones, I. (eds) (2003). Negotiating Environmental Change: New Perspectives from Social Science. Cheltenham: Edward Elgar. Retrieved from: www.e-elgar.com/shop/gbp/negotiating-environmental-change-9781840646733.html.

Cernansky R. (2021). Solving Fashion's Biggest Issues: Overproduction and Overconsumption. Vogue. Retrieved from: www.voguebusiness.com/sustainability/solving-fashions-biggest-issues-overproduction-and-overconsumption.

Clothing Manufacturers UK. (2020). WHAT ARE RECYCLED FABRICS AND TEXTILES? Retrieved from: www.clothingmanufacturersuk.com/post/what-are-recycled-fabrics-and-textiles#:~:text=Recycled%20fabrics%20are%20becoming%20a,and%20saves%20plastic%20from%20landfill. www.commonobjective.co.

Charpail, M. (2017). Environmental Impacts of the Fashion Industry. SustainYourStyle. Retrieved from: www.sustainyourstyle.org/en/whats-wrong-with-the-fashion-industry.

Documentary: Eco-Age & Andrew Morgan (2021). Fashionscapes: A Circular Economy. Retrieved from: www.fashionscapes.co.uk/films/fashionscapes-circularity.

Dottle, R. and Gu, J. (2022). The Global Glut of Clothing Is an Environmental Crisis. Bloomberg. Retrieved from: https://illuminem.com/post/b46b7c86-bd4c-4f8a-96f9-22d9490a903b.

Ellen Macarthur Foundation (2017). A New Textile Economy: Redesigning Fashion's Future. Retrieved from: https://ellenmacarthurfoundation.org/a-new-textiles-economy. www.fashionrevolution.org. www.fibershed.org.

Frost, C. (2021). Materials Evolution A/W 23/24. Stylus. Retrieved from: https://uniquestyleplatform.com/blog/category/seasonal/a-w-22-23/. www.regenorganic.org.

United Nations Climate Change (2021). Fashion Industry Charter for Climate Action. Retrieved from: https://unfccc.int/climate-action/sectoral-engagement/global-climate-action-in-fashion/fashion-industry-charter-for-climate-action/fashion-industry-charter-for-climate-action-resources.

United Nations Department of Economic and Social Affairs. Transforming our World: The 2030

Agenda for Sustainable Development. Retrieved from: https://sdgs.un.org/2030 agenda.

(Please note all Stylus content is subscription only).

BRAND REFERENCES

https://chromat.co.
www.eileenfisher.com.
https://jeffreyheiligers.com/collections/flatpack-couture.
www.ikea.com.
www.hm.com.
www.isseymiyake.com.
https://eu.patagonia.com.
www.adidas.co.uk/stan_smith.
www.stellamccartney.com.
https://unhiddenclothing.com.

CHAPTER **2**

The Responsible 9 Framework

#2 = Circular Services

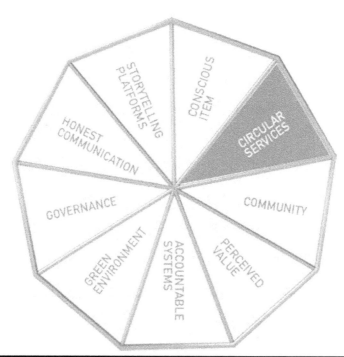

THE RESPONSIBLE 9 FRAMEWORK: #2 = CIRCULAR SERVICE

DOI: 10.4324/9781003285915-3

INTRODUCTION TO THE CHAPTER

An important consideration connected to the purchase of sustainable products, or the **CONSCIOUS ITEM**, as called in **The Responsible 9 Framework**, is what happens to the product when it is no longer needed or wanted. Customers are becoming more interested in different processes and services that deal with the post purchase of the product.

THE PRODUCT LIFE CYCLE: THE POST PURCHASE NECESSITY

Turning waste and deadstock into new items

Like other industries, the fashion industry is responsible for a lot of waste. However, emerging and established brands are starting to see the commercial value in creating products from materials that were once considered waste and deadstock and of no value in the fashion system. Upcycling and the creation of interesting new products from deadstock now resonate with the more environmentally aware sustainable consumer, who in the past might not have found upcycled garments appealing. These repurposed items have a back-story that the fashion brand can tell, and the conscious consumer can proudly share, post purchase.

FIGURE 2.1 Upcycled garment. Credit Shutterstock/Iryna Imago

FASHION INDUSTRY EXAMPLES

London-based luxury fashion designer **Priya Ahluwalia** has become known for her innovative use of material that might otherwise have gone to landfill. In 2021, the directional designer started working on a project with technology giant **Microsoft** called **Circulate**. The system uses AI (artificial intelligence) to help with the upcycling production methods, it invites everyone to donate used clothing so that those items can be upcycled and become part of Ahluwalia's next collection.

MINI CASE STUDY

Ahluwalia further explains the vision and process behind Circulate:

Ahluwalia partnered with Microsoft to create Circulate, a new and innovative experience and platform designed to bring new life to loved but unwanted clothing.

The brand has created a digital platform that invites the UK fashion community to contribute to an upcoming collection, and in return receive points that can be redeemed on the website.

Circulate highlights various "open calls," where the Ahluwalia team requests specific garments that will help make up future looks for the brand. The customer then uploads photos and videos of their own garments to see if they're a match for a future collection. These images are then analysed using AI technology. The AI acts as quality control, by analysing these images (in a matter of seconds), and confirms the garment details like fabric and colour, and ultimately to confirm whether the garments are a match for the collection or not.

Once the garment passes this digital inspection and has been confirmed as useful for a future collection, the customer then receives a prepaid shipping label to send their garment to the Ahluwalia studio.

Assuming that the clothing passes the brand team's in-person inspection, the customer is then awarded points that can be used towards future Ahluwalia purchases, and the knowledge that you have helped make the fashion industry more responsible.

Source: Priya Ahluwalia

Luxury conglomerate **LVMH** has an online marketplace called **Nona Source** for unused leathers and fabrics from brand's it owns such as Dior, Givenchy, and Louis Vuitton. Nona Source is a viable solution that addresses the challenges and opportunities of circularity, a key pillar of LVMH's environmental strategy.

MINI CASE STUDY

LVMH further explains the vision and process behind Nona Source concept:

Nona Source is the first online resale platform for "re-sourcing" exceptional materials from the Group's Fashion & Leather Goods Maisons. Designed by experts from LVMH via its DARE intrapreneurial program (Disrupt, Act, Risk to be an Entrepreneur), Nona Source supports LVMH's environmental strategy by rethinking sourcing and supporting the circular economy.

A revolution in sourcing, Nona Source offers emerging creatives and brands across Europe access to their high-quality fabrics and leathers at competitive prices, to encourage creative re-use of material, which would otherwise remain as deadstock.

Developed with a sustainable vision, Nona Source favours local distribution. Because stocks are located in France, the platform will for the time being deliver within Europe and the UK.

An all-digital experience, Nona Source provides an innovative solution for creatives. The catalogue proposes a wide variety of prestigious materials, from lace to leathers in different compositions, weights, colours, and patterns. Only exclusive patterns or branded fabrics are not available. All materials are carefully selected and re-valued at competitive prices. Product characteristics are presented in minute detail thanks to high-quality visuals, videos to translate the touch and feel experience, plus displays on wooden mannequins for fall and drape visualisation. Thanks to high-fidelity colour data and a digital sensorial experience to faithfully characterise these luxury materials, professionals can purchase rolls, skins or panels, depending on available quantities, without cutting or sampling.

FIGURE 2.2   Nona Source Showroom Paris @La Caserne. Credit
             Nona Source

FIGURE 2.3   Storage of fabric rolls. Credit Nona Source

CIRCULAR RANGES AND PRODUCTS FROM PLASTIC

Plastic is another material commonly used by the fashion industry that raises sustainability concerns. It is recognised that plastic has a severe environmental impact. The disposal of plastic is particularly problematic as it is not biodegradable, taking up to 1,000 years to break down in the environment. Moreover, if it is incinerated, it releases toxic gases. While most plastic can be recycled, this is a complex and expensive process, so most plastic is not. As of today, some fashion companies have begun to reduce and even eliminate their use of plastics in their manufacturing and supply chains. As covered in Chapter 1 (**CONSCIOUS ITEM**), there are also companies innovating with plastic, one company is **Aquafil** who are also working with post-consumer plastic to create **ECONYL.**

Circular products and ranges are now being offered by some of the leading brands, whereby a product can be remade. An example of this is **Napapijri's** "Infinity" Jacket which is 100% recyclable and circular, the jacket's main material is Nylon 6, which is made from ECONYL. The success of the Infinity jacket led the brand to launch their Circular Series, a range of fully recyclable jackets which have been recognised with the prestigious

FIGURE 2.4 mixed nylon waste. Credit Econyl/Aquafil

CRADLE TO CRADLE CERTIFIED® Gold certification (See Chapter 7, **GOVERNANCE** for more information on this), the world's most advanced standard for safe, circular, and responsible materials and products.

INCREASING THE LIFESPAN OF A GARMENT THROUGH AFTERCARE

Customers are moving away from a culture of disposable fashion products; they want items that have longer life and this is now becoming a signal of value. Product lifespan is becoming a key driver in purchasing decisions.

How consumers care for their garments is an important consideration when examining the environmental impact of the garment. Awareness of the effects of over washing and other factors such as the renewed interest in the second-hand resale market (featured in the sections below), is also making consumers think about the importance of keeping items in a wearable and potentially sellable condition.

In order to educate customers and help them to keep their items in a wearable condition for longer, some fashion brands are now dedicating space on their websites or in their stores to provide detailed information on how to look after and care for the items being sold. Some fashion brands are now selling sustainable washing capsules or providing links to local

FIGURE 2.5   Repair as a key priority. This photo shows Zalando's care and repair service. Credit Zalando

cleaning and repair companies. This reinforces the fashion brand's sustainable credentials and also creates a new product category and revenue stream for the brand.

FASHION INDUSTRY EXAMPLES

Swedish fashion brand **Monki** launched a sustainability campaign called Monki Cares; in the video campaign models offer advice and display a hotline number to call for more guidance on how to be more environmentally friendly. American outdoor clothing brand **Patagonia** provides specific care tips on its website which further supports the consumer after they have purchased from the brand. Detailed advice is provided on washing, ironing, and dry cleaning, there is also an informative section on Microfiber Pollution Prevention.

MINI CASE STUDY

Stella McCartney partnered with textile care association Clevercare to produce a witty 1950's infomercial style campaign to teach people how to care for denim and the importance of understanding wool's self-cleaning properties.

The luxury brand also promotes "five easy ways to adopt a sustainable laundry routine," those are:

Think twice about washing
Wondering how often should you wash your clothes? Washing them regularly uses an incredible amount of water; often, methods such as airing and brushing your pieces are enough to keep them clean. Consider spot cleaning for any small stains.

Keep it cool

Wash care labels indicate the highest temperature allowed for cleaning specific items without compromising their quality. A simple way to extend the life of your clothes is to wash them at a lower temperature and hang instead of tumble dry. Studies recommend washing at 30°C rather than 40°C, as this small change in temperature reduces electricity consumption by approximately 40% and provides better care for your clothing.

Take it outside

Tumble drying accounts for 60% of the energy used during laundering. We recommend hanging your clothes up to dry whenever possible – it's better for the environment and for your pieces. Washing cotton garments at lower temperatures and then air-drying them reduces the total lifecycle energy consumption by two times.

Crease free, the easy way

Think of ironing only when really necessary. Often, you can avoid creases and folds by taking hang-dried laundry in the bathroom while showering. The steam will naturally remove creases, saving effort and energy from ironing.

Go green when you dry clean

When it comes to dry cleaning, the best option is to look for an eco or green dry cleaner. The chemicals used by most dry cleaners can harm air quality, the health of employees, and your own well-being. To avoid dry cleaning altogether, remember that cashmere, cotton, and most wools are easily hand-washed in the sink or on a delicate cycle.

Source: Stella McCartney

FIGURE 2.6   Image of person checking care label. Credit Shutterstock/ Kmpzzz

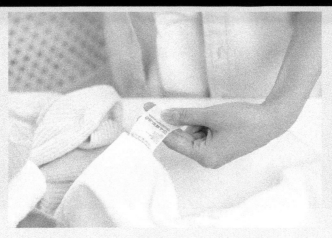

REPAIR

"Make do and mend" and home crafting schemes support those wanting to prolong the life of their product, whether it be due to sustainability concerns or because they want to save money. As mentioned above, conscious consumers are turning away from cheaper (often deemed disposable) items and instead are purchasing garments they think will last longer and hold their value. Even if those items might need repairing or refurbishing.

Things that aren't new aren't necessarily old, and ready to discard and fashion brands are now realising there is a massive opportunity to add in additional services, such as repair spaces and educational workshops to engage with a growing group of mindful consumers.

Repair services and workshops reinforce a consumer belief that the product offered by the brand is of a good quality and worth holding on to; it is also potentially another revenue stream for those brands.

FASHION INDUSTRY EXAMPLES

The Restory is a UK company that provides an on-demand service of modern aftercare for luxury fashion. The company repairs and refreshes shoes, bags, and leather goods.

In February 2022, fashion retailer **Uniqlo** launched a repair service within its flagship New York store. For a small fee, the retailer's

FIGURE 2.7   The process of repairing a shoe. Credit Zalando

experienced in-house alterations staff will mend small tears and busted zips, while more extensive jobs are offered a one-to-one consultation to discuss requirements.

MINI CASE STUDY

British menswear brand **RAEBURN DESIGN** has brought sustainable design to a mainstream fashion audience. The brand's **RÆMADE** range pioneers the reworking of surplus fabrics and garments to create distinctive and functional pieces. The brand's creative fashion studio in Hackney, East London, UK regularly hosts monthly events, discussions, and workshops on the subject of sustainable design.

"I think as a designer you have an obligation to consider what you are doing and why; ultimately we want to make strong, responsible choices that provide our customers with a completely unique and desirable product."

Christopher Raeburn, Creative Director. RAEBURN DESIGN.

Moreover, every decision the brand makes as a business is underpinned by their 4 R's as explained by the company below:

RÆMADE, RÆDUCED, RÆCYCLED, and RÆBURN

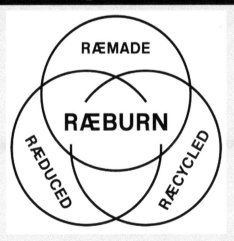

FIGURE 2.8. RÆBURN-ETHOS_LOGO. Credit RAEBURN DESIGN

RÆMADE

Paramount to the RÆBURN philosophy since 2001 is RÆMADE, reworking surplus materials, products, and artefacts into completely new designs. Every RÆMADE piece is a limited edition, proudly cut and reconstructed in England.

RÆDUCED

Designs developed at the RÆBURN Lab are considered for their impact on the environment. Whether reworking surplus materials, minimising carbon footprint with local manufacturing, or simply producing smaller batches, waste can be **RÆDUCED**.

RÆCYCLED

Seeking the most sustainable materials around the globe, and working with responsible manufacturing partners is key to the RÆBURN brand. RÆCYCLING pre-existing materials and harnessing green technologies is fundamental to our production process.

Source: RAEBURN DESIGN

FIGURE 2.9   RAEBURN DESIGN LOGO. Credit RAEBURN DESIGN

Additionally, The Lab E20 was designed in partnership with RAEBURN DESIGN, Get Living, East Village, FutureCity, and Tuesday Design. The Lab E20 is a 3,000 sq. ft. co-creative hub in Victory Plaza, Stratford. It is part retail, part workshop, part studio, installation space, and film room. The space forms a creative call to arms for others; and is aimed to be a springboard for positive change.

FIGURE 2.10   RÆBURN E20. Credit Ben Broomfield

MINI CASE STUDY

Arc'teryx has created and launched **ReBird**™ which is a series of initiatives in upcycling, resale, care, and repair, that guides Arc'teryx users, supporting them in the move towards a more circular way of operating.

Additional insights into ReBird and their approach to circularity at Arc'teryx are detailed by the brand below.

- We practice responsible product creation and delivery. Our hope is to place the promise of circularity at the centre of our business practices moving forward. We're not there yet, but we're excited for what's to come.
- We are working to take responsibility for the land we occupy and the product we produce. We believe in holding ourselves to high standards: we set and achieve annual sustainability objectives based on scientific targets. We are building a circular business model based on our moral obligation to serve our planet.
- Our product durability keeps product on your back and in your hands longer, and out of landfills. Care and repair, ReGear, and upcycling are an added promise of premium service as elevated as the original product itself.

- Our approach to circularity is known as ReBird and is currently comprised of 3 programs:

  - **Care & Repair: our ongoing global warranty offering.** Our products are made to last, and offering Care & Repair services allows us to extend their lifespan even further. We are building out physical ReBird Service Centres into our retail stores as part of our commitment to extending the life of our products.
  - **ReGear: the resale of previously used and repaired products, product samples, and more.** Our resale program is available in the US and Canada, online via Arcteryx.com. We are looking to expand our resale capabilities into NAM retail and beyond North America once we can scale our operations for trade-in and repair to support resale expansion. Trade-in is valued against a standard 20% of the original MSRP of each item.
  - **Upcycling: creating products out of end-of-life raw materials, offered under the ReBIRD program.** We are hoping to extend learnings from internal design testing as well as workshops, in order to determine how best to utilise post-consumer materials that are far beyond repair but still offer an opportunity to be refurbished and created into something new.

This ethos and commitment is communicated very clearly throughout **Arc'teryx**'s New York flagship which opened in 2021.

Source: Arc'teryx

FIGURE 2.11   ReBird Service Centre Arcteryx New York store. Credit Arc'teryx

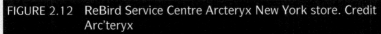

FIGURE 2.12 ReBird Service Centre Arcteryx New York store. Credit Arc'teryx

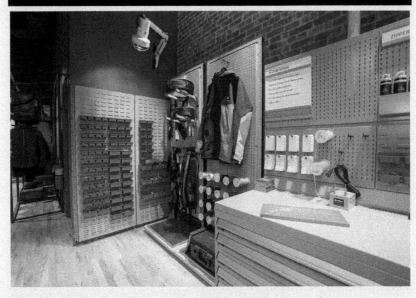

FIGURE 2.13 ReBird Service Centre Arcteryx New York store. Credit Arc'teryx

BUY AND GIVE BACK SCHEMES

Schemes that allow the customer to return items in exchange for vouchers or discounts on new collections are starting to become popular in the new retail landscape and are connecting well with the new budget conscious, circular shopper. These schemes are also a clever way to keep the consumer loyal to a specific fashion brand, while further promoting positive brand associations, reinforcing the notion that the fashion brand cares about the environment and understands the importance of the circular economy.

Within the industry there is a concern about encouraging donations in order to push the consumer to buy again, as this action could be seen as something that actually encourages more consumption. However, at least these buy-back schemes are now helping to promote recycling in a commercially desirable way to many consumers that might not have considered recycling their item otherwise. It is likely that financial incentive schemes will be a key driver to mainstream mass recycling for future fashion businesses.

FASHION INDUSTRY EXAMPLES

In 2020, British brand **Mulberry** introduced a second-hand and buy-back scheme. In this scheme, customers are given a gift card worth 25% of the original selling price when they return the item. The second-hand bags Mulberry receives are then sent for restoration at their factory in Somerset. After this process the brand then sells the revived second-hand items in their flagship store in Bond Street or on their website.

In 2018, French brand **APC** launched their recycling program. The scheme allows customers to return old APC products in exchange for store credit, the amount given depends on the item's condition. APC then ships the garments to a recycling facility to be broken down into fibres; those fibres are then used to make new garments.

Global fashion business **H&M** picks up tonnes of unwanted clothing per day as part of its in-house recycling program. Customers bring in unwanted items from any brand and are given redeemable vouchers to spend on new products. The fashion company then either donate or recycle these items into lower quality products.

People Tree has a partnership with the Give Back Box. After a new item of People Tree clothing has been purchased, customers can reuse the packaging and send unwanted clothes and household items to charity, free of charge.

PRESERVING THE ARCHIVE

Some luxury fashion brands are putting resources into building spaces and in some cases even museums in which to house their past collections. Fondation Pierre Bergé, Yves Saint Laurent opened two museums in 2017, in Paris and Marrakech, to celebrate the work of its founder Yves Saint Laurent. In

2011, The Gucci Museum opened in Florence. Celebrating historical products also helps to showcase a brand's heritage, products like pieces of art, to be kept and admired, the opposite of fast fashion.

In the expert insight following, Professor Andrew Groves discusses the importance of fashion archives for sustainable fashion practice and explains why he started the Menswear Archive at the University of Westminster.

Expert insight from Professor Andrew Groves: Archives as a sustainable design practice
Director Westminster Menswear Archive, University of Westminster

Over the past decade, the value of garment archives in the fashion industry has increased, not only as a means for fashion brands to reinforce their brand history with consumers, but also as a more sustainable method of design research and development. However, the fashion industry has long employed garment archives as a method for conducting object-based research. Massimo Osti, who founded C.P. Company in 1971 and Stone Island in 1982, amassed an archive of over 33,000 garments that was integral to his design process. Utilising predominantly military or utilitarian workwear, he would enlarge details such as pockets by photocopying them and then pinning them to an archive garment. Using a collage-based approach to design, he was able to generate designs more rapidly and communicate to factories the desired level of construction quality he wished to achieve.

Over the past 50 years, Osti's approach quickly became a standard industry within menswear with designers such as Nigel Cabourn, Neil Barrett, and Paul Harvey building their vast private collections that have been indispensable to their design processes. It has also resulted in the establishment of several specialised commercial archives to satisfy the industry's demand for research access to source garments. Such establishments include Modateca Deanna in Reggio Emilia, Italy, Artifact NYC in New York, and the Vintage Showroom in London. However, while large fashion brands are willing to disclose their use of their own archives as a source of inspiration, the use of commercial archives to a research designer, industrial and military clothing is rarely acknowledged. The invisibility of this practice means that students may not realise that this is a legitimate means of fashion research.

Due to this reluctance to discuss the process, many may believe that it consists solely of copying a pre-existing design. Yet while this may be one use, it is much more likely that a designer will use archival material to inform new design outcomes by integrating the aesthetic qualities, materiality, and cut and construction of a garment. Prototyping a collection from scratch is a time-consuming, expensive, and material-intensive endeavour that requires a substantial quantity of raw materials. The use of object-based research through garment archives expedites this process internally, allowing for quicker decisions to be made, especially when a company's production and sampling may be located overseas. In addition, it accelerates communication with factories by using existing garments as references for existing materials or processes, enabling designers to build upon previously established manufacturing techniques.

I founded the Westminster Menswear Archive in 2015 in order to incorporate this object-based research into the fashion design curriculum at University of Westminster. The archive houses over 2,000 garments and fills a significant gap in the UK's existing collections of dress by focusing on menswear design. The archives are open to any students, researchers, or designers who wish to view them. For those who are unable to visit in person, www.mensweararchive.com provides an online catalogue with images of the garments.

The Westminster Menswear Archive is utilised by designers from some of the world's biggest and most influential brands, allowing students to observe their research processes and appreciate the significance of studying material culture as part of their design process. It has also resulted in radical changes in the way students think about their design processes and improved their outcomes by providing them with access to exemplary examples of design that enable their work to build on the design and manufacturing techniques developed by previous generations. As a result, it supports a more sustainable approach to research and design that generates better outcomes for all.

FIGURE 2.14.   Professor Andrew Groves in the UoW Menswear Archive. Credit Jamie McGregor Smith

FIGURE 2.15 UoW Menswear Archive. Credit Jamie McGregor Smith

SECOND-HAND MARKET (RESALE)

The biggest incentive to buy second hand is actually affordability, as second-hand products are often sold at a lower price. It has now become vitally important for fashion brands to incorporate alternative business models such as pre-owned into their existing offers in order to connect with the budget conscious, circular minded shopper.

The buying and selling of second-hand items removes the need for the continued creation of new items, therefore resale is often seen as being a sustainable option. However, the operations and the processes that support resale also need to be considered, resale is certainly not the only answer.

The second-hand market sits at all levels of the fashion industry, from the luxury sector to the high street. Through resale programs fashion brands can further connect with their customer, allowing them to shop and engage with the brand at a different stage of the product life cycle.

Second-hand marketing is growing rapidly; some statistics are forecasting that the resale market will be twice as big as fast fashion by 2030. Fast fashion is predicted to lose many of its consumers who are soon likely to want to buy fewer items and focus on products that are better in quality and therefore have a higher resale value.

FIGURE 2.16   Secondhand clothing. Credit Shutterstock / Iamjohnholt

Expert insight from Felix Kruger

Felix Kruger, Partner and Associate Director, Fashion & Luxury at the Boston Consulting Group, explains the opportunity around pre owned consumption.

The desire to reduce one's negative environmental impact is growing, as is the number of new clothing lines marketed as "sustainable." But what about when you buy something brand new? What are your alternatives?

Second-hand buyers are a rapidly growing segment of the global luxury market. Some luxury brands and retailers did not consider the second-hand market in the past, but as new players enter and consumer interest grows, this is becoming an increasingly interesting route for them.

A recent BCG survey (2020) of 7,000 people from six countries, fuelled by customer data from Vestiaire Collective, revealed new insights into the trend. It forecasts that the global used market will grow at a compound annual growth rate (CAGR) of 15% to 20% over the next five years.

Second-hand luxury sales are increasing due to a variety of factors, including increased online sales, shifting consumer preferences, and growing concern about the sustainability of luxury goods, particularly among younger consumers. These trends were already in motion prior to the COVID-19 outbreak, but the pandemic, and the resulting economic slowdown, has amplified them.

Moreover, in this new post COVID context, social media and digitisation are becoming increasingly influential in driving purchases and providing consumers with easier access to personalised premium second-hand services. These new channels help emphasise the value of heritage storytelling in shaping a brand's identity.

Customers are shopping second-hand to fill their wardrobes with unique, cost-effective items in a sustainable manner. They will do so in the coming years as well. There are numerous advantages for brands that capitalise on this trend. Therefore, brands at all levels of the market should assess these shifts and, equally important, recognise how second-hand consumers may evolve to become buyers of full price, in season luxury items.

Brands can capitalise on the expanding market in a variety of ways. They stand to benefit from the new circular economy just as much as their customers, but in order to reap the full benefits, they must first understand where the opportunities are.

The pre-owned consumption is an unmissable opportunity for brands and it is here to stay.

FASHION BRAND EXAMPLES

eBay is a global commerce platform that connects millions of buyers and sellers in more than 190 markets around the world. eBay states that they "exist to enable economic opportunity for individuals, entrepreneurs, businesses and organisations of all sizes."

Depop is a fashion marketplace app where consumers can discover unique items. They position themselves as a "global community buying, selling and connecting to make fashion more inclusive, diverse and less wasteful." In 2021, American company Etsy bought Depop, for a reported $1.6bn (£1.1bn).

Founded in 2009, **Vestiaire Collective** launched with the aim of offering a high quality resale site in which members can buy and sell luxury fashion in a trusted environment. In March 2021, luxury French group, Kering took a 5% equity stake in the company further highlighting the interest in luxury resale in the longer term.

The RealReal is an online marketplace for authenticated, used luxury goods. The company markets itself as having a "rigorous authentication process, overseen by experts." The company also offers extra support to consumers by offering a free in-home pickup, drop-off service, virtual appointments, and direct shipping services.

Expert insight from Gemma A. Williams: Changing consumption patterns in China

Gemma A. Williams is a globally-focused writer and curator with a particular interest in the China market and Chinese designers. She is the Editorial Director at luxury Chinese publication, Jing Daily.

In a recent survey from Daxue consulting in 2022, almost 90% of Gen Z and Millennials had altered their shopping decisions due to environmental sustainability concerns at least once over the previous six months, whilst over 32% had adjusted their shopping behaviour once a month.

Although there are still reservations around second-hand clothing, the resale sector has been growing steadily. Again, tech has been instrumental there; platforms like Plum, Ponhu, and Feiyu are enabling users to offer their preloved goods. According to a study by the Beijing-based China Center for Internet Economy Research, the resale market surged to $154 billion in 2020.

Physical second-hand stores have opened up and citizens have become more accustomed to the concert of donating and repurposing unwanted items at stores or collection bins now located in most major cities.

THE SHARING ECONOMY (RENTAL)

The sharing economy has taken traditional behaviours such as sharing, swapping, lending and renting, and with the help of technology, made them more in tune with the modern consumer. Before the Internet, renting an item was feasible, but could take a lot of time and customers would have to hunt out specific and suitable stores for the right items. Renting items also appeals to customers who cannot afford to own a product or do not have sufficient need to do so; and in line with the times, it also fosters a spirit of sustainability.

The renting and borrowing of items removes the need for the continued creation of new items, and products are worn time and time again by different users, therefore rental, like resale, is often seen as being a sustainable option. However, something to consider, is that some of the operations and processes themselves might not necessarily be more sustainable than the full price, in season selling model. The following chapters and other parts of **The Responsible 9 Framework** need to be considered and used

FIGURE 2.17 Clothing for rent. Credit Shutterstock / Piotr Swat

by rental (and resale) businesses too, if they also want to be seen as being a truly responsible business in the longer term.

FASHION INDUSTRY EXAMPLES

Thelittleloop is a UK children's clothing rental subscription platform offering shared clothes for growing infants. Its credit system gives a fixed monthly plan (available at three levels) that provides a range of clothing from partner brands. Customers can keep the items as long as they wish, gaining the credits back once the clothing is returned. Between rentals, items are carefully reconditioned and repaired.

Rent the Runway (RTR) is an American e-commerce platform that allows users to rent, subscribe, or buy designer apparel and accessories. It was founded by Jennifer Hyman and Jennifer Fleiss, who launched the company in November 2009. RTR offers apparel, accessories, and home decor from over 700 designer partners and has built in-house proprietary technology and a one-of-a-kind reverse logistics operation.

THE CONSUMER AS THE INVESTOR

The consumer is already starting to buy brands based on what they are worth in the second-hand market, the product's value is incorporated into their purchasing decision. Moreover, when considering the amount of unworn clothing in wardrobes all over the world, it could be agreed that the resale opportunity is potentially massive and the movement to second-hand has only just begun. Simply put, new cost conscious but sustainably enthused consumers are realising that they don't need more; they need to wear or sell what they already have.

The shopper is starting to see that items purchased can now also be worthwhile investments, and ones that can potentially offer an income stream if they are sold in the future.

FASHION INDUSTRY EXAMPLES

MINI CASE STUDY

Californian brand **Patagonia** has a "Worn Wear" scheme, which helps its customers care for the garments they buy from the brand. The program provides resources to support responsible care, repair, and resale through their "Worn Wear" in-store events.

Worn Wear is further explained on Patagonia's website:

Worn Wear is Patagonia's hub for keeping gear in play.

Why extend the life of gear? Because the best thing we can do for the planet is cut down on consumption and get more use out of stuff we already own.

One of the most responsible things we can do as a company is make high-quality stuff that lasts for years, so you don't have to buy more of it.

Buying used extends a garments life by about two years, which drastically reduces both our reliance on virgin resources and our generation of waste.

Trade in, Get Paid, if you have an old Patagonia item that is just sitting around, we'll give you credit towards your next purchase on a used or new garment. Start a trade-in below to learn more.

_____

Source: Patagonia

MINI CASE STUDY

Global sportswear giant **Nike** has launched Nike Refurbished. The company now sells like new, less worn, and aesthetically flawed shoes. Each pair of shoes is refurbished by hand before being put back on sale.

Shoes that are too damaged to be refurbished will still be recycled or donated to community groups.

Nike footwear that cannot be sold as new is then turned into a Refurbished product. This includes pairs returned or exchanged because they weren't quite right, or shoes with small imperfections coming from a manufacturing facility.

The Nike Refurbished process is further explained by the company:

> How **It Works**
> **We Inspect It:** Our experts examine footwear that cannot be sold as new like returns, exchanges, or shoes with a slight imperfection.
> **We Grade It:** If it's eligible for resale, it's given a grade: Like New, Gently Worn, or Cosmetically Flawed.
> Our Grading System:
>
> 1. Like New: Perfect or near perfect condition. The shoes have no signs of wear or flaws.
> 2. Gently Worn: These shoes are in great condition with viable light wear or cosmetic flaws.
> 3. Cosmetically Flawed: No sign of wear, but slightly imperfect (like a stain, a mark, discoloration, or fading).
>
> **You Wear It:** After being carefully cleaned, Refurbished shoes are sold at select stores at a reduced price.
> **Like New. For less.**
>
> _____
>
> *Source: Nike*

THE NEW CONSCIOUS PRIORITY

Shoppers are becoming increasingly mindful of their purchases, choosing products that are sourced responsibly, that are good for the environment, and that last for longer. Fashion brands need to adapt to the growing interest in ethics and sustainability if they want to remain relevant to their consumers. Fashion brands also need to educate their consumers to help them make sustainable decisions, they need to teach shoppers about how they can recycle products at the end of their lifespan and ensure that old clothing isn't going to landfill by offering incentives if brought back to them.

Brands need to continually be thinking whether their whole product offer is connecting with the more environmentally aware and concerned consumer, failure to meet the needs of this new type of shopper will have huge implications for any fashion brand. This topic is addressed by Laura Coppen and Daniel Newton, from German retailer Zalando in the expert insight on the following page.

Expert insight from Laura Coppen
Head of Circularity at Zalando and Daniel Newton Senior Expert Circularity at Zalando.

Zalando's overall sustainability vision is "to have a net positive impact on people and planet," they state "we are committed to making our business and the industry better, to be a business that does not simply do less bad, but fundamentally makes the world a better place for generations to come."

It is clear that we, as a business, cannot infinitely grow on a planet with finite resources. To deliver on both our ambition to triple the business by 2025 and sustainability vision, we must decouple our growth from resource use in the longer term. Circularity is an enabler of our net positive vision, built off three key guiding principles;

1. Eliminate waste and pollution.
2. Circulate materials and products.
3. Regenerate natural systems.

Our focus with circular design and circular business models provide a desirable and viable alternative to the industry's current linear model.

We launched our first circularity strategy in 2021 and now work holistically across all four circularity stages:

1. Design and Manufacture: How a product is designed to eliminate waste and cycle through multiple use-phases.
2. Use: How a product is used and maintained through care and repair advice, products, and services.
3. Re-Use: How the next life/lives of a product is enabled, through resale, sharing, and rental.
4. Closing the Loop: How a product is recycled or returned to the earth at the end of its useful life.

Use stage problem:

If we zoom into the Use Stage of the product life cycle which covers how a product is used and maintained within its original intended purpose, usually with the same owner (e.g. through care or repair actions), and is a key focus area in addressing the waste challenges and driving a circular economy. It is estimated that 45% of garments are thrown away due to stains, up to 90% of which could be removed with professional cleaning. In fact, it is estimated that 82% of textiles that are considered waste could be cleaned, repaired and resold again.[3] The result is that today, a garment is worn an average of just 7 times and each garment is kept for half as long as it was 15 years ago. Zalando internal research on the attitude behaviour gap of customers has found that 58% of consumers feel care and repair is important to them, but just 23% of them actually take action to repair their fashion items. A lack of knowledge on how to repair fashion items at home, particularly among young people, coupled with a lack of convenient, quality, and cost-effective services, advice, and tools represents an opportunity for Zalando in the Care & Repair space.

Zalando's care and repair service:

To close this particular gap, Zalando launched an innovative care and repair pilot in Berlin, in October 2021, partnering with tech company Save Your Wardrobe. Customers can enter a one-stop shop for care and repair services connecting to local, trusted, and high-quality repair, shoe cleaning, and alteration service providers. We partnered with Fairsenden, a German zero emissions delivery startup who utilise reusable packaging for the pick up and drop off of care and repair customer requests.

Customers highlighted the quality of the physical repair service, both in terms of the outcome and the skill required to conduct such a level of output. One customer "intentionally chose a very difficult item to repair" and afterwards they "couldn't even tell the hole was there at all." This highlights the quality of the local partners we are working with, but also the fact that perhaps some consumers are not aware of the capabilities of seamsters, perhaps accelerating the throwaway culture that is impacting the longevity of use of their items. Customers also emphasised the convenience of the model, with one stating they have "been waiting for a service like this." Our research suggests that 50% of consumers have at least one item at home that requires repair, however they don't repair based on the time and effort required. Zalando aims to help customers keep their loved items in use for as long as possible making it convenient and fun to do so. Our service is the start of a journey to learn more about customer needs, iterate and eventually scale up the successes.

FIGURE 2.18   Zalando's care and repair service. Credit Zalando

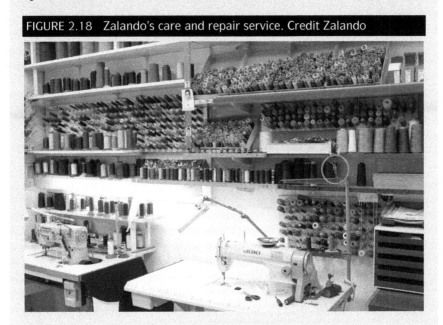

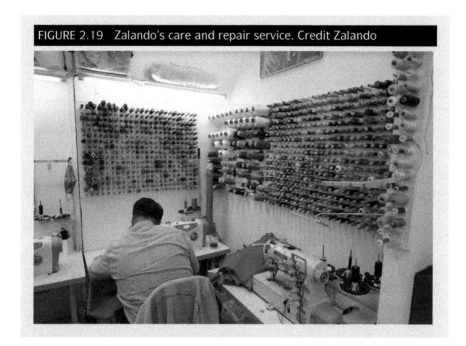

FIGURE 2.19   Zalando's care and repair service. Credit Zalando

This chapter has provided insight into how important it is for fashion brands to incorporate a CIRCULAR SERVICE. Key takeaways include:

- Fashion brands need to look at innovative ways to work with waste and this also resonates well with the customer.
- Repair should be offered to customers, further supporting product longevity and the customers renewed interest in maintaining their items for longer.
- Buy back schemes should be developed by fashion brands in order to communicate to the customer that a fashion brand's product has value even at the end of its life. This then further incentivises the customer to choose the best option.
- Flawed and refurbished items have a value too, these can be sold at a discounted price to the new sustainably minded customer who has the ability to mend items.
- The second-hand market in fashion will continue to grow, therefore the selling of older, often pre-used product should be embedded in standard fashion business practice.
- The sharing economy will continue to be important so rental options should be considered in order to connect with the customer who doesn't value ownership and who wants access to a product at a cheaper price for a limited time.
- The customer will get more powerful and peer-to-peer networks will be commonly used, therefore fashion brands needs to acknowledge this change and connect with their customers by altering their own practice and behaviour.

FURTHER READING

Clodfelter, R. (2014). *Retail Buying: From Basics to Fashion*, 4th edition, Fairchild Books.

Ellen MacArthur Foundation (2017). A New Textiles Economy: Redesigning Fashion's Future, Ellen MacArthur Foundation.

Ellen MacArthur Foundation (2021). Circular Design for Fashion, Ellen MacArthur Foundation.

Gardelti, M. (2019). *Sustainable Luxury and Social Entrepreneurship Stories from Pioneers*, Routledge.

Ottman, J. (2012). *The New Rules of Green Marketing*, Berrett-Koehler.

Posner, H. (2015). *Marketing Fashion*, London, Laurence King Publishing.

Renewal Workshop Report, Leading Circular: Pathways for Evolving Apparel and Textile Businesses from Linear to Circular.

Solomon, M.R. and Rabolt, N.J. (2008). *Consumer Behaviour in Fashion*, 2nd edition, Prentice Hall.

Varley, R. (2014). *Retail Product Management Buying and Merchandising*, 3rd edition. Routledge.

Varley, R., Radclyffe-Thomas, N., and Webb, W. (2018). Patagonia: Creative Sustainable Strategy for a Reluctant Fashion Brand. Bloomsbury.

WEB MATERIAL

Amed, I. et al. (2019). The End of Ownership for Fashion Products? Retrieved from: www.mckinsey.com/industries/retail/our-insights/the-end-of-ownership-for-fashion-products.

BCG Global (2020). The Consumers Behind Fashion's Growing Secondhand Market. Retrieved from: www.bcg.com/press/2november2020-the-consumers-behind-fashions-growing-secondhand-market.

BCG (2022). Consumer Segments Behind Growing Secondhand Fashion.

Chen, C. (2021). The Resale Gold Rush Rolls On. The Business of Fashion. Retrieved from: www.businessoffashion.com/articles/retail/the-resale-gold-rush-rolls-on/.

Crocker, R. et al. (2018). Unmaking Waste in Production and Consumption: Towards the Circular Economy. Bingley: Emerald Publishing Limited. Retrieved from: https://books.emeraldinsight.com/page/detail/unmaking-waste-in-production-and-consumption/?k=9781787146204.

Dean, C. (2020). Waste – Is it 'Really' in Fashion? Fashion Revolution. Retrieved from: www.fashionrevolution.org/waste-is-it-really-in-fashion/.

Edie. (2022). Allbirds Launches Shoe Resale Platform as Part of Circular Economy Efforts. Retrieved from: www.edie.net/allbirds-launches-shoe-resale-platform-as-part-of-circular-economy-efforts/#:~:text=?-,Allbirds%20launches%20shoe%20resale%20platform%20as%20part%20of%20circular%20economy,lifetime%20of%20products%20by%202025.

Edited. (2021). The Guide to Sustainable Sportswear. As Edited.com is a paid subscription website, there is something very similar on the website of Ecoage, 2019, available at: www.eco-age.com/resources/sustainability-and-sportswear.

Ellson, A. (2018). Clothes Worth £12.5bn are Thrown in the Bin. The Times. Retrieved from: www.thetimes.co.uk/article/clothes-worth-12-5bn-are-thrown-in-bin-b8rqfrcg2#:~:text=Britons%20binned%20clothes%20worth%20£,almost%20£500%2C%20research%20found.

Fashion Revolution (2021). The Fashion Transparency Index 2021. Retrieved from: www.fashionrevolution.org/about/transparency-index-2021/.

Fish, I. (2022). Freight Prices Fall as Consumers Cut Back on Fashion. Drapers. Retrieved from: www.drapersonline.com/news/freight-prices-fall-as-consumers-cut-back-on-fashion?tkn=1.

Heinrichs, H. (2013). Sharing Economy: A Potential New Pathway to Sustainability. GAIA-Ecol. Perspect. Sci. Soc. Retrieved from: www.researchgate.net/publication/263058344_Sharing_Economy_A_Potential_New_Pathway_to_Sustainability.

Hobson, K. and Lynch, N. (2016). Diversifying and De-growing the Circular Economy: Radical Social Transformation in a Resource-scarce World. Retrieved from: www.sciencedirect.com/science/article/abs/pii/S0016328716300246/.

Jing Daily. Luxury Resale is China's Next Retail Battleground. Retrieved from: https://jingdaily.com/luxury-resale-is-chinas-next-retail-battleground/.

Lamberton, C.P. and Rose, R.L. (2012). When Is Ours Better Than Mine? A Framework for Understanding and Altering Participation in Commercial Sharing Systems. Retrieved from: https://journals.sagepub.com/doi/10.1509/jm.10.0368.

Light, A. and Miskelly, C. (2015). Sharing Economy vs Sharing Cultures? Designing for Social, Economic and Environmental Good. Interact. Des. Archit. Retrieved from: www.semanticscholar.org/paper/Sharing-Economy-vs-Sharing-Cultures-Designing-for-Light-Miskelly/286cccacaf30bf22a4a8d154d9302af8f41ff1d3.

Martin, C.J. (2016). The Sharing Economy: A Pathway to Sustainability or a Nightmarish Form of Neoliberal Capitalism? Retrieved from: https://ideas.repec.org/a/eee/ecolec/v121y2016icp149-159.html.

Mellor, S. (2021). Changing Fashions: Retailers are Dealing with Deadstock More Openly. Fortune. Retrieved from: https://fortune.com/2021/04/29/retail-deadstock-unsold-clothes-fashion-supply-chain-covid/.

BRAND REFERENCES

https://ahluwalia.world.
www.apc.fr.
www.arcteryx.com.
www.depop.com.
www.hm.com.
www.ebay.co.uk.
www.mulberry.com.
www.monki.com.
www.napapijri.com.
www.nona-source.com.
https://eu.patagonia.com.
www.peopletree.co.uk.
www.stellamccartney.com.
www.the-restory.com.
www.uniqlo.com.
www.raeburndesign.co.uk.
www.renttherunway.com.
https://thelittleloop.com.
www.therealreal.com.
https://us.vestiairecollective.com.
www.zalando.co.uk.

CHAPTER 3

The Responsible 9 Framework

#3 = Community

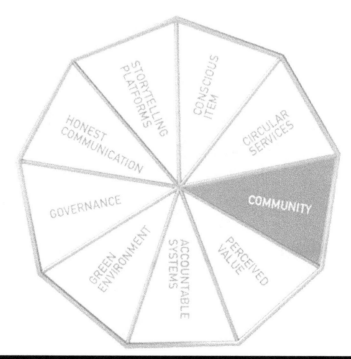

THE RESPONSIBLE 9 FRAMEWORK: #3 = COMMUNITY

DOI: 10.4324/9781003285915-4

INTRODUCTION TO THE CHAPTER

It is often stated that a business is only as good as its people, and that a business' greatest asset is its employees. Whilst this is undoubtedly true, a business is more than simply a sum of its individual people, it is about the community and culture it co-creates and fosters with its employees. When employees know they are working within a community of people who share a common purpose and values, their effort and output becomes more meaningful and their purpose within the organisation becomes more defined.

While the leadership team within a fashion business sets the direction, culture, and values it is the employees that touch, implement, and grow the community, not leadership. All employees, from the shop-floor sales staff, the people who design, garment makers, through to the management team all play their role in growing a business' community.

Community and the company's culture are key elements of any business. One of the driving forces underpinning community and galvanising culture within a fashion business is the role and actions the business is doing to connect to important social issues.

Fashion businesses need a clear and responsible approach to their culture and values so that the community that work inside it are engaged and feel a sense of worth and purpose.

FIGURE 3.1   Diversity in the workplace. Shutterstock/ Ndab Creativity

In this chapter the book will examine the tools and strategies businesses are using to grow and foster community, these include:

- Corporate Social Responsibility (CSR).
- Mission Statements.
- Diversity within the workforce.
- Equal representation within advertising.
- Volunteer programs.
- Further education.

Expert insight from Craig Crawford

2019 Tabbie award-winning author and founderprenuer of Crawford IT, (https://crawfordit.com) a London-based consulting firm specialising in the digital transformation of brands.

People are the priority – not the corporation, not the product, not the promotion, not the profit, but the people. Without the people none of these things would exist.

Throughout my career I've been fortunate to work in a variety of corporate cultures. And each of these has been very different by design. It's important to note that corporate culture by design drives success. When everyone understands the company's DNA, what the corporate strategic goals are, and how they as employees are expected to behave and contribute, everyone wins.

As a designer for the Gap (Gap Inc.) in the first half of the 1990s, I had the privilege of working for the original founders of the company, Don and Doris Fisher. The Gap had a very familial culture. It was founded by the Fisher's in 1969 as a "jeans and record" store – a place where the generation "gap" (teenagers) could spend their time and money. Headquartered in San Francisco, diversity and inclusion were part of the brand's DNA. All races, sizes, religious creeds, and sexual orientations were welcomed and embraced. I remember speaking to my Human Resources representative about the condition in my contract that Gap Inc.'s insurance would not pay for sexual transition surgery. I spoke about this not because I desired a transition, but as someone who grew up on a farm in Virginia, I was surprised that this would be discussed as a line item in my contract. Thirty years later gender re-assignment is now a mainstream topic of conversation.

As part of the New York Gap product development team, I was given the freedom and licence to explore technology, new ways of working, and new ways of manufacturing that we would vet as a group. We wore Gap clothes to work; jeans and t-shirts were our uniform. This was a mandate actually, to ensure that we loved what we created.

We interacted the way a family does: we shared our personal ups and downs, helped each other when work seemed overwhelming, celebrated successes together, and leaned on one another when personal adversity loomed (I remember consoling one co-worker when she ended a relationship because she wanted children and he did not. It was a tough decision for her as they were very much in love. Later she was my shoulder to cry on when my seven-year-old goldfish died. I laugh at this now, but I was distraught, and felt foolish at "being so attached to a fish." She saw nothing strange in that and reminded me he "had been my child.")

At the Gap we had fun. Our work structure was "unstructured" – of course we had seasonal deadlines, but there was no email (we faxed things LOL!), no defined reports, very little administrative bureaucracy. If we needed something, we asked for it. We enjoyed ourselves. We worked hard. We became friends. I am still very much in touch with many of my former Gap colleagues as we have moved on to live and work in other parts of the world.

When I began working for Liz Claiborne, Inc., the corporate culture was very different. Liz Claiborne created her collection in the 1970s when women were entering the workplace. She realised that women had little choice of career apparel – either dress like a man on Wall Street or wear frilly lacy Laura Ashley attire. No surprise then that we didn't even have "casual Friday." We were required to wear suits. Out with the casual Gap wardrobe and in with the new career gear.

Not only did we have email, but we were also issued blackberry devices and told that the expected response time to an email was no longer than 15 minutes. You can imagine what that did to a meeting. Everyone sat half participating while wildly answering emails! We had weekly, monthly, quarterly, and annual reporting structures.

The corporation was in acquisition mode, and during my decade there we acquired more than 40 brands to our portfolio. The then CEO Paul Charron hailed from Procter & Gamble, where they believed a woman would always be loyal to her soap powder, and so the only way to get another woman's detergent budget was to buy that detergent brand. The same logic was applied at "Liz."

For a fashion brand, we were so corporate that other brands referred to those of us that worked there as "Claibornauts." We were united in our quest, understood what was expected of us and got on with it. Over time, as we acquired new brands and with them new cultural expectations, Liz Claiborne, Inc. relaxed a little. We embraced dress down Friday, and ultimately casual attire every day, provided we were dressed "on portfolio." We were the first American fashion brand to embrace 25 paid days off (a nod to our acquisition of Mexx based in the Netherlands). We learned from those we brought into the portfolio of brands.

"If you need total structure, rigidity, process and the rest of it, this isn't the business for you. If you can't handle ambiguity, don't join Burberry." – anonymous Burberry associate from the anthropological study, Burberry: Staging a Culture of Creativity, Design and Innovation.

One of the reasons I left New York and moved to London to join Burberry, was Burberry's unique culture. I had experienced both a relaxed family style corporation and a more structured corporate environment during my New York career. Burberry was a blend of both, and a European locale.

We were clear on who we were – born from a cloth – and we knew where we were going. We understood the next generation luxury consumer was the millennial and we knew digital was the way forward. Armed with our strategic objectives, and empowered to "trust and connect" each other, we all had opportunities to contribute to the brand's upward trajectory.

We used to say, "Globalise because we have to, regionalise because we can." We provided collaboration platforms to connect everyone: head office to regions, store associates to head office, supply chain to head office, consumers to the brand, and the brand to our consumers. We were transparent in our journey and were delighted to have everyone celebrate and be part of it.

"We're empowered because we are confident. It's about trust. We've built a structure of people who are connecting. We have a great young team that knows they have been empowered." – anonymous Burberry executive from the anthropological study, Burberry: Staging a Culture of Creativity, Design and Innovation.

At Burberry, we had no roadmap; we invented our roadmap. This meant constant change and bringing everyone along. We all rolled our sleeves up, delivered, and then the next day asked ourselves, "what's next?"

Our culture at Burberry was so unique that we were told by the anthropological team studying us that more employees met their significant other at Burberry than any other company they had studied. We embraced diversity and inclusion. Same sex partners were allowed to take maternity leave. Gender reassignment openly occurred. We embraced our individuality – my nail varnish and manicures were as lauded as my digital contributions. I remember apologising to the then CEO Angela Ahrendts during a meeting that my nails were chipped. "Don't worry Craig," she said, "I have a teenage daughter. I know it's cool to have chipped nails."

Ask any who worked at Burberry under CEO Angela Ahrendts, and Chief Creative Officer Christopher Bailey, what they miss about Burberry, and I bet they will answer "the people."

A brand is the manifestation of the people who create and maintain it.

CORPORATE SOCIAL RESPONSIBILITY (CSR)

Corporate Social Responsibility, often shortened to the abbreviation CSR, refers to a company's commitment to manage the environmental, social, and economic effects of its business operations. Being socially responsible is a critical part of a fashion business' survival. Corporate Social Responsibility is articulated in initiatives or strategies, depending on a business' goals. Clear CSR initiatives that are acted on improve employee engagement and ultimately how they feel about the company they work for.

Businesses, including fashion businesses, are often guided by a concept known as the triple bottom line theory (TBL) developed by John Elkington in 1998.

The TBL model amalgamates three central components:

- People
- Planet
- Profit

FIGURE 3.2   Triple bottom line theory (TBL) developed by John Elkington 1997. Authors own

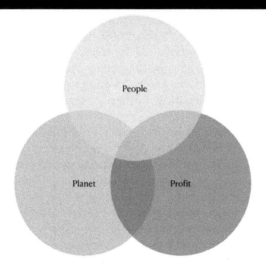

The model suggests that fashion businesses need to focus on the social and environmental aspects of operating as well as profits, in order to trade as a socially responsible retailer (Elkington, 1997).

INTRODUCING THE CITREC FRAMEWORK FOR CSR

In 2020, Lisa Nan developed the **CITREC Framework** to further explain what modern and relevant CSR strategies should include. Nann believes the implementation of CSR programs requires effort from both companies and its stakeholders; her framework provides a tool to help companies implement their CSR strategy within the company culture.

FIGURE 3.3 CITREC Framework, Nan 2022. Authors own	
1. COOPERATION	CSR cannot be achieved by the company alone, but with the help and cooperation of suppliers, consumers, employees and even the government.
2. INTEGRATION	CSR must be integrated in the company's decision making, strategy and all employee's day to day activity. It shouldn't be thought of as a surplus but an integral and essential part of the business' activities to gain competitive advantage.
3. TRANSPARENCY	CSR requires full and honest disclosure, both achievements and challenges must be transparently communicated. A transparent disclosure will allow fair measurement.
4. RESILIENCE	There is not a fixed structure for CSR, every company has its own definition and approach, it requires creativity and resilience. The transition towards sustainability oftentimes requires to disrupt the original system and it demands high responsiveness and adaptivity from the company.
5. ENGAGEMENT	Actively engaging all stakeholders and community through creating a constructive dialogue, helps to advance together as society as whole. CSR needs always to be revisited and challenged.
6. CONSISTENCY	Social and environmental responsibility should be viewed as a long term goal rather than an end point. To pursue effective and radical changes on social and environmental issues companies need to consistently address the matters. Sustainable culture is something embedded within the company, inseparable and will exist until the company exists.

Nann, 2020

FASHION INDUSTRY EXAMPLES

UK retail chain **Marks & Spencer** has a sustainability initiative named "Plan A," this impressive CSR strategy has been in place since 2007. Essentially, this is a detailed sustainability action plan, which started out as 100 separate commitments to achieve within five years, however now it is continually updated, and is one of the leading CSR strategies for any fashion retailer. Marks & Spencer works with their customers and suppliers to combat climate change, reduce waste, use sustainable raw materials, trade ethically, and help customers to lead healthier lifestyles.

Source: Marks & Spencer

Though not a fashion brand the **IKEA** sustainability strategy, named People & Planet Positive, is a really interesting one to draw inspiration from. It was launched in 2012 with clear and concise goals to transform the whole IKEA business, the industries in the IKEA value chain, and life at home for people across the world.

IKEA have stated that they want to have a positive impact on people and the planet. They are attempting to balance economic growth and positive social impact with environmental protection and regeneration.

Many of IKEA's Global sustainability challenges and calls for action are described in the UN's Sustainable Development Goals (SDGs). They guide IKEA in developing the IKEA business and set ambitions as to how the company engages with partners. All of the goals are connected and IKEA uses them as a compass to mobilise change in their working practice.

Source: IKEA

MINI CASE STUDY

Kering owned Luxury brand **Gucci** has a ten-year plan named Gucci Equilibrium which is focused around the three pillars of environment, people, and innovation. It extends to all of its suppliers and relates to every aspect of the brand's day-to-day business, right down to which products are used in cleaning processes.

On their website the brand states the following:

Gucci Equilibrium is our commitment to generate positive change for people and our planet.

Powered by creativity and collaboration, we are reducing our environmental impact and protecting nature, while also prioritising inclusivity and respect, so that everyone in our global #GucciCommunity is free to express their authentic, diverse selves.

As we celebrate our 100th anniversary, we are moving forward into the coming decades with an ongoing commitment to reinforce our culture of purpose, demonstrating our values through innovative pathways towards social and environmental sustainability.

Gucci Equilibrium unifies the principles we uphold and the actions we pursue to treat our world and each other better, for our collective future.

All fashion businesses should have a clear CSR strategy, this needs to be fully visible to the community within the business, and also includes both current and potential consumers. Fashion businesses need to engage in important social issues to further connect their brand or brands to the conscious consumers and employees, so that they in turn support, trust, and respect the organisation. CSR initiatives have become incredibly powerful business tools in helping a company position itself favourably in the eyes of its consumers and to provide a purpose and defined culture within the community.

Expert insight from Lisa Nan
Researcher and Journalist at Jing Daily.

There is no one right way companies can practise CSR and no end point. CSR policies are constantly revisited and developed when new matters arise.

I have outlined five key steps to easily implement contemporary and relevant CSR policies inside a company culture.

1. **Open dialogue**
   Voice to stakeholders – Companies need to ensure all employees have a voice and collect opinions from suppliers, investors, and consumers. This is due to the fact CSR initiatives are achievable only through the collaboration of all the stakeholders. By doing so, every single stakeholder feels ownership of it and contributes to it.
   Learn from competitors – Directors and managers, in any sector, are now openly publishing and disclosing their sustainable actions and impacts. A lot can be learned from competitor companies with mature CSR systems, good and bad!
2. **Objective – define CSR**
   Through open dialogue all stakeholders contribute to the definition of the company's CSR.
   Examination of impact – Identify key areas the company has substantial impact, in terms of both environmental and social.
   Classification by importance – The company classifies the key social and environmental issues which concern its stakeholders and shares those concerns and analyses how the company's social responsibility works, adds value to the organisation, and fits with its strategy. To begin the company can choose one to three major areas to act on.
   Positive Impact – Develop solutions to tackle the selected environmental and social issues and identify departments and stakeholders involved to bring the positive impact.
   Set objectives – Having identified the solution for a positive impact, the company needs to set an objective within a timeframe.
3. **Action – give people responsibility**
   Once the strategy has been settled, one of the most important phases is to put the plan into practice.
   As we gave ownership to all stakeholders to define the company culture and its CSR, they are also accountable for the execution of it. Directors and managers need to embed CSR in an employee's day-to-day task and help suppliers to implement CSR policies.
   CSR initiatives are not only the sustainability department's duty, we must avoid the silo mentality and encourage cross-department collaboration to achieve the desired results.

I suggest the creation of small teams of three to four people from different departments, each team assigned with a theme and given full power. It will be very interesting to see the creativity coming from the collaboration of people from different positions and interests.

A shared vision where CSR is seen as a competitive advantage for the company will drive stakeholders' motivation to act on it.

4. Impact – measure progress

For any plan and strategy, it is fundamental to set ways to measure progress. Although CSR might result intangible, there is still the need of finding suitable metrics to measure the performance, evaluate improvements, and generate momentum towards sustainability.

5. Communicate progress

The communication of the company's CSR progress is a very important step, it contributes to the normalisation of the practice in the sector. The communication must be two ways: the company must align its vision and mission both internally and externally, any incoherency will damage the company's reputation.

Internally, employees need to be constantly updated regarding the company's CSR policies, milestones achieved need to be celebrated and employees' contribution rewarded.

Externally, CSR initiatives and reports need to be shared on important and suitable social media platforms and its own website. More than the achievement it is worth sharing the process and the good practices.

FIGURE 3.4   CSR.Credit Shutterstock / designium

MISSION STATEMENTS

A Mission Statement defines the core purpose of the organisation, it is presented in a short statement which is visible to those that work inside the company as well as its customers. Many fashion brands now incorporate sustainability into their Mission Statements, further highlighting the importance of environmental responsibility at the business' core.

When used effectively, the Mission Statement acts as a blueprint or reference point for a business, facilitating key decisions. Ultimately the business needs to ask itself, does this decision support our Mission Statement or not. If not, the decision potentially creates confusion within its community and runs the risk of destabilising its culture.

The Mission Statement provides a reference point and window into the business that allows the customer to form an opinion about the brand, and ultimately enables them to make informed purchase decisions. When the Mission Statement is consistent with the brand's commercial activities it can drive and increase customer engagement and loyalty, and when it is not, it runs the risk of alienating its customer base.

Below are mission statements from some of the leading fashion businesses:

- **Patagonia** – Build the best product, cause no unnecessary harm, use business to inspire and implement solutions to the environmental crisis.
- **Nike** – To bring inspiration and innovation to every athlete in the world. If you have a body you are an athlete
- **Tiffany and Co** – To maintain an ethical business that is qualitative and sustainable.
- **Timberland** – Our mission is to equip people to make a difference in the world. We do this by creating outstanding products and by trying to make a difference in the communities in which we live and work. We demonstrate this philosophy across all facets of our company from our products to our employee involvement in our communities.
- **Stella McCartney** – To bring conscience to the industry through our shared values and activist non-conformity.
- **Lululemon** – Creating components for people to live longer, healthier, fun lives. We make technical athletic apparel for yoga, running, dancing, and most other sweaty pursuits.
- **The Reformation** – To bring sustainable fashion to everyone.

DIVERSITY IN THE WORKPLACE

Diversity is about recognising, respecting, and valuing differences based on ethnicity, gender, age, race, religion, disability, and sexual orientation.

Being diverse is an essential element of social sustainability and needs to be a fundamental value and culture driver inside any fashion business.

FIGURE 3.5   Mission Credit Shutterstock / Jo Panuvat d

FIGURE 3.6   Diverse workforce. Shutterstock / Ndab Creativity

The acceptance and celebration of everyone's unique qualities, insights, voices, opinions, and experiences are key to building a viable and thriving sustainable business.

A diverse workforce can help a business better understand the impact its brand and operations are having on different communities and parts of society both locally and globally, providing a business with a more rounded viewpoint of society.

Nike's NYC office headquarters house a 4,000 sq. ft. basketball court capable of seating 400 spectators. This impressive sports facility is free to use for Nike employees, brand ambassadors, local leagues, and high-school teams. Nike created the space in order to better connect and serve its local community. This initiative further aligns Nike's role as a leader in the world of basketball, whilst also providing a mechanic for Nike to connect and engage with all of its stakeholders, and it provides a safe and healthy platform for its community to play basketball and exercise.

Expert insight from Mathew Dixon
Director Fashion and Luxury Practice at The MBS Group.

Building diverse and inclusive teams within fashion brands has become one of the highest corporate priorities in recent years. This isn't a topic that should be just bolted onto the responsibilities of Human Resources, but instead should be deeply embedded in the business values, at the very heart of a company. However, diversity goes much further than just driving better ethnic or gender equality. It is imperative that company diversity policies cover LGBTQ+, social mobility, neuro diversity and embrace the disabled community to create a truly inclusive environment. After all, these groups form a significant percentage of the company's customer base, so why wouldn't their voices be heard within corporate decision making?

Building an inclusive culture within a company is critical to its ongoing modernity and future success. There is significant research that show that brands with higher levels of diversity outperform the average across a variety of indicators, including EBITDA. Those companies that have dynamically-built working environments where teams and colleagues are free to authentically express themselves, see far greater job satisfaction, engagement, creativity, and productivity, with a significantly lower staff turnover. In a talent market where brands are fighting to employ the brightest minds, a proudly diverse and inclusive working culture is a huge advantage within talent acquisition, making people want to work within the business.

Building a diverse mindset within a fashion brand must start at the very top. In recent years companies have been hiring a new role, the Chief Diversity Officer, to lead better practice at board level. Company boards are changing from a traditional white male dominance to striking a greater balance between gender and ethnicity. The industry has made positive strides on this in recent years, especially after the rise of the Black Lives Matter movement, however there is still a long way to go. Few companies have members of the disabled community in senior management roles, despite one in five people in the UK being disabled.

A simple method to understand whether a company board is diverse is to ask the question "Who is not in the room?"

Successfully driving diversity and inclusion is not a simple task, especially for legacy brands that have worked, often very successfully, for many years, and requires investment. Just as companies had to pivot and embrace digital transformation, they must now do the same around creating a diverse mindset. Good examples of this include rethinking how businesses hire staff by removing candidate names from CVs to eliminate unconscious bias and building networks within local communities to tap into often overlooked sources of new talent. At a senior level, companies have demanded non-male shortlists to address gender imbalances when hiring board members. This is creating positive change, and now in the UK, 40% of FTSE 100 board positions are now held by women, compared to just 12.5% nine years ago. However, research has shown that other minority groups are still woefully represented and similar action is required to drive equality.

Despite the fashion industry still being at the start of its journey to drive diversity and equality, it is a topic that companies are taking seriously. Brands such as Ganni, Tommy Hilfiger, Calvin Klein, and Lululemon are leading the way with significant internal investment and prioritising diversity at the very top of their business agenda. Such brands are inspiring others to follow, and it is heartening to see the scale of initiatives being introduced and the increased investment being devoted to driving inclusive working environments. It is an investment that will drive a better business in the long term as diversity is an imperative component of modern leadership and is critical to authentically engage with the customer.

EQUAL REPRESENTATION IN MARKETING AND ADVERTISING

Historically, the fashion industry has been guilty of promoting examples of racially insensitive, or offensive, themes and imagery in their advertising. Many fashion brands have promoted unrealistic standards, exclusive and alienating to most.

The faces portraying fashion have a history of being exclusively white with no room for diversity in front of the camera or behind the scenes. The lack of diversity in fashion has led to people perceiving their bodies and their identities as not good enough. It has also alienated certain ethnicities from applying to work for businesses, who they perceive as a place "not for them" and has further exasperated a singular viewpoint within a business' community.

Social values are now shaping purchase decisions more than ever, fashion brands need to implement strategies to incorporate different ethnicities in their promotional campaigns. Fashion brands need to show their support for underrepresented communities. Consumers want to connect with a fashion brand that is inclusive and supportive, regardless of their age, ethnicity, or sexual identity. This is explained further in **HONEST COMMUNICATION**, which is #8 in **The Responsible 9 Framework**.

VOLUNTEER PROGRAMS

Many fashion brands have implemented programs which allow staff to volunteer in their working hours for causes they care about in their communities. Giving the workforce opportunities to volunteer can improve morale and connect one's business to local groups. Today's workforce wants to find a sense of purpose at work, and one way to do that is by increasing options to give back to the local community.

Unlike some partnerships with charities and causes, which can increase costs to a business, developing volunteer programs has the potential to save a business Human Resource costs through increasing employee satisfaction, reducing employee turnover, and as a vehicle in driving recruitment. This reduction has the potential to influence the pricing strategy as overhead costs can be potentially reduced thus lowering product margins and mark-ups.

FASHION INDUSTRY EXAMPLE

A great example of this in action can be seen with **Timberland**, where employees get allocated hours of paid time to volunteer in their communities. This approach also reinforces a fashion brand's genuine commitment to improving the lives and well-being of others.

This is further explained on the Timberland website:

> Timberland first launched its Path of Service™ employee volunteer program in 1992 to give all employees a chance to engage in the community on company time. Since then Timberland employees have served over 1,000,000 hours in communities worldwide and we're still counting. Employees are always encouraged to serve in ways that speak to their passions.
>
> *Source: Timberland*

The Reformation provides their staff with four paid days off per year to volunteer. Two of which are company-wide service days and the other two are left for employees to volunteer for causes the employee is passionate about. The brand also regularly highlights volunteer opportunities to make giving back a little more doable. In addition, the company also celebrates staff birthdays by donating to TreePeople, an organisation that supports urban forests in LA by planting a tree in their name.

Source: The Reformation

THE ROLE OF EDUCATION

Education can play a leading role in helping shape the mindset and perspective of tomorrow's fashion leaders. Whether students are enrolled in their first post-secondary course or if they are currently employed and are further developing their knowledge and skills, it is vitally important that the education system ingrains the ethos of inclusivity. Students have a huge role in shaping the future communities and cultures that they will work in, and ensuring that the industry, business, and community alike, embrace diversity and celebrate individual identity of all types.

Expert from Liliana Sanguino Ramirez
Associate Professor, at Parsons School of Design.

From my own experience in different fields, it is my belief that "identity" is the greatest asset that each, every, and any one of us holds.

Discovering who we are, understanding our own identities and exploring how they can relate to other people's identities is key for everyone's development. This is true for each of us – and vital for students joining a university to become the fashion designers of the future.

Each student commencing this academic and creative journey commits to a process of discovery, recognition, and clarification of their own unique identity, aesthetic, and ethos, to better understand and respond to the times we live in. This is achieved through exploring their own individuality and also by recognising others also have a unique identity, aesthetic, and ethos too.

Contemporary fashion awareness, diversity, ethics, and social responsibility remain of the utmost importance and should be embedded in the curriculum at all times. This is an exciting time to affect changes in the fashion industry and it really ought to start from the education institutions. This is the proper place to begin radical change, to rethink industry, and place the new generation at the helm.

FIGURE 3.7   The girl in this image is Yina Panchi, a designer from the Emberas People, reserve Karmata Rua in Colombia, Credit David Grandorge

This chapter has provided insight on how important it is for fashion brands to develop a community. Key takeaways include:

- When employees within the business know they are working with a community of people who share a common purpose and values, their effort and output becomes more meaningful and their purpose within the organisation becomes more defined.
- All employees; the shop floor sales staff, the people who design, garment makers, through to the management team play their role in growing a business' community.
- Fashion businesses need a clear and responsible approach to their culture and values within their business so that the community that work inside it are engaged and feel a sense of worth and purpose.
- Being diverse is an essential element of social sustainability and needs to be a fundamental value and culture driver inside any fashion business.

- Giving the workforce opportunities to volunteer can improve morale and connect one's business to local communities.
- For the customer the Mission Statement provides a reference point and window into the business that allows the customer to form an opinion about the brand, and ultimately enables them to make informed purchase decisions.
- Education can play a leading role in helping shape the mindset and perspective of tomorrow's fashion leaders.

FURTHER READING

Berners-Lee, M. (2019). *There Is No Planet B: A Handbook for the Make or Break Years*, Cambridge University Press.

Craig, J. (2010). The Face of Fashion: Cultural Studies in Fashion, London: Routledge.

Gardetti, M. (2019). The UN Sustainable Fashion Goals for the Textile and Fashion Industry, Springer.

Gardetti, M. (2019). Sustainable Luxury and Social Entrepreneurship Stories from Pioneers. Routledge.

Varley, R., Radclyffe-Thomas, N., and Webb, W. (2018). Patagonia: Creative Sustainable Strategy for a Reluctant Fashion Brand, Bloomsbury.

WEB MATERIAL

Amed, I. et al. (2019). The State of Fashion 2020: Navigating Uncertainty. McKinsey. Retrieved from: https://bftt.org.uk/state-of-fashion-2020/.

BCG Global (2022). The Five Digital Building Blocks of a Corporate Sustainability Agenda. Retrieved from: https://web-assets.bcg.com/be/28/2262959d4ff8ba21 ade6f9f4a151/bcg-the-five-digital-building-blocks-of-a-corporate-sustainability-mar-2022.pdf.

Crane, A., Palazzo, G., Spence, L.J. and Matten, D. (2014). Contesting the Value of Creating Shared Value. California Management Review. Retrieved from: https://journals.sagepub.com/doi/10.1525/cmr.2014.56.2.130.

European Commission (2018). Corporate Social Responsibility & Responsible Business Conduct. Retrieved from: https://single-market-economy.ec.europa.eu/industry/sustainability/corporate-social-responsibility-responsible-business-conduct_en.

Elkington, J.S.H. (1997). Cannibals with Forks: The Triple Bottom Line of 21st Century Business. Oxford, United Kingdom. Retrieved from: www.wiley.com/en-gb/Cannibals+with+Forks%3A+The+Triple+Bottom+Line+of+21st+Century+Business-p-9781841120843.

Farra, E. (2021). This Is What's Missing in Fashion's Inclusivity Movement. Vogue. Retrieved from: www.vogue.com/article/whats-missing-in-inclusivity-movement-adaptive-fashion-disabled-community.

Ferreira, P. and Real de Oliveira, E. (2014). Does Corporate Social Responsibility Impact Employee Engagement? Journal of Workplace Learning. Retrieved from: www.emerald.com/insight/content/doi/10.1108/JWL-09-2013-0070/full/html.

Freeman, R.E. (1984). Strategic Management: A Stakeholder Approach. Boston, United States: Pitman. Retrieved from: https://research.monash.edu/en/publications/strategic-management-a-stakeholder-approach.

Graafland, J., Van De Ven, B., and Stoffele, N. (2003). Strategies and Instruments for Organising CSR by Small and Large Businesses in the Netherlands. Journal of Business Ethics. Retrieved from: https://link.springer.com/article/10.1023/A:10 26240912016.

Greenwood, M. (2013). Ethical Analyses of HRM: A Review and Research Agenda. Journal of Business Ethics. Retrieved from: https://link.springer.com/article/10. 1007/s10551-012-1354-y.

Heugens, P., Kaptein, M., and Van Oosterhout, J.H. (2008). Contracts to Communities: A Processual Model of Organisational Virtue. Journal of Management Studies. Retrieved from: https://onlinelibrary.wiley.com/doi/abs/10.1111/j.1467-6486. 2007.00738.x.

McKinsey (2021). State of Fashion 2022. Business of Fashion. Retrieved from: www. mckinsey.com/~/media/mckinsey/industries/retail/our%20insights/state%20 of%20fashion/2022/the-state-of-fashion-2022.pdf.

BRAND REFERENCES

www.burberry.com.
www.gap.co.uk.
www.gucci.com.
www.nike.com.
https://eu.patagonia.com.
https://us.pg.com.
www.thereformation.com.
www.tiffany.co.uk.
www.timberland.co.uk.
www.stellamccartney.com.

CHAPTER 4

The Responsible 9 Framework

#4 = Perceived Value

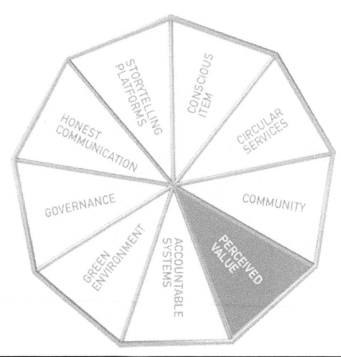

THE RESPONSIBLE 9 FRAMEWORK: #4 = PERCEIVED VALUE

DOI: 10.4324/9781003285915-5

INTRODUCTION TO THE CHAPTER

As outlined within the introduction, traditionally price relates to the cost that a customer must pay for a product. Historically, there were typically four key considerations for organisations that drove the price strategy of a product. These can be summarised as:

1. Product costs of the business to develop, manufacture, transport, and market a product.
2. Mark-Ups and profit margin of the product to cover operational overheads of the business itself, distributors, and end-sellers.
3. What the target consumer is willing to pay for the product.
4. Competitor pricing.

As fashion brands further align and connect their environmental and responsible corporate initiatives with their core brand proposition, a fifth key consideration centred around a business' integrated CSR initiatives, should be added as a key consideration for determining price strategy. While fashion brands continue to align CSR initiatives into their brand proposition, there has also been a seismic shift in today's conscious consumer's motivation and buying behaviour, in driving what they are willing to pay for a product, shifting from one influenced by low-cost pricing, to one driven by the holistic brand value of the product or brand and transparency of costs.

This chapter explores different types of CSR initiatives that are influencing price strategy, how businesses are using these initiatives to drive consumer purchase decisions and in-store traffic, and how the new conscious consumer is beginning to reward companies that have both a transparent pricing strategy and those that provide greater value than simply the product itself.

TRANSPARENT PRICING – THE IMPORTANCE IN COMMUNICATING THE TRUE COST TO THE CONSUMER

Price typically refers to the cost of an item or service that consumers must pay for the item or service, and the consumer needs to feel satisfied that the price is appropriate before they make their purchase. The pricing strategy needs to reflect the brands position in the competitive landscape and the resulting price, or recommended retail price (RRP), should cover the product costs of creating, developing, and transportation of the item and the profit margin to be achieved.

The approach to price is being closely examined by fashion businesses, as they realise modern consumers want additional detail, including the complete cost breakdown, to justify the RRP before they buy. This consumer

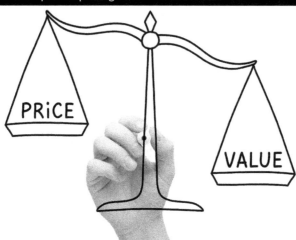

FIGURE 4.1   Transparent pricing Shutterstock/Ivelin Radkov

wants to know that they are not being overcharged for this garment, whilst they also want to understand the environmental impact of that garment being made and delivered.

Their purchase decision is increasingly driven by their perceived value of the garment, which in part, is driven by a need to understand the true cost breakdown. These costs include the materials used, hardware (e.g. zippers), labour costs (and ensuring factory workers were paid a fair living wage), governmental import and export duties, and transportation requirements and costs. The consumer then takes onboard these inputs and asks themselves, "is the price of this garment fair value, and in its creation and transportation, does it deliver against their set of personal values and beliefs on responsible environmental practices?"

Proactive fashion brands are now starting to reveal the true cost of items and are logically breaking down the price of each item clearly on their website and in their marketing materials. Moreover, a clear and transparent fashion marketing and communication that helps a customer to understand why a garment is a particular price can genuinely connect the brand and the customer together and increase brand interaction.

Conscious consumers now truly appreciate brands speaking to them in an honest and intelligent way as highlighted by expert Mytro Angelidou in the following insight. Giving the consumer a clear price perspective can then help them make an informed purchase, which in turn can lead to genuine longer-term engagement and loyalty.

Expert insight from Mytro Angelidou

Mytro Angelidou is co-founder of Sinister Sisters, a Brand Development, Sales and PR agency and incubator representing emerging designers and is also a Lecturer in BA(Hons) Fashion Business, Istituto Marangoni.

The context of the COVID-19 pandemic reinforced consumer views on sustainability, shifting their buying decisions to brands that are transparent in their production practices and ecological footprint and are also politically and socially active. The negative impact of the fashion industry on people and the environment has become a focal point for the conscious consumer, particularly among younger generations like Millennials and Gen Z, who are willing to pay a premium for sustainable products and shop from brands that support social and environmental causes. To respond to the shift in the consumer mindset, brands have been creating products in greener ways which often means facing the challenges of pricing while maintaining margins and applying prices that the consumer will tolerate.

Essential criteria for pricing a sustainable product include material selection, green and ethical production and distribution, end-of-use of the product that enables circularity and donations to charitable causes. Brands and designers need to consider the entire product value chain when setting prices for such products.

Materials: The main cost of sustainable products is at the beginning of the value chain, which includes growing and harvesting raw materials, weaving, sewing, and dyeing the products. These stages also have the most significant environmental impact. Therefore, critical decisions early on, like fabric sourcing, need to be considered as green and ethical production costs are higher. Retail prices must reflect these decisions to maintain profit margins.

Manufacturing: The location of manufacturing will also impact the cost of the product. Re-shoring strategies that move production near or even on-shore to minimise risk, lead times, and carbon footprint and for transparency purposes come with increased costs.

End-of-life: Product end-of-life that enables circularity is another crucial factor in product design and material selection. Investment in technology, like Digital IDs, is used for traceability and can provide information on the product's composition to facilitate recycling. Such investments also need to be added to the mark-up.

Social impact: Finally, the brand's social impact is another crucial factor: fair wages for people across their supply chain and charitable donations. It is becoming a norm for brands to donate part of their sales to charities and other credible causes to increase their social impact and align with consumers' expectations.

The prices of eco-friendly and sustainable products in fashion can be 150–200% higher than non-sustainable. Although consumers are aware of the environmental and social importance of buying sustainable products, prices are often significantly higher than consumers are willing to pay. Wider adoption of sustainable practices across the supply chain will bring costs down in the long run. In the meantime, these additional costs would need to be absorbed by the brands to promote and support sustainable consumption.

FASHION INDUSTRY EXAMPLES

Californian online retailer **Everlane** is synonymous with timeless styles at affordable prices. It is also a brand that is at the forefront in its aim for radical cost transparency. The true cost behind all of its products, including materials, labour, and transportation are clearly visible on the website and marketing materials and communicated to the consumer in a very straightforward and clear way. Interestingly, Everlane also communicates that there are costs that they can't accurately account for – like design, fittings, wear testing, rent on office and retail space, but the brand says that they believe the customer deserves to know exactly what goes into making the products.

CONNECTING WITH CREDIBLE CAUSES ALIGNED TO YOUR BRAND PROPOSITION

Connecting to credible causes is a movement that is increasingly adopted by many fashion brands and has become a key driver of pricing strategy. More and more fashion brands all over the world are beginning to announce their long-term support and alignment with charities and important movements both locally and globally. The most successful of these initiatives occur when the cause is inherently connected to the brand's proposition and the connection between brand and cause is genuine and authentic. Many of these fashion brands see their connection to a cause as intrinsic to their

FIGURE 4.2   Connecting with charities. Credit Shutterstock/Rawpixel.com

underlying business and if executed successfully, have numerous benefits to the organisation in the form of (but not limited to):

- Creating awareness, and reinforcing a brand's proposition with both its current and potential customer base.
- Driving purchase through increased perceived value.
- Enhancing employee engagement, satisfaction, and recruitment.

The connection to an authentic cause has a key role within the pricing strategy as the partnership with the cause can impact on both the originations costs, which needs to be accounted for and recouped within an organisations margin (which in turn drives decisions on price), but as importantly it can influence the consumers' willingness and desire to pay the price for a product. The greater the perceived value, the greater the willingness for the target consumer to pay the asking price.

Expert insight from Lucy Litwack
CEO of Coco de Mer a female-owned, run, and focused lingerie and pleasure business.

At the heart of everything I do is a purpose, so when I was given the opportunity to purchase Coco de Mer, the company for which I had been CEO for three years, I knew it was my chance to grow a brand with a clear and definite message – the importance of female pleasure.

As a female-owned and female-led business, championing women's causes underpins every one of our goals at Coco de Mer, and we believe in going that extra mile to empower all women. People are at the heart of what we do. From the teams we work with to the clients we provide for, we strive for inclusivity, diversity, and openness. To provide a safe space for discovery, growth, and enjoyment. In essence, we exist to shine a light on the extraordinary power, potential, and importance of female pleasure.

I became involved in the fight against Female Genital Mutilation (FGM) five years ago after reading survivor Waris Dirie's memoirs. Her story brought home the horror of what was happening to so many girls worldwide and inspired me to do whatever I could to help. I reached out to Waris through her Desert Flower Foundation and we decided to create a campaign that would raise awareness and funds, by working together using both of our platforms. So, Waris became the face of Coco de Mer's Icons collection – with a film and photo campaign to bring the long-overdue conversation to the table. To break the silence and help to eradicate a ritual that unnecessarily harms countless women and girls.

As a brand focused on the importance of female pleasure, the fight against FGM felt like a natural cause for Coco de Mer to champion. Given that FGM is a direct disabler of the pleasure we celebrate, as a team we committed to advocate for, and support, the NGOs and activists who work so tirelessly in this space. Initially, I was concerned that, as an outsider who was not a victim of this cruel practice or part of this culture, my desire to help might not be wanted. I could not have been more wrong. They welcomed me with open arms. What a generous and warm-hearted community – and, despite what they have suffered, the levels of fun and laughter know no bounds. I have made lifelong friends in this group of incredible people.

What is FGM? The WHO describes FGM as any procedure that injures the female genital organs for non-medical reasons. It is the deliberate, non-medical removal or cutting of the female genitalia. It has no health benefits and can be very harmful. On another level, it is about power and control. Control over women, over their bodies, over their sexuality. I absolutely believe that a woman must have the right to choose what happens to her own body. Body Autonomy is a fundamental human right for all women, no matter where they are from or where they live. And that is why the fight against FGM is so close to my heart.

Sustainability of all walks is at the very core of Coco de Mer, and we are committed to creating a positive impact on society and the world in which we live. Respect, honesty, openness – they are all marks of empowerment, and should be a given for everyone, regardless of who or where they are in the world. For over 20 years, we have fostered enduring relationships to make better, more sustainable products within the arena of conscious luxury. By being a transparent brand that supports responsible practices and proudly uses its platform to speak up for social justice, we ensure Coco de Mer is a force for good in every way.

I became aware of two issues as I started to support this cause:

One, the fact that the West thought that FGM was a "cultural practice," a "tradition" that we didn't understand and therefore shouldn't interfere.

Two, that it was an issue "only" in the African world.

How many crimes must be committed against women in the name of tradition before this is acknowledged? Why does the reverence for outdated tradition persist as humankind grows better informed, more globalised, and apparently more knowledgeable? Flouting reason and even law.

FGM is not purely a woman's issue. Or an African issue. It is a humanitarian issue. It's child abuse and it's gender inequality.

It is also a global problem. 21 out of every 1,000 women in London have undergone FGM. This abuse happens in almost every country in the world.

Education is key to bringing change. We need to empower girls and teach boys. Together, they can stop future generations from facing the same inhumanity.

As we know, men of true quality do not fear equality. On the contrary, the world desperately needs present fathers, loyal brothers, loving partners, strong husbands, and vulnerable leaders to sharpen other men.

We need to break the silence and create safe spaces where FGM and sexual pleasure can be discussed openly amongst the most vulnerable communities. To break down taboos and lift women up.

Corporate partnerships provide an excellent way of reaching new audiences. We can raise greater awareness using combined platforms and resources.

I am a trustee of The Five Foundation, the global partnership to end FGM. We work at a systemic level to advocate for better funding streams for women on the African continent and beyond.

A shared purpose unites us, a woman's fundamental human right over her own body. And until all women have access to education and independence, they will not be in a position to stand up to these harmful traditions.

As a brand that considers everyone equal and worthy of pleasure, it is our duty to advocate for change, empower education, and be the voice for those who cannot speak up.

FIGURE 4.3 Waris Dirie x Coco de Mer Desert Flower Foundation film "Break The Silence: End FGM. Credit Rankin and Coco de Mer

CHARITABLE DONATIONS

One of the most popular implementations of connecting with causes within an organisation, and adopted by many fashion brands, is giving a share of profits to a cause. This share of profit, can be in the form of yearly, quarterly, or monthly payments or it can be delivered at the point of purchase, when a percentage of the sale price is donated. In some cases, brands have developed dedicated capsule collections centred around a specific cause or charity where a significant percentage of the sale price is donated to the charity. Another emerging tactic for brands giving to charities at checkout is called "Rounding Up," which enables customers to round up the amount they have been charged to the nearest whole number. The additional money charged then goes to a specific charity communicated at checkout by both point-of-sale materials and the staff.

When these partnerships with a charity or cause are clearly communicated to the consumer, the association helps build genuine connection between the responsible shopper and the fashion brand, and through this approach, the consumer learns that the fashion brand they are choosing to buy from also cares about the same important causes. Simply put, it demonstrates to the consumer that the fashion brand is not just focused on selling the item itself, or generating profit, but is also focused on making a positive impact on society, which in turn increases the reputation and perceived value of the brand. More broadly, corporate giving also makes a business look good to the public, as it functions as another marketing channel: being a philanthropic business is a great way to raise the profile of your organisation and improve your reputation amongst your audience.

FASHION INDUSTRY EXAMPLES

A great example of a fashion brand that has built a long-term relationship with a charity is **Ralph Lauren**. Pink Pony is their worldwide initiative developed to support the fight against cancer. The campaign first began in 2000, and its mission is to reduce disparities in cancer care ensuring that access to quality treatment is available to everyone at an earlier, more curable stage. When a consumer buys a product from the Pink Pony range, 25% of each item's purchase price is donated to American cancer charities in Ralph Lauren's fight against cancer.

"When someone we love has cancer, we are all affected—husbands, wives, mothers and fathers, sisters, brothers, and friends. This is our effort in the fight against cancer." Ralph Lauren

American brand **Patagonia** supports more than 1,000 grassroots environmental organisations around the world. In 2002, Patagonia founder Yvon Chouinard also established the non-profit corporation "1% for the Planet," an alliance of businesses that donate 1% of their total annual sales to grassroots environmental groups.

> It's also so important that we stay in this together. One lesson that I've learned, and that this pandemic is certainly teaching us, is that we're not in isolation. The problems we're facing now have to be solved on a global basis and can only be solved by people working together and staying tough together — like all of you in the 1% for the Planet community.
>
> Yvon Chouinard, 2021, Founder of Patagonia
> and Co-Founder of 1% for the Planet

PANGAIA, founded in 2018 by a group of designers, scientists, and technologists, has worked with The SeaTrees project which is restoring and protecting 26 hectares of degraded mangrove forest in the West Papua region of Indonesia. For every piece of PANGAIA clothing sold a mangrove tree is planted. Local Indonesian villagers are employed to plant a diverse mix of mangrove species, creating jobs, healthy ecosystems, and habitats. The region's current mangrove estuaries are 75% deforested, which is why restoration is so important.

Another great example of a brand continually connecting with credible causes can be found with Luxury British brand **Stella McCartney**. As an example, the brand launched a capsule collection supporting Greenpeace's campaign to stop deforestation in the Amazon, which is fuelled by industrial agriculture and meat production. The Stella x Greenpeace capsule embodies a shared commitment to protecting the planet and wildlife alongside the capsule collection, the Stella McCartney Cares Foundation also donates to Greenpeace to support its campaign to stop deforestation in the Amazon.

FIGURE 4.4   PANGAIA Logo. Credit PANGAIA

In 2021, French brand **Kenzo** partnered with the World Wide Fund for Nature (WWF) and donated a portion of sales from a capsule collection to the charity (the world's leading independent conservation organisation). The collaboration forms part of a broader partnership between Kenzo and the WWF, which works to improve the sustainability of Kenzo's cotton supply chain and freshwater footprint.

Many brands attempted to support business and individuals over the COVID-19 pandemic. For example, American brand **Michael Kors** released a special edition LOVE T-shirt to help the World Food Programme (WFP). All profits from the T-shirt went to support relief efforts directed at providing vital nutrition to help keep underprivileged children healthy over lockdown. While this was an important thing to do, it also had the added bonus of connecting the brand to local communities and potentially its future consumers.

Bottletop have a #TOGETHERBAND Campaign, which aims to share the UN's 17 Global Goals through creativity and culture. One-hundred percent of profits from the sales of #TOGETHER products go to charities that advance the Sustainable Development Goals. All of their #TOGETHERBANDs are handmade at their atelier in Nepal by a collective of women who have been rescued from human trafficking. They are made from Humanium Metal and 100% Parley Ocean Plastic®.

Expert insight from Erica Charles

Program Leader, Glasgow Caledonian University, London. Brand Ambassador for Save the Children from 2010–2016.

Due to an increasingly competitive marketplace, the last ten years has seen a movement away from the traditional charity shop concept. Looking at different ways to reach new audiences has become critical for a charity's survival. Arguably, led by Mary Portas and Save the Children, a new wave of charity retailing came to the forefront in the early 2000s, where charities created concepts that strategically pursued both social and commercial impact.

Established in 2009, the premium charity shop concept Mary's Living & Giving Shop for Save the Children, put community and sustainability at the heart of their business. Mary Portas wanted to revolutionise the way charity shops were perceived, as well as create an outlet for premium brands and retailers to dispose of their excess and old stock without damaging the value of the brand. Mary encouraged Save the Children to invest in the core principles of retailing – location, store design, visual merchandising, competitive pricing, customer service, and quality stock – which resulted in attracting a more affluent consumer and providing a space where some of the world's most recognised designer and premium brands and retailers felt comfortable donating stock – high value end-of-life fashion.

For years burning stock to protect intellectual property and prevent illegal counterfeiting has been common practice in the fashion industry; and by 2030, fashion brands will significantly contribute to the 134 million tonnes of textiles a year that will be discarded (burned or destined for landfill). As consumers increasingly look to brands that are more socially and environmentally responsible, businesses need to do more to connect with consumers, build trust, and gain loyalty. Donating end-of-life stock to charity shops, is one way by which brands can provide a positive response to the ever-increasing environmental challenge, and have more of an affinity with the more conscious consumer.

Motivations for brands donating to charity shops reach beyond environmental benefits. The majority of stock donations received are done so from brands that feel a true emotional connection to the cause. However, there are some brands who want to be seen as being responsible and doing good, and they use their donations primarily as a vehicle for their own purpose – a guilt-free exercise to support their cause-related marketing campaigns. Equally, some brands will openly seek a financial return on their donation as UK brands that donate stock to approved UK charities can qualify for tax deductions; therefore, benefitting financially by donating stock that no longer serves their business.

Whatever the motivation, the reality is that without generous donations from brands and retailers, charity shops would struggle to exist, and the 339 million tonnes of textiles that currently gets diverted to these shops would end up in landfill costing councils millions in landfill tax, and the environment in terms of carbon emissions. Sales from these donations also raise the much-needed unrestricted funds that enable charity response teams to be first on the ground during a humanitarian crisis. This can literally be the difference between life and death for many.

This chapter has provided insight on how important it is for fashion brands to develop transparent pricing strategies. Key takeaways include:

- It is critical for fashion brands to understand the importance of aligning themselves to causes that their customer also cares about.
- A fashion brand's commitment to important causes should be ongoing and not seen as a one-off exercise.
- At the point of purchase, customers can be given the opportunity to add an additional amount to give to a charity.
- A fashion brand should consider using some of its marketing budget to promote important causes.
- Fashion brands should loan charities their staff for set periods in the year in order to show genuine commitment. This can also further align their values with their employees.

- Specific limited-edition ranges could be offered which wholly promote a credible cause and also specifically give money back to this cause.
- With price transparency becoming an expectation of some customers, fashion brands should consider explaining their pricing strategy in an honest and detailed way.
- Brands should support charity shops, by donating old or unwanted stock to them.

FURTHER READING

Berners-Lee, M. (2019). *There Is No Planet B: A Handbook for the Make or Break Years*, Cambridge University Press.

Berman B.R. and Evan J.R. (2013). *Retail Management: A Strategic Approach*, 12th edition. Pearson.

Clark J. (2015). *Fashion Merchandising Principles and Practice*. Palgrave, Macmillan.

Goworek, H. (2007). *Fashion Buying*, Oxford: Backwell Pub. Ltd.

Jackson, T. and Shaw, D. (2001). Mastering Fashion Buying and Merchandising Management, Basingstoke, Palgrave Macmillan.

Kendall, G.T. (2009). *Fashion Brand Merchandising*, Fairchild Books, Conde Nast Publications Inc.

Varley, R., Radclyffe-Thomas, N., and Webb, W. (2018). Patagonia: Creative Sustainable Strategy for a Reluctant Fashion Brand, Bloomsbury.

West, D., Ford, J., and Essam, I. (2010). Strategic Marketing: Creating Competitive Advantage. Second Ed., Oxford: Oxford University Press.

WEB MATERIAL

Austin, J., Stevenson, H., and Wei-Skillern, J. (2006). Social and Commercial. Entrepreneurship: Same, Different, or Both? Entrepreneurship Theory and Practice. Retrieved from: www.researchgate.net/publication/307773106_Social_and_Commercial_Entrepreneurship_Same_Different_or_Both.

Ayres, I. and Nalebuff, B. (2003), In Praise of Honest Pricing, MIT Sloan Management Review. Retrieved from: https://sloanreview.mit.edu/article/in-praise-of-honest-pricing/.

Bain, M. (2022). Fashion's New Approach to Setting Prices. Business of Fashion. Retrieved from: www.businessoffashion.com/articles/technology/fashions-new-approach-to-setting-prices/.

Bagwell, L.S. and B.D. Bernheim. (1996). Veblen Effects in a Theory of Conspicuous Consumption. American Economic Review. Retrieved from: https://www0.gsb.columbia.edu/faculty/lhodrick/veblen%20effects.pdf.

Balachander, S. and A. Stock. (2009). Limited Edition Products: When and When Not to Offer Them. Marketing Science. Retrieved from: https://pubsonline.informs.org/doi/abs/10.1287/mksc.1080.0401.

Basmann, R.L., D.J. Molina, and D.J. Slottje. (1988). A Note on Measuring Veblen's Theory of Conspicuous Consumption. The Review of Economics and Statistics. Retrieved from: https://econpapers.repec.org/article/tprrestat/v_3a70_3ay_3a1988_3ai_3a3_3ap_3a531-35.htm.

Baye, M.R. and J. Morgan. (2009). Brand and Price Advertising in Online Markets. Management Science. Retrieved from: https://faculty.haas.berkeley.edu/rjmorgan/Branding.pdf.

BCG (2020). A New Era And A New Look For Luxury. Retrieved from: www.bcg.com/publications/2020/new-era-and-new-look-for-luxury.

Bell, A. (2021). White Paper: Future Consumer 2023. WGSN. Retrieved from: www.wgsn.com/en/blogs/introducing-your-future-consumer-2023.

Brown, L. (2002). The Eco-economic Revolution: Getting the Market in Sync with Nature. Retrieved from: www.proquest.com/openview/c53d35707d23a4e97685a2d810562282/1?pq-origsite=gscholar&cbl=47758.

Deshpande, S.S. (2018). Various Pricing Strategies: A Review. Journal of Business and Management. Retrieved from: www.iosrjournals.org/iosr-jbm/papers/Vol20-issue2/Version-8/K2002087579.pdf.

Dottle, R. and Gu, J. (2022). The Global Glut of Clothing Is an Environmental Crisis. Bloomberg. Retrieved from: www.bloomberg.com/graphics/2022-fashion-industry-environmental-impact/?leadSource=uverify%20wall.

Faith, D.O. and Agwu, E. (2018). A Review of the Effect of Pricing Strategies on the Purchase of Consumer Goods. International Journal of Research and Management, Science and Technology. Retrieved from: https://papers.ssrn.com/sol3/papers.cfm?abstract_id=3122351.

Fierra, A.G. and Coelho, F.J. (2015). Product Involvement, Price Perceptions, and Brand Loyalty. Journal of Product and Brand Management. Retrieved from: www.emerald.com/insight/content/doi/10.1108/JPBM-06-2014-0623/full/html.

Gourville, J. and Soman, D. (2002). Price and Psychology of Consumption. Harvard Business Review. Retrieved from: https://hbr.org/2002/09/pricing-and-the-psychology-of-consumption.

Hachibiti, M. (2020). How COVID-19 Shapes The Ethical Consumption In Germany. Mintel. Retrieved from: www.mintel.com/blog/covid-19/watch-how-covid-19-is-shaping-ethical-consumer-behaviour-in-germany.

Henkel, R. (2021). Unsold Fashion: What Happens to Merchandise when Stores are Closed? Fashion United. Retrieved from: https://fashionunited.uk/news/business/unsold-fashion-what-happens-to-merchandise-when-stores-are-closed/2021033154736.

Howard, J.A. and Sheth, J.N. (1996). The Theory of Buyer Behaviour. Journal of American Statistical Association. Retrieved from: www.researchgate.net/publication/235361430_The_Theory_of_Buyer_Behavior.

Kahneman, D., Knetsch, K. and Thaler, R. (1986a). Fairness as a Constraint on Profit Seeking: Entitlements in the Market. American Economic Review. Retrieved from: https://web.mit.edu/curhan/www/docs/Articles/15341_Readings/Justice/Kahneman.pdf.

Larson, R.B. (2017). Promoting Demand Based Pricing. Journal of Revenue and Pricing Management. London. Retrieved from: https://ideas.repec.org/a/pal/jorapm/v18y2019i1d10.1057_s41272-017-0126-9.html.

Moore, K. (2019). Report Shows Customers Want Responsible Fashion, But Don't Want To Pay For It. What Should Brands Do? Forbes. Retrieved from: www.forbes.com/sites/kaleighmoore/2019/06/05/report-shows-customers-want-responsible-fashion-but-dont-want-to-pay-for-it/.

Neal, W.D. (1998). Satisfaction is Nice, but Value Derives Loyalty. Marketing Research. Retrieved from: www.proquest.com/openview/cc0a5457f9329fad3a02bd13a364246f/1?pq-origsite=gscholar&cbl=31079.

Rosmarin, R. (2020). Sustainability Sells: Why Consumers and Clothing Brands Alike are Turning to Sustainability as a Guiding Light. Retrieved from: www.insider.com/guides/style/sustainability-as-a-value-is-changing-how-consumers-shop.

BRAND REFERENCES

www.stellamccartney.com.
https://eu.patagonia.com.
www.ralphlauren.co.uk.
www.kenzo.com.
https://bottletop.org.
https://pangaia.com.
www.coco-de-mer.com.
www.michaelkors.co.uk.

CHAPTER 5

The Responsible 9 Framework

#5 = Accountable Systems

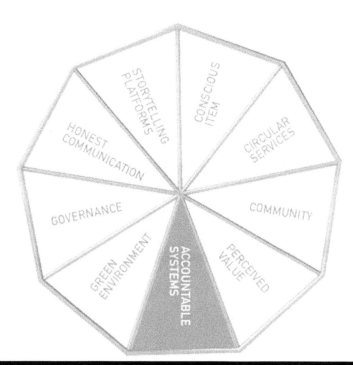

THE RESPONSIBLE 9 FRAMEWORK: #5 = ACCOUNTABLE SYSTEMS

DOI: 10.4324/9781003285915-6

INTRODUCTION TO THE CHAPTER

This chapter examines different sourcing options, digital solutions within the supply chain, sustainable transportation considerations, and innovations in sustainable packaging. Historically packaging was very much connected to product attributes, as online sales continue to grow, protective packaging has become both a priority and concern for fashion brands, therefore, now moves to **#5 ACCOUNTABLE SYSTEMS** in **The Responsible 9 Framework**.

RESPONSIBLE SOURCING AND SUPPLY CHAIN

Sourcing refers to acquisition of raw materials or finished products within a fashion supply chain. Responsible sourcing is critical across the fashion industry as this would consider social, ethical, and environmental factors in its process. In the context of the global retail environment, most fashion brands source from developing and low labour-cost countries (low-cost country sourcing) to achieve larger quantities at a lower cost.

The supply chain refers to the chain of activities that is involved in a product's journey from raw material to the customer. The larger the brand, the bigger and more complex this chain is likely to be. A responsible supply chain considers the environmental and human impact of their products' journey through the supply chain, from raw materials sourcing to manufacturing, storage, delivery, and every transportation link in between. Ensuring every part of this chain is more environmentally and ethically conscious has now become critical for fashion brands who want to be seen as being responsible and environmentally respectful.

FIGURE 5.1   Supply chain.Shutterstock / travel mania

UPSTREAM AND DOWNSTREAM

The supply chain can be divided into two parts: upstream and downstream. Upstream refers to all the activities within the supply chain up until the manufacturing of the product, until it leaves this unit. Downstream refers to all the activities within the supply chain from the moment the products leave the manufacturing facility to be eventually transported to the warehouse, retailers, and the customers.

Traceability and accountability have become key words in this vital activity. As discussed throughout earlier chapters, knowing where their items come from, how they are made, and the journey the product has taken to get to them, is rapidly becoming a leading priority for consumers of all ages.

Additionally, if the fashion brand is able to state it has a responsible sourcing and supply chain strategy in place it is likely to improve or reinforce its brand reputation.

THE CHALLENGES WITH THE SUPPLY CHAIN

There are many challenges within the supply chain, fashion brands are still struggling to understand how to better manage the process, as highlighted by Archana Chandrasekar, in the expert insight below.

Expert insight from Archana Chandrasekar

Archana Chandrasekar is a Lecturer at the University of Westminster and Istituto Marangoni. Chandrasekar has extensive first-hand knowledge of working with Indian factories and is also a Design Consultant for emerging brands.

The deep layers of the fashion supply chain

The supply chain in the fashion industry is like an onion with different layers. If one of the inner layers is rotten, it is impossible to find out until or unless you peel off the rest of the layers. If one of the layers down the supply chain ignores the basics of sustainability, it is exceedingly difficult to point it out unless you investigate layer after layer with a magnifying glass. The inner layers of the fashion industry can be overly complicated to manage by a head office unless they are all owned by the same company (vertically integrated), which most brands cannot afford to have. Let us assume that a brand wants to produce a simple, "sustainable" bright cobalt blue cotton dress with orange thread embroidery. From a customer's perspective, if the composition on the label says "100% Organic Cotton," they assume that the dress is sustainable. However, even for a simple dress like this, the layers involved are many.

The deepest layer is the fibre, which with an organic tag gets away without exposing the real problems of the soil erosions and water usage involved with any cotton production. "World cotton production is projected to grow 1.5% p.a. to reach almost 30 Mt in 2029" (OECD Agriculture Statistics, 2022). Is organic cotton sustainable enough when the demand for cotton is so large that to produce it, there will be negative ecological consequences? The Global Change award winner 2020, Galy has paved the way for lab grown cotton using biotechnology which could be a sustainable solution for the future of cotton. It is imperative that brands and customers move away from the psychological desire for fibres like cotton and start considering other sustainable alternatives.

Then comes the layer where the cotton fibre is transported to the mill for weaving. The transport involved here as well as the distance covered are factors that could increase the carbon footprint. The energy usage of a machine loom that would weave these fibres to fabric contributes to the overall carbon footprint as well.

The next stage is to achieve the bright blue cobalt colour in the fabric without the local rivers turning blue or harming the health of the workers involved. This is a layer that has been exposed in the past for the damages it is causing to the people and the planet. There are several environmental laws requiring an environmental permit to operate in most countries that have set a standard such as the environment agency in the UK, but in most countries where the dyeing takes place for the fashion industry, there are loopholes and practices that ignore these laws (RiverBlue, 2016).

After this comes the embroidery unit (supplier) layer. Will the embroidery supplier choose a sustainable thread for the embroidery? What about the orange dye that colours the thread? Beyond the topic of dyeing, this thread also must be dye fixated with processes using mordants that guarantee there is no bleeding of colour on the final garment. These mordants have to be alum or iron based to comply with environmental laws. If the customer washes the garment and ends up having the orange colours spread to the blue cobalt dress, it is a definite return and a stain (pun intended) on the brand's image. What is the brand's priority here? Colour fastness or sustainable dyeing methods?

This example is that of a simple garment without complex layers within the supply chain, yet there are factors that are not visible to the customers that are embedded within these layers. Can the garment be labelled as sustainable without guaranteeing sustainability at every layer of its supply chain? Will the customers start taking legal actions in the future against the brands for covering up the truth between the layers? There is still much to do.

THE NEED FOR ACCOUNTABLE SYSTEMS

Fibre production has doubled in the last 20 years from 58 million tonnes in 2010 to 109 million tonnes in 2020 and is expected to grow. This growth will have a significant impact on the planet and people if a more responsible transformation is not put in place. Fair and ethical production methods are also in question considering events like the Rana Plaza disaster in Bangladesh that killed 1,134 workers when an unfit factory collapsed (more information of this tragic event is discussed in the Fashion Revolution Case Study below). More and more customers want to know where their clothes are being made and where they come from due to the exposure from media investigations on the pitiable working conditions of the labourers.

Sperl (2020), developed three simple steps for fashion brands to consider when implementing social and environmental practices to help them achieve a greener and more responsible process.

1. Research the most environmentally responsible raw materials (also see Chapter 1-**CONSCIOUS ITEM**).
2. Embrace auditing to ensure fair production. When choosing a new manufacturer or supplier background checks are key. When choosing a factory, as a brand the following questions need to be answered:

   • Is the factory already audited and "approved" by a reputable authority?
   • Are there any subcontractors involved? If yes, have they been audited?
   • What are the working conditions like? (Go and see, find evidence).
   • Have any non-compliances ever been identified? If yes, how has the factory responded to these?

3. Traceability: map out social and environmental impact along the whole supply chain, consider each and every step.

Sustainability does not mean anything if it cannot be traced, there needs to be evidence of the steps a company is taking. The reason why it is hard for larger brands to disclose supplier information is because their supply chain is so large and complex that it is easy to lose sight, as explained by Chandrasekar in the expert insight on pages 107–108.

UNACCEPTABLE PRACTICE EXPOSED

Activist groups **(also see #7 GOVERNANCE in The Responsible 9 Framework)** and media attention (see Introduction) have helped to expose unethical practices inside the fashion industry and in particular revealing the lack of transparency in the supply chain.

MINI CASE STUDY

Fashion Revolution is a not-for-profit global fashion activist movement that has helped draw attention to the vital importance of transparency in the supply chain. The organisation was created as a response to the Rana Plaza disaster in Bangladesh in 2013; the fourth largest industrial disaster in history when a garment factory collapse killed 1,134 people working inside it.

Fashion Revolution represents both the industry and public, it has the vision of "a global fashion industry that conserves and restores the environment and values people over growth and profit." Fashion Revolution campaigns for reform across the whole of the fashion industry with a focus on the need for greater transparency in the fashion supply chain. It calls on customers to ask the question to brands of "who made my clothes" which became a global trend on social media platforms such as Twitter in 2018.

On their website and in their communication Fashion Revolution lists the reasons why it is crucial to have full transparency in the fashion supply chain. They highlight that during the manufacturing process clothes are touched by many pairs of hands before they ever reach the shop floor. Fashion Revolution also explains that a fashion brand might place an order with one supplier, who carves up the order and subcontracts the work to other factories. They go on to further explain that this happens regularly across the industry and makes it extremely difficult to monitor human rights and environmental impacts.

No fashion item should be declared or labelled as sustainable, until it can be clearly evidenced that workers throughout the supply chain were paid a living wage. Furthermore, brands should not just develop a limited edition line that is heavily promoted, misleading customers into thinking that this is the whole philosophy of the company. As the complex consumer becomes more aware and demanding, they will expect to see honest business practice in every element of the product offer.

Source: Fashion Revolution

EMISSIONS

Emissions are gases and other particles that are released into the atmosphere as a result of burning fuels and other processes. The most common types generally come from automobiles, power plants, and industrial companies. Many fashion companies are working on reducing their carbon emissions in order to be more environmentally accountable.

Within the fashion supply chain, the emissions occur mainly during synthetic and man-made fibre production stage, manufacturing stage, and distribution stage.

CARBON NEUTRAL

A fashion company can say it is carbon neutral if the amount of CO_2 emissions they put into the atmosphere are the same as the amount of CO_2 emissions they remove from the atmosphere. Sometimes the term "net zero" is used when discussing emissions, it is the same as carbon neutral, the "net total" of your emissions is then zero. Most international climate goals are aiming for net zero by 2050.

FIGURE 5.2   Net Zero. Shutterstock / GVLR

CARBON NEGATIVE

A fashion company can go further than carbon neutral and become carbon negative. A company can be carbon negative if the amount of CO_2 emissions they remove from the atmosphere is larger than the amount of CO_2 emissions they put into the atmosphere.

SUSTAINABLE TRANSPORTATION

Sustainable transportation refers to any means of transportation that has a low impact on the environment. Some fashion brands are turning to electric vehicles to bring down their emissions. The major benefit of electric vehicles is the contribution that they can make towards improving air quality in towns and cities. With no tailpipe, pure electric vehicles produce no carbon dioxide emissions when driving. This reduces air pollution considerably.

While considering long distance transportation, air freights are the worst in terms of emissions. Shipping can be considered as a slightly more sustainable alternative to air freights. However, shipping still contributes to a high level of emissions.

INNOVATIONS

New technologies are presenting promising opportunities for improvement across the supply chain. For example using blockchain technology in the supply chain has the potential to improve transparency and traceability as well as reduce administrative costs. In the expert insight on the following page, James Clark, Author and Senior Postgraduate Lecturer at London College of Fashion, UAL, discusses the impact of relationships within supply chain management and the complexity of data management. Clark explains how blockchain technology could potentially be a solution to avoid mistakes and errors during data handling and management.

Expert insight from James Clark: The information chain

James Clark is a Senior Postgraduate Lecturer at London College of Fashion, UAL. He is the author of the acclaimed Fashion Merchandising: Principles and Practice *and is a chapter contributor to* Fashion Management: A Strategic Approach.

Global supply chains are huge, complex, and fast paced acting as the mechanism to link organisational strategies, operations, trading tactics, stakeholders, and decision making into a seamless chain of processes and relationships. To reflect this, supply chain management can be defined as seeking to facilitate the "management of upstream and downstream relationships with suppliers and customers in order to deliver superior customer value at less cost to the supply chain as a whole" (Christopher, 2011, p. 3).

Implicit in the definition is that a supply chain manages relationships that are internal and external to a business. Relationships can be inefficient and where the lead time from product design to retail reduces and the fluctuations in demand patterns intensify then the smallest error can magnify as its effect travels through the chain. Logically, if relationships can be made to be efficient then the supply chain can become more efficient, and demand can be better serviced through higher quality and lower cost operations.

Relationship management places a different focus on supply chain operations. Rather than being simply a logistical chain operation, supply chains are a logistical and information chain operation. Accurate data and data information flows have become the lifeblood of the supply chain. Data is handled globally, across different time zones, time periods, stakeholder type, and in different configurations. It could include sales data, shipping data, inventory data, cost data, purchase order data. The combination of data type and use is then multiplied across the number of products in a range across its total lifecycle.

Complex data interpretation and use across a multi-dimensional model needs that data to be visible. Supply chain visibility through tools such as barcodes, global trade item number (GTIN) codes allows technology to track product as it moves through the chain. For example, Global Positioning System (GPS) tracking combined with radio frequency identification (RFID) chips facilitates information flows as to where a product is (in the factory, in transit, in a warehouse, in a store) and data about the product (the number of units shipped, its value). This makes the supply chain more efficient as relationships can use factual real time data to make decisions.

Data within the supply chain management involves sales, shipping, inventory, cost, purchase information to name a few.

However, there are still flaws. Data needs to be input and updated throughout the chain and multiple users of data can lead to error. Each user is devolved and there is room for delay in data input and even data manipulation. Emerging blockchain technology is fast becoming a route to eliminating these flaws. Blockchain enables faster, cost-efficient inventory management by improving inventory visibility, stakeholder information flows, and aiding financial planning to support the cash flow of the chain.

In short, a blockchain is a decentralised form of digital ledger that records verifiable, tamperproof transactions among multiple stakeholders. For a supply chain, blockchains are private linked networks limited to known stakeholders that allow the automation of activities while protecting against error and in some cases malicious attack.

For example, errors in the form of mistakes in inventory data, lost or inaccurate shipments, and duplicated financial transactions are impossible to detect and correct in real time. Errors such as these are also difficult to correct, particularly if a shipment is in transit. This is because global supply chains are complicated and the origin of the error and its implication on different aspects of the chain may not be obvious or easy to correct.

Blockchain value lies in its chronological encrypted blocks of information and actions that integrate all stakeholders with their own copies of the blockchain totality. In effect, the blockchain is a complete, trustworthy, and tamperproof audit of activities in the supply chain. Therefore, all stakeholders share their data allowing each one to use common, complete, and verifiable information when making its own decisions within the chain.

The benefits to the supply chain of blockchain in practical logistical operations focuses on accurate real time inventory information flows that allow each step in the chain to be triggered, actioned, and financed instantaneously with trust that factual data is at its heart. For supply chain management this operational trust creates efficient relationships that go a long way to satisfying Christopher's definition of the function that delivers superior customer value at less cost to the supply chain as a whole.

QR CODES

A QR code (short for Quick Response Code) is a machine-readable optical label that contains information. They are also a useful way to track and manage product inventory.

FASHION INDUSTRY EXAMPLES

American brand, **Reformation**, partnered with FibreTrace to help with transparency with their customers. Using QR technology, Reformation can now verify each step of their garment's lifecycle. FibreTrace tags textiles with a unique pigment that can be tracked throughout apparel supply chains and authenticated in the finished goods. Through its partnership with Fibretrace, Reformation also deepens its commitment to supply chain and raw material traceability to deliver on providing the consumer with increased brand transparency. The project aligns with Reformation's goal of becoming climate positive by 2025.

PANGAIA also uses QR codes and have even developed Digital Passports on all of their products, which are printed on each item's care label, allowing the sustainable shoppers to unlock the entire lifecycle of their purchase. The QR codes also provide information on the product's environmental impact, including data on the carbon and water usage needed to create it. This is all information that the conscious consumer wants to see, QR codes are a really effective tool to get this information directly to them, more specific information on this is discussed in the following mini case study.

MINI CASE STUDY

PANGAIA has partnered with connected products innovator EON to power "digital passports" for its products to accelerate greater transparency, traceability, and circularity in the industry and inspire responsible consumer choices. Powered by a QR code and cloud-hosted digital twin, the digital passports bring to life each garment's unique journey and offer customers access to product-level impact reporting in a more interactive way.

The digital passports, which are printed directly onto PANGAIA care labels, unlock a bespoke digital experience when scanned by a customer's phone. Designed to simulate the user-experience of social media platforms, the experience takes the customer on a journey from the product's origin through to its purchase, transportation, and aftercare. This includes provenance information and mapping of the dyeing, production, and distribution facilities. Whilst PANGAIA already takes steps to report on its products' impact and sustainability credentials, the digital passports will, for the first time, bring together all product-specific data into one place in a fun and engaging way for the consumer.

The digitised product experience will enable PANGAIA to update their customers in real-time as the breadth of their impact reporting evolves. For example, carbon and water impact data could be added retrospectively to a digital passport if the results of a full Life Cycle Assessment were pending.

FIGURE 5.3   PANGAIA care label. Credit PANGAIA

FIGURE 5.4   PANGAIA care label. Credit PANGAIA

As PANGAIA is still at the start of its own circularity journey, digital passports are also helping bridge the gap until the brand can offer customers a fully circular model. As well as being a signal of authenticity, visibility around lifecycle data and aftercare guidance will encourage current and future owners to extend the life of their products and keep them in circulation at the highest value possible, for longer. By providing digital passports and leveraging EON's CircularID™ Protocol, PANGAIA is also paving the way for a more circular textile industry. Pioneered by EON, the Protocol is working to ensure that circular resale, recycling, and sorting partners can access the data they need to identify, steward, and manage products and materials from one product lifecycle to the next.

Source: PANGAIA

Attire the studio, a start-up brand founded by Xenia Adonts, is another great example of a company that communicates openly and transparently with its customers. Under each product, the customer is able to see the whole cost structure of the garment. A QR code inside the garment provides the customer with information about the particular supplier. The company works only with certified organic material and certified factories. This provides customer proof of the brand's dedication towards sustainability.

ON-DEMAND MANUFACTURING

On-demand manufacturing is a method of producing goods only when needed, only in the amounts required, and most commonly when ordered by the customer. The on-demand manufacturing model immediately solves two issues, it removes the challenge of what to do with unsold clothes and additionally, with this model, there is no need to predict volumes that need to be manufactured in advance.

Artificial intelligence (AI) can be used to predict customer purchasing behaviour based on data analysis from previous sales and customer decisions. This can be an important tool in the on-demand manufacturing model.

Some fashion brands are beginning to implement on-demand manufacturing models, which is helping to reduce their risk, cost and, importantly, their waste from overproduction. Transitioning to an on-demand manufacturing model can give fashion brands more production flexibility and removes the additional costs that come with creating a product before it is sold. The three key ways that the process of production is transforming is discussed further by Joanne Yulan Jong.

Expert insight from by Joanne Yulan Jong

London based ESG sustainability and brand consultant, author of The Fashion Switch, *and founder of the award-winning agency Yulan Creative. She has 25 years of experience developing fashion brands in the UK and internationally, 12 years of these working with luxury brands such as Giorgio Armani in Milan.*

With economies worldwide acknowledging that uncertainty will continue and sustainability becomes ever more important, things have to change. Technology and data are the keys to unlocking the future to create a transparent and intelligent supply chain.

Here are three key ways the process of production is transforming.

1. Harness the power of AI to predict with accuracy what customers want. In other words, no longer creating and producing ranges and orders based on retrospective data.
2. Combining technologies and hybrid cyber-physical systems powered by AI – enabling transparency, agility, and efficiency. These systems then will consume and generate huge volumes of data helping to improve them further.
3. Automated, smart, and fast manufacturing that enables the made-to-order business model. This requires highly advanced technology connected to cutting machines and sewing systems and robots. This intelligent supply chain means the elimination of traditional overproduction, reducing waste and increasing margin.

Smaller brands have already pioneered this on-demand approach to sustainable fashion. UK company Unmade was one of the first to harness technology, beginning as a direct-to-consumer business making one-off high-end knitwear items. Over time they refined their technology and streamlined it into a B2B service called UnmadeOS. Their technology now enables clients to connect their supply chain to the world of on-demand. This idea of an intelligent supply chain is exactly what the industry was calling for and they have already collaborated with sports brands Rapha and New Balance. www.unmade.com/unmade-os/ It's not a new approach but takes time and massive investment to develop at scale.

The speed of that change will depend on the generous sharing of this cutting-edge technology, knowledge, scale, and resources. Only then can the fashion industry proudly say that it serves people, the planet, and profit.

PACKAGING

Historically when examining a product's credentials the packaging would have been an important attribute. However, in **The Responsible 9 Framework:** Packaging now belongs in **#5 ACCOUNTABLE SYSTEMS** as it connects more with the process of getting the product to the customer.

The pandemic in 2020 forced bricks and mortar retail stores all over the world to close, people were forced to stay at home and therefore ordered even more online. Many of the products arriving at the customer's door were coated in protective plastic and excess materials.

Media reports on global plastic pollution have given rise to several social media trends around boycotting plastics in packaging. Consumers have started realising that they are, unintentionally, adding to the plastic and environmental crisis. Many are actively trying to reduce the amount of plastic and excess materials they accept in packaging opting for more sustainable alternatives; showing sustainability is growing far beyond the product itself.

Packaging used traditionally was often about opulence and excess, fashion brands would use tissue, multiple boxes, ribbon, and bags adding glamour to the purchase of the product. However, this excessive approach

FIGURE 5.5 of Certified Sustainable Packaging -Shutterstock / Doctor Victor Wong is quickly becoming outdated as packaging designers now understand the importance of producing a responsible offer. Consumers are now starting to expect brands to use sustainable packaging, brands that don't could actually also miss out on sales.

Certified Sustainable Packaging is an accreditation within the packaging industry. Packaging is given either a bronze, silver, gold, or platinum mark helping to make sustainability in packaging a more visible issue, and help brands choose their packaging strategically and in line with their core values (also featuring in Chapter 7 **GOVERNANCE**).

FASHION INDUSTRY EXAMPLES

In 2022, **Marni** introduced packaging that met the FSC standards (see Chapter 7 **GOVERNANCE**). The visually eye-catching boxes and shopping bags are composed of 50% recycled paper and 100% recycled cardboard, of which 60% come from pre-consumer waste and 40% from post-consumer waste.

Source: Marni

Many brands are still sending online orders to their customers using two boxes, this is often unnecessary, especially if the item in the packaging is for the person receiving it.

Nike have a range of trainers named Space Hippie, this is an exploratory footwear collection inspired by life on Mars, where materials are scarce and there is no resupply mission. The trainers are created from scraps, the brand states that the Space Hippie range is the result of sustainable practices meeting radical design. Nike ships their Space Hippie sneakers range in a single recyclable branded box that cancels the need for a double box. Highlighting that there is no need for two boxes; a shipping box and then a branded box for the shoes.

Source: Nike

Gucci offers carrier bags that are now made from sustainably sourced beater-dyed paper from **FSC-certified** forests (see Chapter 7, for more information on FSC certified, **GOVERNANCE**), with cotton ribbon handles used in order to provide a more sustainable alternative.

British brand **Mulberry**'s packaging uses innovative CupCycling technology that transforms disposable coffee cups into waste, and then into beautiful paper and carrier bags. Mulberry have stated: "In one year of using this process, our partners at the James Cropper paper mill repurposed over 1.5 million coffee cups for Mulberry Green paper that would otherwise have been sent to landfill." All additional Mulberry paper and card is FSC certified.

Source: Mulberry

BIODEGRADABLE SUSTAINABLE PACKAGING SOLUTIONS

Biodegradable things can be broken down naturally by the organisms in an ecosystem, essentially the material naturally breaks down into smaller components, such as sugars and gases.

FASHION INDUSTRY EXAMPLES

There are a number of companies working to develop more environmentally friendly packaging, for example **The Better Packaging Company** has developed courier bags that are fully compostable. The funny slogans on the packaging state "I'm a real dirt bag," cleverly conveying the benefits of this sustainable packaging alternative.

Innovative packaging solutions company **Notpla** offers a seaweed-based paper that transforms a wasted resource into a quality product. The paper is designed to capture the essence of the ocean and is synthetic-free with no synthetic sizing agents or coatings.

REUSABLE PACKAGING

Fashion brands are starting to address excess use of packaging with innovative materials and containers that could be repurposed. However, there is still a huge opportunity for fashion brands to adopt reusable packaging in order to connect with the environmentally conscious shopper who demands less or zero waste.

FIGURE 5.6   Biodegradable packaging. Credit Shutterstock / Maples Images

FASHION INDUSTRY EXAMPLES

Innovative American packaging company **Boox** loans out reusable blue Velcro plastic boxes (Boox Box), to brands that work with them. Customers can use the packaging to make returns to the brand, or they can send the packaging back empty so it can be cleaned and used again. Boox's boxes can be used around 200 times before being reduced into plastic chips and remade again into new boxes, so fully circular themselves.

Boox also has another product called the Boox Baag which is also designed to be reused hundreds of times. Boox Baag was developed specifically as a solution for items such as clothing.

PACKAGING FREE

Some retailers are also experimenting with packaging free spaces inside their stores. Zero waste shops will help to eradicate unnecessary and wasteful packaging. The customer is required to bring their own containers – whether that's bags, bottles, or boxes – to avoid as much waste as possible.

FASHION INDUSTRY EXAMPLES

American department store chain **Nordstrom** ran a Package Free Pop-In 2021, where consumers could shop across verticals including beauty, homeware, and kids from brands offering products vetted by Nordstrom's sustainability experts to ensure it meets a certain standard. Shoppers were encouraged to bring their own bags and containers when shopping at the Package Free pop-In.

UK Department store group **Selfridges** offer a "naked click & collect," which essentially is all products purchased just minus the box, in order to remove unnecessary packaging from their in-store collections.

Beauty brand **REN** has launched an initiative to reduce cosmetics packaging waste. The British brand has partnered with a number of other brands including Biossance, Youth to the People, Herbivore, and Caudalie, on the We Are Allies campaign. The campaign is led by REN's CEO, Arnaud Meysselle, and has the goal of producing only planet friendly packaging by 2025.

SOLUTIONS

Avery Dennison is a materials science and manufacturing company specialising in the design and manufacture of a wide variety of labelling and functional materials. Their expertise and global scale enables them to deliver innovative, sustainable, and intelligent solutions to customers all over the world. The company and some of their innovative solutions are further explained by Amy Lee in the next expert insight.

Expert insight from Amy Lee
Senior Manager, Trends and Insights Apparel at Avery Dennison.

For too long, the fashion space has been profitable at the expense of livelihoods and the health of the planet. The impacting trauma has touched us as a collective global community, triggering a movement for change that has been growing and growing for decades.

Every improvement that we want to realise as an industry is rooted in connection. We can start with connecting with each other – our teams, our companies, and our wider networks. From there we can connect our processes, opening up opportunities to put change into action.

Transparency is essential in exposing the challenges and tasks at hand. What we don't know, we can't improve. By connecting hardware, products, people and places, we are empowered to tackle anything from safety in the workplace, forced labour and fair wages, to environmental impact, inefficiency, and waste. Connection is loaded with opportunity.

The human need for connection was felt particularly strongly through the shared experience of a global pandemic, which is still so fresh in our minds and present in our lives. Consider that this need is systemically intertwined with digital technology. Never before have we needed such a strong "phygital" existence to live happy, healthy lives and run sustainable, profitable businesses.

Also notable is the mindsets of emerging generations. Those experiencing adolescence in a world that is so intricately connected on a global scale are receiving an influx of information at an unprecedented rate. While misinformation is rife, this anytime-access to news and data is seen to be giving young people a heightened sense of urgency for behavioural and process change, as well as a natural intuition for authenticity. Those who capture the attention and spending power of this audience by delivering on transparency and meaningful action will be a step ahead.

Digitally, we can connect our entire ecosystem of the fashion industry and beyond. Take the transformational opportunities of artificial intelligence through prediction and automation. Automation poses a positive shift in our workforces through re-training and upskilling individuals so that their purpose is more purposeful, safe, and valuable than ever before. Meanwhile, smart factories can get to work optimising for speed, efficiency, and agility – a prerequisite for operating in the midst of ongoing disruption. The goal not being to simply sell more, but to sell better.

Prediction offers solutions to a whole host of industry challenges, including the harvesting of data to generate demand signals. Demand-driven manufacturing is coming. Fashion businesses are already building the digital infrastructure required to make only what is needed, in the quantities in demand, delivered in the right moment. Connected products have the power to generate meaningful – even educational – interactions. Not only can brands and retailers leverage connection to enable closer relationships with their audiences, but they can create feedback loops to inform design, merchandise planning, logistics, circular infrastructures and more.

As an industry, we are learning that stakeholder interactions can not happen in silos. Each event has a knock-on effect on something else, which is why it is so critical to look deeply and holistically at the end-to-end process of creation and consumption.

Avery Dennison's "#caretobethechange" campaign goes some way to addressing this connectivity so badly needed in apparel supply chains. The care label is a small but essential touchpoint on a garment that acts as a platform for sharing information. Its role is destined for connection. With legislation coming down the track that will allow brands and retailers to communicate care and content digitally, the opportunity to support new business models and sustainable infrastructures, as well as foster meaningful human engagement will be paramount to success.

With investment – together with the right partnerships – we can build the capabilities needed to innovate and accelerate the shift to an earth-positive, human-centric reality. As individuals, we must not underestimate the power of connection as a means to shape and create what we want the future of retail to look like.

FIGURE 5.7   Avery Dennison Care Label. Credit Avery Dennison

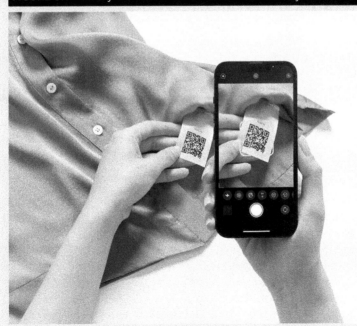

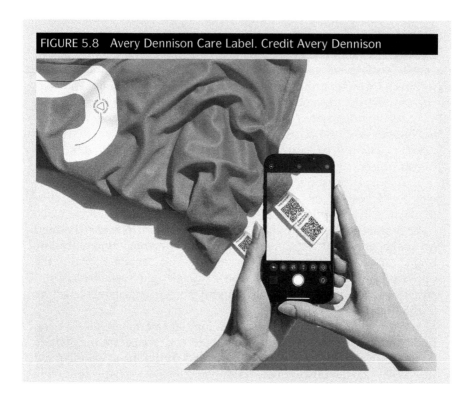

FIGURE 5.8 Avery Dennison Care Label. Credit Avery Dennison

This chapter has provided insight on how important it is for fashion brands to develop a circular system. Key takeaways include:

- Sourcing refers to the acquisition of raw materials or finished products within a fashion supply chain, it is key that fashion brands source responsibly.
- Fashion brands should work towards having a responsible supply chain that considers the environmental and human impact of their products' journey through that supply chain (from raw materials sourcing to manufacturing, storage, delivery, and every transportation link in between).
- Traceability and accountability are important in both the upstream and the downstream supply chain.
- Blockchain technology in the supply chain has the potential to improve transparency and traceability as well as reduce administrative costs.
- Real-time data management within the fashion supply chain allows companies and brands to monitor all activities in both upstream and downstream sections as well as providing an opportunity to correct mistakes and adopt solutions.
- An excessive approach to packaging is outdated and fashion brands now understand the importance of producing a responsible solution that is in line with their sustainability commitments.

- Innovations such as Avery Dennison's Care Label and EON's digital passports will become essential components on products that act as a platform for sharing information.

REFERENCES

Christopher, M. (2011). *Logistics and Supply Chain Management*, 4th edn. Pearson: Harlo.
Movie: RiverBlue (2016). Directed by DAVID MCILVRIDE & ROGER WILLIAMS (Film). Paddle Production.

FURTHER READING

Ellen MacArthur Foundation (2021). Circular Design for Fashion, Ellen MacArthur Foundation.
Frings, G. (2013). *Fashion from Concept to Consumer*, Prentice Hall.
Gardetti, M. (2019). The UN Sustainable Fashion Goals for the Textile and Fashion Industry, Springer.
Janjarasskul, T. and Krochta, J.M. (2010). Handbook of Sustainability Research. Scientific Publishing, Frankfurt.
Varley, R., Radclyffe-Thomas, N., and Webb, W. (2018). Patagonia: Creative Sustainable Strategy for a Reluctant Fashion Brand, Bloomsbury.

WEB MATERIAL

Burns, S. (2020). Why Product Customization Will Position Your Brand To Win In 2020. Forbes. Retrieved from: www.forbes.com/sites/stephanieburns/2020/01/10/why-product-customization-will-position-your-brand-to-win-in-2020/.
Chen, C. (2022). Fashions 5 Most Promising Supply Chain Innovations. Business of Fashion. Retrieved from: www.businessoffashion.com/articles/retail/fashions-5-most-promising-supply-chain-innovations/.
Deloitte (2019). The Deloitte Consumer Review: Made-to-order: The Rise of Mass Personalisation. Retrieved from: https://www2.deloitte.com/content/dam/Deloitte/ch/Documents/consumer-business/ch-en-consumer-business-made-to-order-consumer-review.pdf.
European Bioplastics (2013). Bioplastics—Facts and Figures. European Bioplastics, Berlin. Retrieved from: https://docs.european-bioplastics.org/publications/EUBP_Facts_and_figures.pdf.
Grewal, D., Hardesty, D.M., and Iyer, G.R. (2004). The Effects of Buyer Identification and Purchase Timing on Consumers' Perceptions of Trust, Price Fairness and Repurchase. Retrieved from: www.sciencedirect.com/science/article/abs/pii/S1094996804701218.
Global Protocol on Packaging Sustainability (2011). Intentions. Journal of Interactive Marketing. Retrieved from: www.readkong.com/page/global-protocol-on-packaging-sustainability-2-0-7021981.
Haws, K.L. and Bearden, W.O. (2006). Dynamic Pricing and Consumer Fairness Perceptions. Journal of Consumer Research. Retrieved from: https://academic.oup.com/jcr/article-abstract/33/3/304/1891884?redirectedFrom=fulltext.
Jabareen, Y. (2008). A New Conceptual Framework for Sustainable Development. Environment, Development and Sustainability. Retrieved from: www.researchgate.net/publication/310662968_New_Conceptual_Framework_for_Sustainability.

James, K., Fitzpatrick, L., Lewis, H., and Sonneveld, K. (2005). Sustainable Packaging System Development. In: Leal Filho, W. (Ed.). Retrieved from: www.researchgate. net/publication/269819087_Sustainable_Packaging_Systems_Development.

Marci, K. (2022). How Fast Fashion can Slow Down. Edited.com. Retrieved from: https://edited.com/blog/how-fast-fashion-can-slow-down/.

McKinsey (2020). Sustainability in Packaging: Inside the Minds of Global Consumers. Retrieved from: www.mckinsey.com/industries/paper-forest-products-and-packaging/our-insights/sustainability-in-packaging-inside-the-minds-of-global-consumers.

McKinsey (2021). Sustainability in Packaging: Inside the Minds of Global Consumers. Retrieved from: www.mckinsey.com/industries/paper-forest-products-and-packaging/our-insights/sustainability-in-packaging-inside-the-minds-of-global-consumers.

OECD/FAO (2020). OECD-FAO Agricultural Outlook, OECD Agriculture Statistics. Retrieved from: www.oecd-ilibrary.org/agriculture-and-food/oecd-fao-agricultural-outlook-2020-2029_1112c23b-en.

Paddison, L. (2021). How Carbon Might go out of Fashion. BBC. Retrieved from: www.bbc.com/future/article/20211105-how-carbon-might-go-out-of-fashion.

Pinatih, D. (2021). Packaging Innovations & Lux Packaging. Stylus. Retrieved from: https://app.stylus.com/cross-industry/packaging_futures_21.

Richards, A.L. (2019). How to Make Activewear Without Killing the Planet. The Business of Fashion. Retrieved from: www.businessoffashion.com/articles/sustainability/how-to-make-activewear-without-killing-the-planet/.

Sherman, L. (2019). How Can New Technologies Help Make Fashion More Sustainable? Retrieved from: www.businessoffashion.com/articles/sustainability/how-can-new-technologies-help-make-fashion-more-sustainable/.

Sperl, A. (2019). Retrieved from: www.businessoffashion.com/articles/sustainability/how-can-new-technologies-help-make-fashion-more-sustainable/.

(Please note all Stylus content is subscription only).

BRAND REFERENCES

https://pangaia.com.
www.hm.com.
www.marni.com.
www.nike.com.
www.notpla.com.
www.selfridges.com.
https://www.renskincare.com.
www.averydennison.com.
www.alibaba.com.
https://shop.boox.com.
www.thereformation.com.

CHAPTER 6

The Responsible 9 Framework

#6 = Green Environment

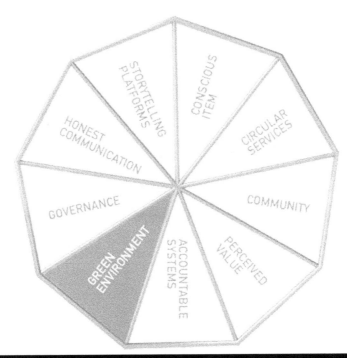

THE RESPONSIBLE 9 FRAMEWORK: #6 = GREEN ENVIRONMENT

DOI: 10.4324/9781003285915-7

INTRODUCTION TO THE CHAPTER

Environmental concern has led many businesses, including fashion businesses, to examine their practices throughout all of their operations, and not just focused on their products, and this also includes the physical retail locations, where brands sell their items.

Many fashion brands are now thinking beyond a product's sustainability credentials and applying sustainable practices across all aspects of the consumer journey. In doing so, fashion retailers are now creating physical stores that are energy-efficient spaces, designed, resourced, and constructed with ethically sourced materials.

From the interior design through to the fittings that a store uses, every aspect of the physical store location has come under scrutiny, as responsible fashion brands strive to develop a greener environment. Brands that are leading the way are now starting to use waste materials in their displays and repurposing them afterward. If fashion brands incorporate environmentally friendly initiatives into their store design, they can grow their sustainability credentials while also reducing costs and creating less damage to the environment.

THE MOVE TO GREEN AND MORE ENVIRONMENTALLY FRIENDLY STORES

Retail buildings are known to use large amounts of energy, with factors such as electricity, air conditioning, and lighting contributing to a brand's carbon footprint and emissions. According to Schneider Electric, retail buildings are the largest consumers of energy among non-residential buildings in Europe, contributing $20 billion each year. Factors such as electricity, air conditioning, and lighting all contribute to a brand's carbon footprint and emissions. Fashion retailers wanting to be considered environmentally responsible are rethinking how they build and run their stores, turning them into **GREEN ENVIRONMENTS**.

Zero Waste is a set of principles focused on waste prevention that encourages the redesign of resource life cycles so that everything can be reused. The goal of Zero Waste is for no rubbish to be sent to landfills or the ocean. Some of the leading fashion brands are now working towards the goal of being Zero Waste throughout their whole business, including their physical retail space. Every aspect of the retail environment is now being examined and debated and these include (but are not limited to):

- Living interiors.
- Clothing hangers.
- Mannequins.
- Lighting.
- Energy.

One of the challenges faced now is the misconception that recycling is the best and first option. Many products that can be recycled actually are not because of the cost and processing time. Other actions need to be considered and taken before something is sent to be recycled. This mindset needs to be applied not just at the product manufacturing and supply chain operations but throughout the entire business, this includes the physical retail environments where products are displayed and sold.

THE 5 R'S HIERARCHY

Shelby Bell developed the **5 R's hierarchy**, in 2020. According to the 5 R's, four actions should be taken prior to recycling, those R's are refuse, reduce, reuse, repurpose, and then recycle. Incorporating this approach into a fashion business' overall approach could greatly reduce waste and recycling efforts will minimise landfill waste.

    Refuse: Fashion brands should refuse to accept waste as much as possible throughout their whole business, such as refusing to buy wasteful or non-recyclable products and refusing unnecessary product packaging options.

    Reduce: Fashion brands need to aim to significantly reduce the use of harmful, wasteful, and non-recyclable products, this applies to all parts of the business, including the garments and the packaging. Reducing dependency results in less waste materials ending up in landfill and the associated negative environmental impacts.

    Reuse: Brands need to attempt to reduce items throughout their business on a regular basis, instead of constantly replenishing.

    Repurposing: For every item that can't be refused, reduced, or reused, fashion brands should attempt to repurpose it, this is also known as upcycling.

    Recycle: Once a brand has gone through the first 4R's, recycling is the most environmentally friendly waste disposal method, however, this should be the last option.

Source: Shelby Bell

LIVING INTERIORS

Incorporating greenery into retail spaces helps create an environment in which customers can relax, take their time, and shop around, while also communicating green credentials. Store interiors now include living plants and walls that help improve air quality and acoustics. Living or "green" walls and roofs can also help to thermally insulate in order to reduce their energy requirements and therefore reduce costs.

FASHION BRAND EXAMPLE

The **Timberland** Carnaby Street store in London, UK, was the brand's first purpose-led store in Europe. The store promotes the brand's sustainability endeavours throughout the whole space. Inside the store, shoppers are educated about the brand and are immersed in Timberland's vision of combining fashion with nature leading towards a greener and responsible future. The store has a full-height living green space with natural elements throughout, it is like a modern exhibition, transparent and honest marketing approaches have been used throughout the space.

As Argu Secilmis, vice president of global marketing for Timberland, further explains:

> "Carnaby Street is an iconic retail experience in London and the perfect location for Timberland to reveal our new purpose-led retail store. This is where nature and fashion come together to create something fresh and bold in the marketplace. We are excited to engage with our community, immerse them in our brand experience, and build a movement together toward a greener future."
>
> *Source: Timberland*

CLOTHING HANGERS

Every aspect of the retail store should be considered when taking a green approach, and this also includes essential items such as clothing hangers. Clothing hangers used to display garments in stores should also have sustainable credentials and shouldn't be overlooked. Typical hangers are made of plastic or metal and have a lifespan of only three months.

British company **Braiform** developed the Re-Use system that has kept billions of plastic hangers and accessories out of landfills. Now part of the Tam Hangers group, their mission, and business model is further explained on their website:

> "We're passionate about green, cost-effective service. That's why we created the Re-Use program: the first-ever closed-loop hanger solution. We partner with major retailers and garment manufacturers to re-use hangers — dramatically reducing the number that ends up in landfills, and the cost to clients.
>
> Hangers in the Re-Use program are recycled at the end of their lifecycle and recycled plastic used in producing new hangers to prevent plastic from ending up in landfills. We currently have the largest hanger production facility in Europe which practices lean manufacturing techniques minimising waste and improving efficiency."
>
> *Source: Tam Hangers*

Another leading firm producing environmentally sustainable hangers is German firm **Cortec**. Their innovative hanger is made from a combination of recycled plastics and meadow grass. The material they use even meets the strict requirements of EN 71–3, which applies to the production of children's toys in the EU.

MANNEQUINS

Mannequins are used throughout stores to display products, as part of a green approach to retail, both their manufacturing and their ultimate end-of-life should also be taken into consideration. Moreover, they should not be sent to landfill sites after a few months of use as has previously occurred.

Pasqual Arnella is a Spanish company that produces mannequins made entirely from paper waste, they supply some of the leading fashion businesses including Patagonia and the British label Ben Sherman. Over the last 50 years, the business has evolved from making papier-mâché figurines and horses as toys for children, to now specialising in the manufacturing of mannequins for fashion retailers. The products are made of recycled paper waste, which comes from cellulose, a completely renewable resource.

ENERGY EFFICIENT LIGHTING

Effective use of lighting is integral to the consumer in-store experience. At the same time, lighting makes up a large share of the average store's energy consumption. LVMH established that 70% of its greenhouse gas emissions were directly attributable to energy consumption at its 4,700 stores with 50% coming from lighting. The luxury group have made installation of LED lighting a priority to reduce its energy usage by 30%.

Adopting energy efficient technologies such as LED lighting is an effective strategy for fashion brands to drive both environmental and economic benefits. According to The Carbon Trust, a 20% cut in energy costs can represent the same bottom-line profit benefit as a 5% increase in sales.

RENEWABLE ENERGY

In addition to energy efficiency measures such as LED lighting, fashion brands continue to step up investments in renewable energy to power their stores and demonstrate their sustainability credentials.

Renewable energy generated from carbon neutral sources such as sunlight, wind, rain, tides, waves, and geothermal heat are now significantly undercutting fossil fuels as a cheaper source of energy.

Fashion brands that recognise the need to shift away from fossil fuels have joined the RE100, a global initiative of major businesses committed to 100% renewable power. Global luxury group, **Kering**, joined the RE100 initiative in 2020, pledging to use 100% renewable electricity by 2022. **Burberry**, one of the most prominent RE100 members, currently sources 93% of its electricity from renewable sources, on track to achieve its target to use 100% renewable electricity in its own operations by 2022.

FIGURE 6.1 Renewable energy - Credit Shutterstock / Eviart

FASHION BRAND EXAMPLES

Ralph Lauren has committed to powering 100% of its globally owned and operated offices, distribution centres, and stores with renewable electricity by 2025. To achieve their goal, Ralph Lauren has announced that they will pursue a combination of virtual power purchase agreements in North America as well as assess a select number of US sites for onsite solar power installations. For the remaining electricity use, the company is planning to purchase green power products, including renewable energy certificates, guarantees of origin, and international renewable energy credits.

Source: RE100

PVH is one of the largest global apparel companies, owning and marketing brands such as Calvin Klein, Tommy Hilfiger, Van Heusen, and Speedo. Alongside its RE100 commitment of powering 100% of its operations with renewables by 2030, they announced an intermediate goal of reaching 50% by 2025. PVH recognizes that progress against climate change starts with external measurements and accountability. The steps they are taking include engaging with suppliers operating the most energy-intensive facilities to set targets and reduce greenhouse gas emissions, working to develop products with lower environmental impact and collaborating with suppliers to drive renewable energy transitions.

Source: RE100

Stella McCartney makes responsible decisions in every part of the business including the way they design and operate their shops and offices. All their new stores are lit using LED lighting, which uses 75% less energy than traditional bulbs and lasts over 25 times longer than conventional options. In the UK, all their locations are powered by wind energy provided by Ecotricity, a renewable energy company focused on developing and building new wind turbines. Whenever possible, the fashion brand also buys their fittings and furniture locally or from auctions.

Additionally, Stella McCartney's UK, London, Flagship store, incorporates handmade, organic, and ethically sourced materials throughout. Transparent and sustainable marketing messages can be seen around the store and these help to further communicate the brand's push to being a green and responsible brand. Further information about the store is explained in Juliet Russell and Philip Mak's expert insight.

Expert insight from Juliet Russell and Philip Mak

Juliet Russel is Head of Sustainability at Stella McCartney. Philip Mak is Global Head of Content and Editorial at Stella McCartney.

Stella McCartney's 23 Old Bond Street flagship in London personifies the conscious luxury pioneer's ethos, reflecting a modern approach to design, innovation, and sustainable practices. The 700-square-metre space was built with customised experiences and multi-sensory engagement in mind, leveraging architecture and art, materials and music, décor and operations to bring the British designer's ethical perspective to life.

"Old Bond Street, it's probably one of the most prestigious retail locations in the world. And for me being born and bred in London and having our business headquarters there and design studio, it's an incredible honour for us. This store really tells the story of the World of Stella McCartney; incorporating sustainability, fashion and luxury," says Stella McCartney.

The store was envisioned by award-winning, London-based design collective Wayward. It is modularly designed to interchangeably evolve and highlight not only Stella McCartney's latest collections, but also provide a textured emotional experience. The Grade II historic 18th-century building's original façade provides a sharp dichotomy with the cutting-edge four-storey interior.

Celebrating Stella's love of nature, guests are greeted upon entry by "Stella Rocks" – a bespoke indoor rockery installation acting as a natural air purifier, consisting of black limestone from a quarry in Stanhope and carefully selected rocks sourced from the McCartney farm in Campbeltown, Scotland. They are surrounded by replanted moss and thyme, sourced through Wayward's plant rehoming scheme. Moving up a level to the first floor, the outdoor urban garden features silver birch trees that sit alongside relocated ferns, wild ginger, and moss.

Stella McCartney believes it is responsible for the resources it uses and its environmental impact, with every effort made to move away from traditional luxury materials in favour of handmade, organic, and responsibly sourced alternatives. Among 23 Old Bond Street's conscious qualities are: LEED accreditation; an oversized skylight maximising natural light; low-energy LED lighting; and 100% renewable electricity from Ecotricity.

It was also the first store in the United Kingdom to use Airlabs' nano-carbon filtration technology, protecting customers and staff from city air pollution, as well as biodegradable and biobased BNATURAL mannequins by Bonaveri. These display models are constructed from BPlast®, a bioplastic material composed of 72% sugarcane derivative for a significant reduction of CO_2 emissions, and coated with BPaint® – a paint made solely from renewable organic substances and free from petroleum derivatives.

Aligned with Stella McCartney's circular ambitions, 23 Old Bond Street also features wall finishes crafted from office paper waste, reclaimed timber plinths, vintage furniture, recycled foam seating, displays made from reused runway show props and repurposed Fur Free Fur lining the lifts. In addition to informative messaging scattered throughout, the space also hosts educational experiences to foster conscious creativity and collaboration.

As Stella McCartney's global flagship, 23 Old Bond Street serves as a living lab for the brand's upcoming innovations and initiatives – paving the way for and enabling circular takeback schemes, rental and repair services, and future exhibits being planned today to protect our planet's better tomorrow.

Though not a fashion brand, retailer **IKEA** is on a very important sustainability journey, pioneering green retail and providing a reference for the fashion industry. In 2019, IKEA opened a store in South East London which when opened was marketed as their most sustainable store to date. The 344,445 sq. ft. store was built using renewable construction materials. The company used many green technologies such as solar roof panels, geothermal heating, and LED lighting in order to further enhance the green retail space. In order to further support their sustainable message, the store only offers customers a limited number of parking spaces, this is done to encourage both customers and employees to commute by public transport. When a product is bought from the store, IKEA then offers the option of electric vans, minicabs, and courier bicycles as home delivery options. Detailed and informative marketing displays are also featured throughout the store to communicate and teach their customers about the different technologies that can be used to make customers' homes more energy-efficient and environmentally friendly.

Source: IKEA

Sustainable accessories brand, **Bottletop**, has a 3D printed store in London, UK which was created by robots using upcycled plastic. The store is zero waste, the flooring of the store is made from reworked rubber tires and the interior is made from 60,000 upcycled plastic bottles. The space embodies the company's core mission to empower people through sustainable design and creative culture.

Source: Bottletop

Expert insight from Patsy Perry

Reader in Fashion Marketing, Manchester Fashion Institute, Manchester Metropolitan University.

Scrutiny of the fashion industry's social and environmental impact is centred on product and supply chain operations, while the physical store has been largely absent from debates and critiques of fashion's sustainability issues. Fashion retailers are developing and implementing various sustainability initiatives, commitments, and strategies around sourcing, supply chain operations, and end-of-life of the products they sell and increasingly using the physical store to communicate around sustainability. However, they have been critiqued for being insufficient as the pursuit of growth is supported by retail marketing that encourages consumers to purchase more, not less, clothing.

The store environment is not only a selling space but also a symbol of brand identity and a place for multisensory brand experiences. Sometimes significant investment is needed to create an effective retail experience and communicate brand position in a competitive marketplace, with the ongoing investment needed for upgrading and refitting from time to time. Physical retail has lower return rates compared to online retail and less shipping and packaging but has impacts from shopfit, furniture, materials, and resource infrastructure. Similar to the challenge of product sustainability in a sector based on planned obsolescence, store interiors also tend to be transient rather than enduring, which increases environmental impact and waste.

Window displays and visual merchandising can be quite elaborate and may feature other items in addition to mannequins and products. These need to be designed, sourced, produced, and transported – all of which have environmental and social impacts – but there is a lack of transparency on their supply chain and what happens at end-of-life when the display changes. Window displays are designed to support specific seasonal campaigns or collections, so by their very nature are temporary and need to be changed on a regular basis to keep the store looking fresh and enticing.

With sustainability such an important priority, fashion retailers are increasingly focusing on physical stores by incorporating responsibly sourced materials within shopfit, window displays and visual merchandising, and rethinking the purpose of selling space.

Shopfit

Some retailers use salvaged or recycled materials to reduce environmental impact and support the projection of their brand image. Patagonia's Manchester store features reclaimed items from nearby industrial locations such as lighting and wood from old factories and tiles from an old police station. Patagonia's approach to shopfit, focusing on utility and longevity, mirrors its approach to product design.

Window displays and visual merchandising

Various items and materials have lower environmental impacts, such as salvage, reclaimed wood, recycled plastic, cardboard, deadstock fabrics, or 3D printed plastic waste. Consideration should also be given to the end-of-life of temporary displays so that items and materials can be repurposed, upcycled, recycled, or disposed of responsibly. Over the years, Hermès has often used leather offcuts from its manufacturing processes to create elaborate sculptures for its window displays.

Selling space

Some retailers are repurposing selling space to support customers in slowing down consumption, extending product lifetimes and reducing waste by offering repair, upcycling, reuse, and rental services or curating immersive exhibitions featuring educational storytelling about sustainability. Arc'teryx set up its first ReBird™ Service Center in its New York store as a physical manifestation of its ongoing initiatives around circularity, which includes complimentary repairs and education around care and repair (this is further explored in Chapter 9, **STORYTELLING PLATFORMS**).

This chapter has provided insight into the value of creating a GREEN ENVIRONMENT. Key takeaways include:

- Green environments reduce carbon emissions, drive real economic benefits, and promote health and well-being of customers and employees.
- Store interiors can include living plants that help improve air quality, well-being, and aid with thermal insulation to reduce energy requirements and therefore reduce costs.
- Fashion brands should consider different sustainable strategies to create green environments, including renewable energy and energy efficiency, zero waste management, and circularity.
- Consideration should also be given to the end-of-life of temporary displays so that items and materials can be repurposed, upcycled, recycled, or disposed of responsibly.
- Physical stores should be energy efficient spaces, designed with ethically sourced materials.
- Renewable energy generated from carbon neutral sources such as sunlight, wind, rain, tides, waves, and geothermal heat is now significantly undercutting fossil fuels as the world's cheapest source of energy.

FURTHER READING

Ellen MacArthur Foundation (2021). Circular Design for Fashion, Ellen MacArthur Foundation.

Frings, G. (2013). *Fashion from Concept to Consumer*, Prentice Hall.

Gardetti, M, (2019). *The UN Sustainable Fashion Goals for the Textile and Fashion Industry*, Springer.

Little, T. (2018). *The Future of Fashion: Understanding Sustainability in the Fashion Industry*, New Degree Press.

WEB MATERIAL

McKinsey (2022). Green Business Building. Retrieved from: www.mckinsey.com/capabilities/sustainability/how-we-help-clients/green-business-building.

Road Runner Smarter Recycling (2020). blog/the-5-rs-of-waste-recycling (Shelby Bell). Retrieved from: www.roadrunnerwm.com/blog/the-5-rs-of-waste-recycling.

Talbot, P. (2021). The Shifting Landscape of Brand Loyalty. Forbes. Retrieved from: www.forbes.com/sites/paultalbot/2021/07/13/the-shifting-landscape-of-brand-loyalty/.

UKFT (2020). UKFT's Compendium of Industry Statistics and Analysis 2020. Retrieved from: https://ukft.s3.eu-west-1.amazonaws.com/wp-content/uploads/2021/11/24095453/UKFTs-Compendium-of-Industry-Statistics-and-Analysis-2020-Executive-Summary.pdf.

WGSN (2021). Big Ideas 2023: Fashion. WGSN: Future Strategies. www.wgsn.com/en/products/fashion.

BRAND REFERENCES

www.ikea.com.

www.stellamccartney.com.

www.ralphlauren.co.uk.

www.pasqualarnella.com.

www.tamhangers.com.

www.timberland.co.uk.

www.cortecvci.com.

www.pvh.com.

CHAPTER 7

The Responsible 9 Framework

#7 = Governance

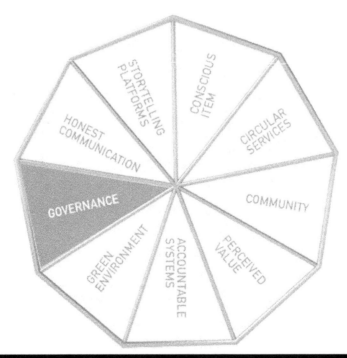

THE RESPONSIBLE 9 FRAMEWORK: #7 = GOVERNANCE

DOI: 10.4324/9781003285915-8

INTRODUCTION TO THE CHAPTER

This chapter introduces number 7 in **The Responsible 9 Framework: GOVERNANCE**. It is important for fashion brands to actively seek support and guidance from outside organisations and groups on their journey to be a genuinely responsible business.

The objective of this chapter is to provide a broad overview and insight into both the larger global initiatives that have been developed that sit across all industries including the fashion industry, and the specific foundations and activities that are being developed internally within the industry itself. This chapter provides a list of a number of organisations and groups that have been included in order to show the breadth that is on offer, they sit across three categories:

- Supportive Organsiations.
- Certification Companies.
- Activist Groups.

In 2015 all **United Nations** member states accepted The 2030 Agenda for Sustainable Development Goals, this agenda sets out a clear and specific plan of action to improve the whole planet and the lives of the people who live on it. This is clearly a very important set of goals, and one that unites countries and policy together. The Sustainable Development Goals have provided a framework with which to help governments all over the world to better understand what needs to happen in order to protect the future of the planet.

The agenda sits across five main categories, People, Planet, Prosperity, Peace, and Partnership. The United Nations further outlines these categories on their website, sdgs.uu.org/2030agenda:

People
We are determined to end poverty and hunger, in all their forms and dimensions, and to ensure that all human beings can fulfil their potential in dignity and equality and in a healthy environment.

Planet
We are determined to protect the planet from degradation, including through sustainable consumption and production, sustainably managing its natural resources and taking urgent action on climate change, so that it can support the needs of the present and future generations.

Prosperity
We are determined to ensure that all human beings can enjoy prosperous and fulfilling lives and that economic, social and technological progress occurs in harmony with nature.

Peace
We are determined to foster peaceful, just and inclusive societies which are free from fear and violence. There can be no sustainable development without peace and no peace without sustainable development.

Partnership

We are determined to mobilize the means required to implement this Agenda through a revitalised Global Partnership for Sustainable Development, based on a spirit of strengthened global solidarity, focussed in particular on the needs of the poorest and most vulnerable and with the participation of all countries, all stakeholders and all people.

The interlinkages and integrated nature of the Sustainable Development Goals are of crucial importance in ensuring that the purpose of the new Agenda is realised. If we realize our ambitions across the full extent of the Agenda, the lives of all will be profoundly improved and our world will be transformed for the better.

The SDGs were developed through extensive work from the United Nations, and outlines 17 key goals, which all countries need to address and take urgent action on; they are:

(1) No Poverty, (2) Zero Hunger, (3) Good Health and Well-being, (4) Quality Education, (5) Gender Equality, (6) Clean Water and Sanitation, (7) Affordable and Clean Energy, (8) Decent Work and Economic Growth, (9) Industry, Innovation and Infrastructure, (10) Reducing Inequality, (11) Sustainable Cities and Communities, (12) Responsible Consumption and Production, (13) Climate Action, (14) Life Below Water, (15) Life On Land, (16) Peace, Justice, and Strong Institutions, (17) Partnerships for the Goals.

Some of these Sustainable Development Goals have already been successfully implemented in developed countries, but certainly not all of the developing ones. Attention now turns to achieving these 17 Goals collaboratively by 2030. Focus is also on specific industries (such as the fashion industry) to improve practice in order to meet the SDG's, however the industry has a long way to go, as highlighted by M. Fernanda Hernandez Franco.

FIGURE 7.1   SDGs -Shutterstock / Mameraman

Expert insight from M. Fernanda Hernandez Franco
Head of Sustainability for a leading Italian multi-brand retailer.

Sustainable fashion shouldn't even be a thing, fashion should be intrinsically sustainable, unfortunately, this is not the case. We are suffering the environmental and social impact of bad business decisions. Products are still untraceable, transparency is not as common as it should be, damaging chemicals are used, there is a big reliance on fossil fuels, bias on communication campaigns, discrimination and lack of human rights are occurring, equality still a challenge . . .

On the topic of gender equality and women's empowerment, the SDG number 5 of the UN is very close to my heart. I think it is very important to spotlight this goal in the industry as we are still very far behind where we should be, which is evident by the shocking statistics at the World Economic Forum in 2022.

Women within the fashion industry are the biggest percentage of clients and of the workforce, from production and corporate, but with a big payment gap, opportunities to grow from the supply chain to c-suit are still few and far between. Moreover, there are the big stereotypes of women's beauty and profile clichés circulated through communication and marketing within the industry. I think it is necessary to set a course from where we are now, take a position and commit to it, defining specific short- and long-term KPIs (Key Performance Indicators). We could encourage equal opportunity businesses, set goals to communicate without biases, engage suppliers and companies to be part of this change, joining forces with NGOs through campaigns and programs, and as customers, support businesses and brands that are working in that direction.

Online shopping is growing and becoming an important reference for consumers all over the world, a fast and easy way to shop. Corporations have a huge responsibility within the environment and society, they should prioritise social engagement as part of their business' mission and commit to shifting actions to prevent climate change, support innovation and regenerative economy.

The market is demanding more information and transparency. Education on sustainability within brands and companies would encourage sustainable consumer behaviour to choose a more conscious approach to fashion consumption.

Considering all this information and the increasing demand from investors from a business perspective for better industry practices, now geared mainly towards Millennials and Gen Z customers, it is time to work hard for a better world, to work as a community, to work with humility. It is time for us to take responsibility as companies and brands, as governments and policy makers, and most importantly as customers to make better and more informed choices.

Fashion is such a fascinating and inspiring industry, it is a source of self-expression, impacts and influences huge masses, thus, if that power could be used for good, a big shift could occur.

> I strongly believe in a business with purpose, profit but with responsibility and commitment to the planet and its people, where we can foster equality, inclusion, innovation, growth, and opportunities for all.

SUPPORTIVE ORGANISATIONS

The **British Fashion Council** (BFC) strengthens British fashion in the global economy as a leader in responsible, creative businesses. It does this through championing diversity, building and inviting the industry to actively participate in a network to accelerate a successful circular fashion economy. **The Institute of Positive Fashion** (IPF) is the engine for industry change and demonstrates the BFC's commitment to climate action. The IPF activates across a global network to convene the industry, government, academia, and other stakeholders to develop industry-wide transformation programs of change to accelerate outcomes.

Through the IPF, the British Fashion Council is working on a strategy to enable the industry to reduce climate and societal impact in line with UN goals. The strategy will comprise adaptation of business models and working practices across the whole industry. The IPF seeks to ensure an equitable industry, balanced with the needs of the planet and society by taking an holistic approach across three key pillars:

- ENVIRONMENT

This pillar focuses on environmental and business governance to drive a more sustainable fashion future.

- PEOPLE

This pillar represents the people, from the product makers to the staff, students, and models who pioneer our brands.

- COMMUNITY and CRAFTSMANSHIP

This pillar supports the talent, skills, and elements of craftsmanship that make up our unique industry and have positive impacts on local communities.

The **Ellen MacArthur Foundation** is an important charity that works to accelerate the transition to a circular economy, to eliminate waste and pollution, and to support the regeneration of nature. The team extensively researches and then works with businesses, academia, policymakers, and institutions to mobilise systems solutions at scale, globally. The Ellen MacArthur Foundation also has an informative podcast about a new way to design, make, and use things; it is called The Circular Economy Show.

The **Environmental Justice Foundation** (EJF) campaigns to reduce the human and environmental costs of cotton production, exposing human rights abuses, pesticide misuse, water-shortages, and calling for supply-chain transparency. EJF has investigated and exposed state-sponsored forced child labour in Uzbekistan resulting in immediate improvements to international supply chains and retailer policies.

Fashion for Good is a global initiative to reimagine how fashion is designed, made, worn, and reused. With an innovation hub in Amsterdam, a startup accelerator in Silicon Valley, and a worldwide network of collaborators and changemakers, it demonstrates a better way for the fashion industry to work; a way in which companies, communities, and the planet can flourish.

The **Fashion Pact** is a global coalition of companies in the fashion and textile industry (ready-to-wear, sport, lifestyle, and luxury) including their suppliers and distributors, all committed to a common core of key environmental goals in three areas: stopping global warming, restoring biodiversity, and protecting the oceans. Launched as a mission given to Kering Chairman and CEO, François-Henri Pinault by French President, Emmanuel Macron, the Fashion Pact was presented to Heads of State at the G7 Summit in Biarritz in 2019.

Fashion Roundtable is dedicated to reimagining a responsible, inclusive, and thriving fashion industry. Their mission is to raise the reputation of the fashion industry, support UK talent and manufacturing, embed ESG (environmental, social, governance) standards and increase investment in innovation. Fashion Roundtable does this by working closely with government, parliament, and key strategic partners, to promote the voice and needs of the sector, educating and influencing decision-makers. They have a unique team drawn from fashion, business, economics, and politics, and offer transformative strategies across the industry. Fashion Roundtable represents the diverse voices of the industry, creating the potential for long-term sector growth.

The **Fifteen Percent Pledge** is a US based not-for-profit organisation that calls to action for major retailers and corporations to create sustainable and supportive ecosystems for Black-owned businesses to succeed. The organisation works with companies to comprehensively re-evaluate their structures, ways of working, funding, and resourcing in order to implement meaningful change and create greater equity for Black businesses.

Global Fashion Agenda (GFA) is a leading global forum on fashion sustainability and centred on the Copenhagen Fashion Summit, an event for industry decision-makers on fashion sustainability. Since 2009, Global Fashion Agenda, a non-profit organisation, has organised and hosted the Copenhagen Fashion Summit, a leading business event on fashion sustainability. Global Fashion Agenda is also known for releasing the annual CEO Agenda and the annual Pulse of the Fashion Industry report in collaboration with The Boston Consulting Group.

The Global Fashion Agenda is a year-round mission to mobilise the international fashion industry and community to transform the way fashion is produced and consumed.

Australian company **Good On You** is a source to get brand ratings, articles, and expertise on ethical and sustainable fashion. The company has a database of thousands of fashion brands, all assessed against their transparent rating system that focuses on the impact on people, the planet, and animals. Potential customers can check a brand's sustainability rating before they decide to purchase from it. This site provides the customer with detailed information about the product and the brand they would not otherwise have access to.

The **Sustainable Fashion Forum** (SFF) educates, empowers, and inspires people to reimagine the future of fashion by asking tough questions that ignite conversation and inspire change. In 2017, the Sustainable Fashion Forum began as a passion project. Today, SFF is a global community of passionate sustainable fashion advocates who believe that they can create change together. Founded on the principles of discovery and education, the Sustainable Fashion Forum is an online platform and offline conference for conscious fashion enthusiasts looking to make a tangible impact in their communities and beyond.

The **Sustainable Markets Initiative (SMI)** was launched by His Royal Highness, Prince Charles at The World Economic Forum 2020. The **Fashion Taskforce** operates as an industry sub-group of the Sustainable Markets Initiative and is chaired by Federico Marchetti, Founder of the YOOX Net-a-Porter Group. Its members come from fashion brands all over the world including: Brunello Cucinelli, Burberry, Chloé, Eon, Gabriela Hearst, Giorgio Armani, Johnstons Of Elgin, Moda Operandi, Mulberry, Selfridges, Stella McCartney, The Dubai Mall, Vestiaire Collective, and Zalando.

The Fashion Taskforce is committed to being leaders and exemplars to the global fashion, textile, and apparel sectors, working to accelerate the transition towards a more sustainable future.

The Sustainable Angle is a not-for-profit organisation and founders of **Future Fabrics Expo**. They initiate and support projects with a focus on sustainability in fashion and textiles and related industries such as food and agriculture. The Future Fabrics Expo was initiated in order to effect positive change within the industry by connecting and promoting innovators and suppliers of sustainable materials with fashion brands.

The materials showcased at the Future Fabrics Expo are all accompanied by educational background information and the seminars and workshops are held to aid fashion brands to have a positive impact upon nature and communities.

The **UK Fashion & Textile Association** (UKFT) is a network for fashion and textile companies in the UK. The association brings together designers, manufacturers, suppliers, agents and retailers to promote their businesses and our industry, both in the UK and throughout the world.

The **World Wildlife Fund** (WWF) is a leading independent conservation organisation. Their mission is to create a world where people and wildlife can thrive together. To achieve their mission, they are finding ways to help transform the future for the world's wildlife, rivers, forests, and seas; pushing for a reduction in carbon emissions that will avoid catastrophic climate change; and pressing for measures to help people live sustainably, within the means of our one planet. The organisation often connects with the fashion industry in order to help highlight issues and improve practice.

CERTIFICATION COMPANIES

Certifications are often presumed to focus solely on environmental issues, however, they can cover a wide range of issues including social, economic, and labour rights. Among the most common certifications used by the fashion industry are those related to fibres, chemicals, circular processes, working conditions, and fair trade. Some certifications apply to supply chains and raw materials while others certify production processes or production management. Additionally, there are certifications for business-to-customer approaches, such as packaging or after-sales services. Certifications vary in their remit and can consider more than one of these or all of them.

The certifications that are adopted by a brand should reflect its key sustainability priorities. Although fashion brands must actively seek outside support in their endeavour to be a truly responsible business, certification should be viewed as one strategy to help them pursue sustainability. In order to prevent greenwashing (misleading claims about sustainability credentials, more information on this topic is in Chapter 8, Honest Communication), it is important to distinguish between what a brand is certifying and what it claims to possess. Unless this is addressed, greenwashing is likely to persist.

B Corp certification – B-Labs is the non-profit business behind the **B Corp certification**. B-Labs measure a company's social and environmental performance from materials to the supply chain and employee treatment in order to determine whether they should receive the B Corp certification. A traditional business considers profit as the bottom line; B Corps add two more key factors; people and planet in order to create a "triple bottom line."

Several Fashion brands have already achieved B Corp status, including; Chloé, Patagonia, Allbirds, Eileen Fisher, and Veja Trainers. However many more fashion brands are now aiming for B Corp certification as this will then help the brand to showcase their entire social and environmental impact.

MINI CASE STUDY

Allbirds, a global footwear and apparel company has impressive sustainability commitment goals, including reducing its per-unit carbon footprint by 50% by the end of 2025.

Allbirds has developed ten public facing sustainable commitments, also known as their Flight Plan; these are broken down into three sections; those being regenerative agriculture, renewable materials, and responsible energy. These are the ten commitments published by the brand:

Regenerative Agriculture:

- 100 percent of Allbirds's wool will come from regenerative sources
- 100 percent of Allbirds's annual on-farm emissions from wool will be reduced or sequestered

Renewable Materials:

- 75 percent of materials used in Allbirds products will be sustainably sourced natural or recycled materials
- Allbirds will reduce the carbon footprint of its key raw materials by 25 percent
- Total raw materials used by Allbirds will be reduced by 25 percent across footwear and apparel products
- Double the lifetime of Allbirds's footwear and apparel products

Responsible Energy:

- Source 100 percent renewable energy for "owned and operated" facilities
- Source 100 percent renewable energy for Tier 1 manufacturing partners
- Achieve a steady state of >95 percent ocean shipping
- Reach 100 percent of customers machine washing on cold and 50 percent of customers hang-drying Allbirds apparel

Source: Allbirds

Hana Kajimura, Head of Sustainability at Allbirds

"When Allbirds launched in 2016, sustainability was a founding principle. As a B Corp and a Public Benefit Corporation, we've always been laser focused on our impact, and specifically our ambition to reverse climate change through better business. That starts with minimising our carbon footprint. Every decision we make is done through the lens of carbon reduction, and we're specifically focusing on regenerative agriculture, renewable materials and responsible energy to help us achieve our sustainability goals. While we've been working diligently to minimise our carbon footprint from the beginning, July 2021 was the first time we announced forward-facing targets for 2025 and 2030. The result is the Allbirds Flight Plan: ten of the most ambitious, science-based sustainability targets in the footwear and apparel industry. Our ten quantitative commitments ladder up to our overarching climate goals. We're aiming for a 50% reduction in our per-unit carbon footprint by the end of 2025, fully inclusive of scope 1–3 emissions. By 2030, we expect to reduce our per-unit footprint by 95%.

    While Allbirds has prioritised sustainability from the start, our Flight Plan holds us to clear milestones that keep us accountable to progress. The success of this plan relies on the participation of all core stakeholders, from suppliers and partners to employees and customers. We fully understand the challenges ahead, and know that these targets will be difficult to meet, but we feel optimistic about our ability to rise to this challenge."

FIGURE 7.2   Allbirds Carbon footprint sticker in Wool Runners. Credit Allbirds

FIGURE 7.3   Allbirds Merino Wool. Credit Allbirds

The **Bluesign** standard indicates that a textile or garment has the smallest possible ecological footprint. It assesses the brand from the bottom up and looks carefully at their resource productivity, consumer safety, water emissions, air emissions, and occupational health and safety standards. This certification is great for assessing a brand's environmental footprint and employment practices.

Certified Sustainable Packaging is an accreditation within the packaging industry. Packaging is given either a bronze, silver, gold, or platinum mark helping to make sustainability in packaging a more visible issue, and help brands choose their packaging strategically and in line with their core values.

Cradle to Cradle Certified is the global standard for products that are safe, circular, and responsibly made. Leading brands, retailers, designers, and manufacturers rely on the Cradle to Cradle Certified Product Standard to ensure the impact of their products on people and planet is a positive one. Cradle to Cradle Certified helps companies to innovate and optimise materials and products according to the world's most advanced science-based measures.

The **Fairtrade Foundation** is a movement for change that works directly with businesses to ensure that trading is done fairly and wholly supportive of their workers. The International Fairtrade System (which the Fairtrade Foundation is a part of) represents the world's largest and most recognised fair-trade system. The Fairtrade Foundation award, The Fairtrade Mark, is a symbol made up of a blue sky that symbolises optimism, and an arm, raised in the air to represent empowerment. The Fairtrade Mark also incorporates the colour green to symbolise growth.

The **Forest Stewardship Council** (FSC) is a non-profit organisation with a set of standards to make sure that forestry is practised in an environmentally responsible and socially beneficial way. The FSC label identifies responsibly sourced forest products, and can be applied to fabrics, clothing, footwear, packaging, and swing tags made from FSC certified materials.

The **Global Organic Textile Standard** (GOTS) is one of the globally most recognised standards. It ensures that throughout the supply chain (from harvesting to sale) the requirements for the organic classification have been met. Moreover, it will look at conditions such as forced labour, fair wages, and exposure to unsafe working conditions

Global Recycle Standard encourages transparency into the accurate amount of recycled materials used in each new product. It is divided into three qualifications. Bronze: means clothing contains less than 30% recycled material; Silver: 75%–95% of recycled material used; Gold: 95%–100% of the product has been made from recycled materials.

The **Leadership in Energy and Environmental Design** (LEED) is the most widely used green building rating system in the world. Available for virtually all building types, LEED provides a framework for healthy, efficient, and cost-saving green buildings. LEED certification is a globally recognized symbol of sustainability achievement and leadership.

MINI CASE STUDY

Through LEED certification, building and interior spaces receive an internationally recognizable, third-party verification that shows the world that a company means business regarding sustainability. Retailers can also use LEED to support CSR reporting. USGBC further explains the benefits of LEED certifications on their website.

- Health: Employees and customers of LEED-certified retail locations benefit from spaces designed to maximise indoor fresh air and minimise exposure to airborne toxins and pollutants.
- Savings: LEED stores operate with lower operating costs. On average, the life-cycle savings amounting to 20 percent of total construction costs represents a ten-fold payback on the upfront investment.
- Responsibility: LEED certification sends a powerful message about a company's values and priorities. By using LEED, retailers actively demonstrate to their employees and customers that they care about human health, community resilience and environmental protection.
- Value: LEED-certified retail spaces attract and retain more customers than non-certified comparable spaces. LEED spaces also report higher sales and operate with lower overhead costs.
- Brand loyalty: LEED certification sends a powerful message about a company's values and improve overall brand experience and increase brand loyalty
- Verification: The LEED plaque on the wall sends the message that you care about your customers and employees and that a third party has verified the sustainability and health aspects of your space. Third-party validation helps guarantee that each project saves energy, water and other resources, reducing overall environmental impact. No cutting corners

Source: USGBC

The **OEKO-TEX Standard 100** is an eco-label certification that is among the most recognised. It ensures customer safety and tests if textiles or garments meet all safety requirements by testing the textiles or garments and their accessories such as zippers, buttons, etc. It also limits the use of banned substances such as heavy metals or azo dyes. Before products are released to the market they are tested to ensure compliance.

   STeP by Oeko-Tex assesses companies based on their working conditions, consideration of the environment, and health and safety during fibre production processes such as spinning, weaving, use of chemicals during the treatment process, and disposal of waste. Once an audit has been carried out by an official representative from OEKO-TEX, the certification is granted for a three-year period before re-assessment.

The **Butterfly Mark** is a third-party accreditation mark created in consultation with the **Positive Luxury Sustainability Council** that identifies the luxury brands that meet the highest standards of verified innovation and environmental performance, offering transparency at points of sale and equipping consumers to make more informed purchasing decisions.

Textile Exchange's mission is to develop, manage, and promote a suite of leading industry standards, as well as to collect and publish critical industry data and insights that allow brands and retailers to measure, manage, and track the use of preferred fibre and materials. The members and leaders from the Textile Exchange aim to achieve five major goals, those being:

1. Encourage greater use of preferred fibres and materials.
2. Increase the integrity of the value chain by implementing standards and certifications.
3. Allow for industry-wide collective impact and action.
4. Raise awareness about the positive, meaningful changes that have been made.
5. Use the Sustainable Development Goals as a lexicon and reporting framework.

By achieving these objectives, the Textile Exchange plan for a transformative change will result in a more sustainable, responsible textile industry.

The **Woolmark** brand represents a commitment between woolgrowers, brands, and consumers on the authenticity and quality of the fibre. As a not-for-profit organisation Woolmark works alongside Australia's 60,000 woolgrowers to research, develop, and certify Australian wool. They encourage and unite the entire supply chain by:

• Connecting, inspiring, and educating.
• Guaranteeing wool fibre quality.
• Collaborating with like-minded brands.
• Championing the wool fibre's eco-credentials.

Connected by the common thread of Australian wool, Woolmark works to create positive change through open and honest conversations across the entire supply chain. They are committed to assisting brands and supply chain partners to be responsible in all areas of operation, from fibre sourcing through to garment making.

The fair-trade certification issued by the **World Fair Trade Organisation** (WFTO) awards the social criteria of a company. It will assess if for example cotton farmers have been paid a base level minimum price for their product. Companies have to adhere to social responsibility standards during processing and manufacturing of cotton.

The **Zero Discharge of Hazardous Chemicals** (ZDHC) helps brands to manage their supply chain in order to reduce the amount of hazardous chemicals that are discharged into water waste. To get a ZDHC Accepted Certificate, organisations need to apply and submit to testing which is done by the ZDHC Foundation.

ACTIVIST GROUPS

The **Clean Clothes Campaign** (CCC) educates and mobilises consumers, lobbies companies and governments, and offers direct solidarity support to workers as they fight for their rights and demand better working conditions. The national branches of the CCC are autonomous organisations of researchers and activists.

The **Ethical Trading Initiative** (ETI) is a leading alliance of companies, trade unions, and NGOs that work together to tackle the many complex questions about what steps companies should take to trade ethically, and how to make a positive difference to workers' lives.

Extinction Rebellion is an international movement that uses non-violent civil disobedience in an attempt to halt mass extinction and minimise the risk of social collapse. In 2020, the group introduced #BOYCOTTFASHION, urging people to not buy fashion for a whole year as the industry plays a big role in climate change. Extinction Rebellion encourages sharing, renting, or buying second-hand clothes, using what is already in circulation.

Fashion Revolution was founded in the wake of the Rana Plaza factory collapse in 2013. Since then, they have grown to become a significant fashion activism movement, mobilising people, brands, and policy-makers through research, education, and advocacy. Fashion Revolution is a global movement of people who aim to make the fashion industry work.

Fashion Takes Action (FTA) is a non-profit organisation founded in 2007 with the goal of promoting sustainability in the fashion industry through education, awareness, research, and collaboration. This is accomplished through programs like the annual WEAR Conference, and the Sustainable Fashion Toolkit, which is a free online platform with hundreds of vetted, credible resources summarised and categorised from global organisations. This is a valuable time-saving resource that includes reports, guidelines, standards, articles, podcasts, case studies, and other materials.

Global Fashion Exchange (GFX) is an international platform promoting sustainability in the fashion industry through inspiring forums, educational content, and circularity initiatives.

Greenpeace is an independent campaigning organisation that uses non-violent direct action and creative communication to expose global environmental problems and promote solutions that are essential to a green and peaceful future. Greenpeace has been calling on major brands to eliminate the use and release of harmful chemicals from their production chain, they also work to rewind habits of unsustainable consumption and production to live within planetary boundaries.

#rewiringfashion is a proposal for the Global Fashion Industry, which was first developed in 2020 and is facilitated by the Business of Fashion. The proposal was developed after a number of ongoing conversations between a growing group of independent designers, CEOs, and retail executives from around the world came together to rethink how the fashion industry could and should work. The forum is led by designer Dries Van Noten, Lane Crawford President Andrew Keith, and Altuzarra CEO Shira Sue Carmi. Some of the issues cited are out-of-sync fashion calendars which the forum states are unsustainable for industry professionals and damaging for sales and a fashion show format that is outdated and does not connect with the customer.

The **Slow Factory** is a school, knowledge partner, and climate innovation lab focused on addressing the intersecting crises of climate justice and social inequity through narrative change and regenerative design.

The **Slow Fashion Movement** is a global community of slow fashion campaigners who aim to transform the fashion industry, which is failing and prioritising short-term economic gain over the long-term health of people and planet. The Slow Fashion Movement believes in empowering people for collective action to create a social tipping point.

As the fashion industry continues to move towards a more responsible future other organisations, certifiers, activist groups. and charities will emerge. It is very important that fashion brands connect with these in order to understand the environmental and social issues and to ensure that they operate responsibly

WEB MATERIAL

www.un.org.
https://globalfashionagenda.org.
https://taskforcefashion.nl.
https://ellenmacarthurfoundation.org.
www.fashionroundtable.co.uk.
www.thesustainablefashionforum.com.
www.thefashionpact.org.
thesustainableangle.org.
www.woolmark.com.
www.wwf.org.uk.
https://ejfoundation.org.
https://sourcemap.com.
www.britishfashioncouncil.co.uk.
https://instituteofpositivefashion.com.
https://15percentpledge.org.
https://goodonyou.eco.
https://fashionforgood.com.
www.bcorporation.net.

https://textileexchange.org.
www.fairtrade.org.uk.
https://fsc.org/en.
www.positiveluxury.com/butterfly-mark.
www.fashionrevolution.org.
https://extinctionrebellion.uk.
www.greenpeace.org.uk.
https://fashiontakesaction.com.
https://cleanclothes.org.
https://slowfashion.global.
https://slowfactory.earth.
www.ethicaltrade.org.

CHAPTER 8

The Responsible 9 Framework

#8 = Honest Communication

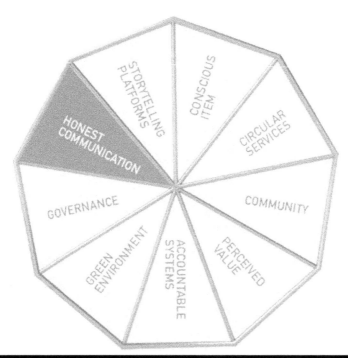

THE RESPONSIBLE 9 FRAMEWORK: #8 HONEST COMMUNICATION

DOI: 10.4324/9781003285915-9

INTRODUCTION TO THE CHAPTER

The next element of **The Responsible 9 Framework** is HONEST COMMU-NICATION, this has purposely been placed at the end of **The Responsible 9 Framework** along with STORYTELLING PLATFORMS (Chapter 9). This has been done because fashion brands should address the responsible elements of their business before building and executing their communication strategy around their products and brand values. In simple terms, best practice would dictate that a fashion business needs to ensure that their core commercial model is sustainable or that they have a roadmap to becoming more responsible, before beginning a dialogue about their green credentials with their existing and potential consumer base. Brands that attempt to engage with their audience around their green credentials, that don't have a fully thought-through sustainable plan, run the risk of being accused of greenwashing and, in turn, alienating their potential consumer base and hurting their brand reputation.

WHAT IS GREENWASHING?

The more sustainable and aware conscious consumer now demands that each fashion brand's communication be open and honest. This consumer holds businesses accountable; they expect that nothing should be hidden, and that everything should be openly discussed. Moreover, this consumer rewards those brands that practise honest communication, and they punish brands that they deem as engaging in deceptive communication and business practice (often referred to as greenwashing).

Greenwashing is a marketing tactic that is used to deceptively persuade the public that an organisation's product or service aims and policies are environmentally friendly. Many brands, including fashion brands, have been called out for providing unclear information about their sustainability credentials, and have been criticised for greenwashing because they are not providing the correct information. The conscious consumer is now turning away from those fashion brands that they see as being dishonest.

GREEN MARKETING AND COMMUNICATION

Green marketing is the practice of developing communication and advertising strategies based entirely on a brand's real or perceived green credentials with a business objective, of profit through sustainable development and practice.

In Jacquelyn Ottman's **The New Green Marketing Paradigm**, she explains how marketing leaders are shifting the rules across consumers, product, marketing, and communications and corporations in a bid to build credible green marketing strategies. Her model, in a clear and concise format, outlines the transition from a conventional and traditional

FIGURE 8.1 The New Green Marketing Paradigm, Ottman, 2011. Authors on table		
Issues	**Conventional Marketing**	**Green Marketing**
Consumers	• Consumers with lifestyles	• People with lives
Products	• Cradle to grave • One size fits all • Globally sourced	• Cradle to cradle • Services • Locally Sourced • Regionally Tailored
Marketing and communication	• Product end benefits • Selling oriented • One way communication	• Values • Educating and Empowering • Creating a community • Word of mouth
Corporate	• Secretive • Reactive • Independent and autonomous • departmentalised • Short term oriented / Profit maximising	• Transparent • Proactive • Interdependent / allied with stakeholders • Cooperative • Holistic • Long term oriented/ triple bottom line

Source: Ottman: 2011

marketing approach towards a more relevant green, sustainable approach, which wholly connects with the new conscious and much more complex consumer.

Jacquelyn Ottman has also developed **The Seven Winning Strategies for Green Marketing**. This concise list was developed from her learnings from working with sustainability leaders over the last 20 years. These seven strategies provide brands, including fashion brands, a clear guide on how to build green marketing solutions by highlighting the approaches and questions they need to answer about their own business and customers, in order to market their items to the more sustainable consumer.

OTTMAN'S SEVEN WINNING STRATEGIES FOR GREEN MARKETING ARE:

1. Understand the environmental and social beliefs and values of your customers and other stakeholders and develop a long-term plan aligned to them.

2. Create new products and services that balance consumers desires for quality, convenience, and affordability with minimal adverse environmental and social impacts over the life of the product.
3. Develop products that offer practical benefits whilst also empowering and engaging consumers in meaningful ways about the important issues that affect their lives.
4. Establish credibility for your efforts by communicating your corporate commitment and striving for complete transparency.
5. Be proactive. Go beyond what is expected from stakeholders. Proactively commit to doing your share to solve emerging environmental and social problems – and discover your competitive advantage in this process.
6. Think holistically. Underscore community with users and with the broad array of corporate environmental and societal stakeholders.
7. Don't Quit. Promote responsible product use and disposal practices. Continually strive for "zero" impact.

Ottman, 2011

Historically, fashion promotional strategies have been developed with the sole purpose of pushing consumers to buy and consume as many products as possible, as highlighted in the Introduction of this book, without any thought of the environmental impact that this practice creates. While we can't ignore a business' right to exist and its core objective to increase sales, traditional marketing communication has without question played a role in today's environmental crisis.

By using Ottman's two models one can begin to look at promotion differently, away from its traditional role as a singular tool to drive product sales, to a role of storytelling where brands are using their communication and promotional strategy to engage with their audience, by educating them on the importance of responsible business practices, and in turn outlining their brands journey to becoming environmentally responsible.

TRANSPARENT COMMUNICATION

Today's consumer has more access to information than ever before, which is due in part to digital innovations such as the internet and social media. These innovations have now enabled consumers to actively and easily search for honest and responsible fashion brands that connect with their own values.

In the past, fashion organisations have been labelled secretive and closed. Now the expectation is for these companies to be honest, collaborative, and open. No longer should processes used inside a fashion business be guarded secrets, instead they need to be clear with full visibility given to the customer. With this fresh stance comes a new approach to communication, fashion brands now need to allocate marketing spend to explain their responsible practices clearly and transparently.

When considering relevant communication tactics and tools, fashion brands also need to ensure that they take their consumer on their business' journey to becoming a more responsible brand or retailer. This process should include everything, the good and the challenging and even the currently impossible; the path needs to be clearly laid out, mistakes must be admitted to and plans should be fully visible and on-going. Consumers are questioning traditional promotional messaging, and fashion brands need to be able to back up their promises with clear evidence and hard facts.

The following expert insight from Peter Rees summarises three critical questions brands need to ask themselves while developing their communication strategy. Peter then goes on to further explain the changing motivations and behaviour of the new conscious consumer.

Expert insight from Peter Rees
Senior Lecturer at London College of Fashion.

Current marketing communications activities, or promotion works across the 3Ms of the Combinations Mix: Message, Market and Method, adapted from Lasswell, 1948.

This framework covers three important areas:

- What do we wish to say? – the content of the communication.
- Whom do we wish to say it to? – the audience or stakeholders targeted.
- What is the best way to deliver the message? – the digital and offline communications tools, techniques, and platforms to be used.

In my experience, this 3Ms model provides a very practical framework for planning and executing effective clear and honest communication campaigns.

The changing consumer

Communications techniques and approaches have changed significantly over the past decade due to different motivations and expectations of target consumers for fashion brands of all sizes. The most significant changes demanded are:

The Green Agenda – Led at first by the Millennial and latterly Generation Z; more and more fashion consumers are confirming the importance that they attach to issues such as: climate change, ethical sourcing, recycling, packaging, ethical production technology, and new fashion business models. Companies can achieve a sustainable competitive advantage by systematically addressing these issues.

A new "Woke" approach – There is a general societal move to consider the ethical and societal responsibilities of governments, business, and the community as a whole.

> Companies that only pay lip-service to topical environmental issues are likely to be held accountable for such superficial "green-washing." The backlash can be severe.
>
> **Personalisation** – Consumers increasingly expect to be treated as individuals, with a personalised marketing mix tailored to their unique, individual needs.

In response to the emergence of the conscious consumer and new behavioral patterns, as summarised by Rees, brands must now develop open and honest communication tactics and strategies. The conscious consumer understands that a brand can't instantly change all their businesses' practices to become fully responsible overnight, but they do want to know that a fashion brand accepts responsibility, acknowledges their sustainable shortcomings, and has a plan and timeline in place to address these issues. Moreover, brands are more likely to successfully engage with this consumer base, if they communicate genuine information about their whole business with integrity and honesty.

A great example of a brand that aims to be fully transparent in its entire approach is British cosmetics company **Lush Cosmetics**, which was founded in 1995 in Poole, Dorset, UK. The company is known to be an ethical company, using only natural ingredients in all of their products, while rejecting the use of preservatives that may be harmful to the human body.

All of the Lush products are fair trade, and none are tested on animals. Lush also communicates exactly who personally and individually has made their products. On some of Lush's product packaging, they even include an illustrated image and name of the person responsible for making the item. In addition, Lush also have their own YouTube channel where they show the production process of different products, giving the consumer full access and visibility of their manufacturing process.

AIDA MARKETING MODEL, LEWIS 1898

A key starting point for fashion brands, when building their communication strategy, is to understand and think through all the potential touch points or interaction points a potential customer may have with their brand, from the very first brand interaction through to sale conversion, sale confirmation, and post purchase survey. Knowing this customer journey allows brands to plan and tailor their communication tactics based on the level of understanding and fluency a customer has with a brand and its values.

One of the most well-known tools that helps businesses understand their customer's journey with their brand is the AIDA model. The AIDA model is a useful academic tool for fashion brands to better understand and examine the movement of the customer. The AIDA acronym stands for Awareness, Interest, Desire, and Action. This AIDA marketing model also now can include the important influence social media is having on the customer and brand relationship.

These are the four stages a consumer goes through during the process of potentially purchasing a product.

- **Awareness:** This specifically relates to how fashion brands make potential customers aware of products. For example, what is their promotion campaign? Which tools or platforms do they use? What should the messages be?
- **Interest:** This considers how fashion brands gain the interest of the potential customer and how they make themselves visible to the potential customer.
- **Desire:** This refers to what makes the fashion brand's product desirable to the customer. How can the fashion brand manage to make an emotional connection with this potential customer?
- **Action:** This final stage is related to what the fashion brands "call to action." For example: Is it easy for consumers to connect with the brand?

The following expert insight by Martin Deal looks at the AIDA model, and explores if it is still relevant for fashion businesses, some 120 years later, to better understand the customer journey.

FIGURE 8.2   AIDA Model. Diagram - authors own

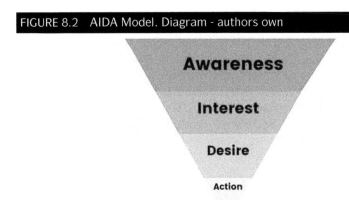

Expert insight from Martin Deal:
Is AIDA still relevant in today's digital world?
Digital Strategist and Senior Lecturer at City University.

The AIDA model was invented by Elmo Lewis back in 1898. As Lewis was an advertising specialist it was considered as a multi-stage process to develop from advertising to sales. It has been widely accepted in the marketing world as a pre-sales model based on the assumption that branding can be influenced by advertising and that purchasing decisions are based on stimuli communicated by advertising.

The main advantage of the model is its simplicity – but how relevant is it in today's environment?

Marketing essentially has three stages – Presence, Communication, and Persuasion.

- **Presence** – getting noticed in a crowded environment.
- **Communication** – creating the right message to the right audience.
- **Persuasion** – making the audience do something.

In the 21st century this is more complex than the AIDA model suggests. With millions of websites and social media platforms vying for the audience's attention, the "Attention" element of AIDA is not a simple matter of advertising.

As domestic consumers, we don't surf the internet when we want to find a product. We have our favourite websites. We concentrate on the 10 to 12 websites we like and ignore the rest of the world. This funnel view has been intensified by using smartphones as our main tool for search. We are protective of our phones as a platform in a way we are not with desktop computers. We block out calls from numbers we do not recognise, and we install apps around our personal interests. We ignore everything else. It is a "I am the centre of my universe" concept. This makes it extremely difficult for an advertiser to invade our smartphone world with their new product. Without "Attention" it is difficult for Interest, Desire, and Action to follow.

Communication is another major hurdle in the digital world. There is so much content available it is difficult to filter it so that a brand stands out. The marketing process of customer segmentation is well established but by its very nature it is more resource intensive. Layered messages to audience segments are extremely difficult in the real world, although in theory it sounds very simple. This is one reason why, in the fashion industry, influencers are so important. They can get that product in front of their niche customer audience.

The AIDA model is linear in concept. Attention leads to Interest. Interest leads to Desire and finally Desire leads to Action. But buying decisions are not so linear in today's marketplace. Very few people start a search on Google at the Attention stage. It is more likely they are at the Interest stage – they have seen the product somewhere and want a closer look at it.

AIDA also does not consider the complexity of our buying decisions. We are not just stimulated by adverts. In today's world we are more likely to be influenced by brand loyalty or satisfaction levels. We are also influenced by peer recommendation – hence the importance of social media as a digital channel. We are also creatures of habit and tend to go back to brands and product lines we trust. There is an element of comfort and safety in staying with what we know.

There has always been a barrier between marketing and sales. The ability to get the consumer to take that final step "Action" in the AIDA model has always centred on certain individuals – salespeople. Getting the customer to buy the product comes down to persuasion. In the digital world we talk about "a call to action" the concept that we can get the customer to do more than just buy the product. They can leave their details, download our app, attend an event and much more. But ultimately, in Lewis' world, we want them to make that purchase. Historically, sales were considered as persuading a customer to purchase something they were not ready to purchase. Today, we teach people that a sale is an exchange of value. If we can convince people that they are getting value, they will buy the product. How many times have you heard of a fashion sale called "an investment piece"?

Over the years there have been many attempts to replace the AIDA model with something more up-to-date. Forrester Research developed their Marketing RaDaR model based on Reach, Depth, and Relationships channels. **Reach** channels generate initial interest – through internet search or media advertising. **Depth** tells the products story via websites and direct sales approaches. **Relationship** channels serve existing customers via social media and email campaigns.

McKinsey & Company have a circular model which they call the **"Customer Decision Journey."** This model throws out the "Funnel Approach" favoured by the AIDA model but instead sees the purchasing decision as a battleground based on four phases. These phases are initial evaluation, active consideration, actual purchase, and post purchase evaluation. They see the goal of marketing is to reach prospective customers at the moments that most influence their decisions. They cite electronics companies having high-definition televisions switched on in stores which creates excitement (interest and desire) about the product, and Amazon offering product recommendations at the point of purchase as examples of this in the real world.

The whole world was affected by the COVID pandemic during the period 2020 to 2022 and the fashion industry has used this period of disruption to create change in the industry and to its approach to marketing. The fashion industry has embraced new technology to create desire and to incorporate the new movements in social responsibility and sustainability. It has recognised that the old "Push Marketing" model, essentially based on AIDA, has now been replaced by a consumer driven marketing approach. The emphasis has changed from consumers following marketing to marketing being guided by consumers.

In 2022, the fashion industry has seen an exponential growth in the use of technology, especially artificial intelligence (AI), virtual and augmented reality, blockchain technology, and mobile commerce. AI is being used to enhance the customer experience and to provide product suggestions, per the McKinsey model. AI also monitors and predicts consumer trends allowing the market to stay "in the moment" with the consumer. Virtual Reality has created a boom in online fashion purchases and the concept of omnichannel purchasing has created excitement in the fashion marketplace. The ability to "try and buy" through VR either online or through the high street store generates the Desire in the AIDA model. Blockchain technology is being used to create efficiencies in the fashion supply chain and to track where products are in the supply chain process, making product choice more relevant to the moment, instead of following the trend. Mobile commerce using smartphone payments is facilitating online shopping with cashless payments. There has also been a major move away from platforms such as eBay and Gumtree to more modern apps such as Vinted and Depop.

Sustainable fashion and responsible retailing are also vital movements with today's consumers and will continue to be so going forward. The use of alternative plant-based fabrics and the use and reuse of textiles is also changing consumers' approach to fashion. There is also a growing appetite for fashion rental outlets as opposed to direct purchase allowing the concept of fast fashion to continue without the consumer feeling guilty about environmental disturbance and depletion of natural resources.

So where does this leave the AIDA model? Is it still relevant in today's digital marketplace? There is no doubt that the digital marketplace and new technology platforms have changed the way the consumer approaches the buying decision. As Forrester and McKinsey have pointed out there are different elements to the simple model invented by Lewis over 100 years ago. But, essentially, irrespective of the new tools being used and the underlying influences such as brand loyalty, recommendation, and experience the consumer still goes through the linear process of Attention, Interest, Desire, and Action.

There is something to be said for the proverb **"If it ain't broke, don't fix it"**!

RESPONSIBLE CONSUMPTION

It is important for fashion brands to ensure that their marketing methods are explanatory, describing the whole business process inside the brand from the creation of the products through to the people who develop them. The consumer wants to better understand exactly what the fashion brand is doing and its impact on the environment to make a more informed and responsible purchase decision, or otherwise known as responsible consumption. Simply put, responsible consumption is consumers considering the environmental impact of their purchase decisions. This ties into the Sustainable Development Goal 12, titled "responsible consumption and production," which is one of the 17 Sustainable Development Goals established by the United Nations in 2015. (For more information on all 17 Sustainable Development Goals please refer to Chapter 7-**GOVERNANCE**.)

The following thought-provoking expert insight by Veronica Bates Kassatly, argues that the current communication strategy of fashion brands "buy mine, it is better on the environment" has not actually addressed the crux of the responsible business challenge. She argues that the industry needs to move to a mindset and communication strategy centred on how much an item has actually been worn in context to the actual items production impact on the environment.

Expert insight from Veronica Bates Kassatly: Challenges around Green Washing

Veronica Bates Kassatly is a former World Bank financial analyst and economist, who currently works as an independent analyst, writer, and speaker in the sustainable apparel industry. Her recent publications include a collaboration with the Geneva Center for Business and Human Rights: The Great Green Washing Machine Part 1: Back to The Roots of Sustainability, *and* The Great Green Washing Machine Part 2: The Use And Misuse of Sustainability Metrics In Fashion.

The underlying theme of all consumer-facing sustainability claims at the present time is permission to shop. The narrative is simple. Don't buy that cotton/wool/viscose buy mine, it's more sustainable. Don't buy cotton/wool/viscose at all, buy my innovative fibres and fabrics, they're more sustainable. Don't buy virgin fibres and fabrics, buy recycled ones, they're more sustainable. Don't buy new, buy second hand, it's more sustainable. Don't buy forever, buy for a few days (rent), it's more sustainable. The common thread in all of this is "buy".

I quote the March 2022 EU Strategy for Sustainable and Circular Textiles:

> *"As clothing comprises the largest share of EU textile consumption (81%), the trends of using garments for ever shorter periods before throwing them away contribute the most to unsustainable patterns of overproduction and overconsumption."*

You will note that absolutely nothing in the current messaging from the sustainable apparel sector addresses this. Nor, for that matter, does the EU circular strategy itself. Indeed, the EU is planning to introduce consumer facing Product Environmental Footprint or PEF labels for all garments. These will tell consumers that something is rated "A" or "Better" for sustainability, without once telling them that the most important determinant of a garment's sustainability is the decision that they themselves will make – how many times they will wear it.

A true and honest sustainability score has a denominator, not just a numerator. Clothes are not sandwiches. They are supposed to be worn more than once. For any given impact, how harmful that actually is, depends on how many times the garment is worn. A dress with a production impact of 1,000 that is worn 1,000 times, has an impact of one per wear. A dress with a production impact of 100 that is worn 5 times, has an impact of 20 per wear. And a dress with a production impact of 24 that is worn once, has an impact of 24 per wear.

Moreover, at the end of 1,000 wears there will be only ONE of the first type of dress to dispose of. There will be 200 of the second, and 1,000 of the third. The difference then is not just at the front end, at the beginning of any garment's life, or the factory gate as so many brands and their funded initiatives would have us believe, but also at the end-of-life.

The mere fact that garments are worn significantly more would reduce the infamous mountains of waste clothing that plague countries as far apart as Ghana and Chile, and that befoul oceans, seas, and watercourses, from Lebanon to Bali. Yet not once is this mentioned in any consumer facing sustainability claims that I have seen. Nor is it included in any proposed legislation that I am aware of.

It is self-evident from all this that some fast fashion brands that declare their sustainability as a function of the fibres and fabrics that they use, the accords that they have signed, or the initiatives that they have joined, could be fundamentally dishonest. As indeed, is any initiative that "certifies" the purported sustainability of these claims.

Moreover, brands whose advertising and marketing encourages consumers to shop consistently and repeatedly – through much vaunted "drops" of new styles, influencer posts, "hauls," discounts for repeat purchases, or the exchange of used items, and so on and so forth, whilst simultaneously declaring its "sustainability" is likewise running the risk of being or perceived as being fundamentally dishonest.

Indeed, when we consider that you cannot, scientifically, compare LCAs produced using different boundaries and different methodologies, and that there is no suite of LCAs for global fibres produced using exactly the same boundaries and methodologies (let alone based on representative and recent data) the magnitude of the deception becomes clear.

It might seem that since everyone else is doing it, and there are currently no repercussions for brands making false and misleading "sustainability" statements – why not join them? The answer is: because of reputational risk. For the past decade "sustainable" fashion has been subject to almost no oversight or accountability, but times are changing.

The insight from Veronica Bates Kassatly highlights how far the industry has to go. However some emerging and leading brands are beginning to discuss responsible consumption behaviour with their audience, and they are starting to weave in the practice of responsible consumption within their communication strategy. An example of this integration is the Patagonia 2011 campaign "Don't Buy This Jacket."

MINI CASE STUDY

Patagonia created a "Don't Buy This Jacket" advert back in 2011 and set a benchmark example for marketing, promoting the term known as responsible consumption.

On their website, Patagonia outlines the thought process behind their campaign:

> Why run an ad in The New York Times on Black Friday telling people, "Don't Buy This Jacket"?
>
> It's time for us as a company to address the issue of consumerism and do it head on.
>
> The most challenging, and important, element of the Common Threads Initiative is this: to lighten our environmental footprint, everyone needs to consume less. Businesses need to make fewer things but of higher quality. Customers need to think twice before they buy.
>
> Why? Everything we make takes something from the planet we can't give back. Each piece of Patagonia clothing, whether or not it's organic or uses recycled materials, emits several times its weight in greenhouse gases, generates at least another half garment's worth of scrap, and draws down copious amounts of freshwater now growing scarce everywhere on the planet.
>
> We're placing the ad in the Times because it's the most important national newspaper and considered the "paper of record." We're running the ad on Black Friday, which launches the retail holiday season. We should be the only retailer in the country asking people to buy less on Black Friday.
>
> But we're in business to make and sell products. Everyone's paycheck relies on that. Moreover, we are a growing business, opening new stores and mailing more catalogues. What do we tell customers who accuse us of hypocrisy?
>
> It's part of our mission to inspire and implement solutions to the environmental crisis.
>
> It would be hypocritical for us to work for environmental change without encouraging customers to think before they buy. To reduce environmental damage, we all have to reduce consumption as well as make products in more environmentally sensitive, less harmful ways. It's not hypocrisy for us to address the need to reduce consumption. On the other hand, it's folly to assume that a healthy economy can be based on buying and selling more and more things people don't need – and it's time for people who believe that's folly to say so.
>
> Nevertheless, Patagonia is a growing business – and we want to be in business for a good long time. The test of our sincerity (or our hypocrisy) will be if everything we sell is

> useful, multifunctional where possible, long-lasting; beauti-
> ful but not in thrall to fashion. We're not yet entirely there.
> Not every product meets all these criteria. Our Common
> Threads Initiative will serve as a framework to advance us
> toward these goals.
>
> Why the provocative headline if we're only asking people
> to buy less and buy more thoughtfully?
>
> To call attention to the issue in a strong, clear way.
>
> _____
>
> *Source: Patagonia*

EQUAL REPRESENTATION IN MARKETING AND ADVERTISING

Historically, the fashion industry has been guilty of promoting examples of racially insensitive, or offensive, themes and imagery in their advertising. Many fashion brands have promoted unrealistic standards, exclusive and alienating to many.

The faces portraying fashion have a history of being exclusively white with no room for diversity in front of the camera or behind the scenes. The lack of diversity in fashion has led to people perceiving their bodies and their identities as not good enough. It has also alienated certain ethnicities from applying to work for businesses, who they perceive as a place "not for them" and has further exasperated a singular viewpoint within a business' community (diversity in the workplace is discussed in Chapter 3, COMMU-NITY, #3 In the Responsible 9 Framework).

Now, as social values are informing purchase decisions more than ever, fashion brands need to implement strategies that incorporate different groups in their promotional campaigns. Fashion brands need to show their support for underrepresented communities as well, they need to be inclusive and NOT exclusive. Consumers want to connect with a fashion brand that is wholly inclusive and supportive, regardless their age, ethnicity, ability, or sexual identity.

MULTICULTURAL AND INCLUSIVE MARKETING

Multicultural marketing refers to a marketing strategy that recognises and targets one or more audiences of a specific culture and ethnicity. Successful marketing campaigns highlight people or groups that may be under or mis-represented. Accurate representation allows for the true target consumers to feel understood and valued.

Cultural inclusiveness addresses and supports the needs of people from diverse cultures, and values their unique contribution. Inclusive mar-keting means creating campaigns and content that reflects the diverse com-munities that a company serves and is open and respectful of all cultures. Truly inclusive marketing can elevate the stories and voices of people that

FIGURE 8.3 Multicultural advertising. Credit Shutterstock / Andrew Angelov

have been typically marginalised or underrepresented, deepen connections with customers, and even influence positive social change.

FASHION INDUSTRY EXAMPLES

Sportswear giant **Adidas** developed a powerful campaign called "I'm here to Create." The hero content component of the campaign showed a meeting of well-known, diverse celebrities including Pharrell Williams, Aaron Rodgers, Lionel Messi, and Von Miller. The narrative was built around Adidas powerfully bringing these influential people to the table to talk about the interplay between creativity and diversity. The content united people across industries, gender, race, politics, sexual orientation, age, and ability.

On Women's Day 2020 **The North Face** launched their first ever "International Women's Day" collection; a collection designed, created, and marketed by an all-female team, which was led by women's rights champion Oryana Awaisheh, while the collection campaign was fronted by musician Jess Glynne, as well as female athletes and explorers from across Europe. What makes the collection even more unique was that the range was the first-ever to be produced at Jerash Garment Factory, an all-female factory in Jordan founded by Awaisheh which provided more than 500 new jobs for women and their families.

Rihanna's Savage X Fenty lingerie line campaigns have helped to break binary stereotypes. Images of the raunchy, unisex collection are anchored in edgily styled, diverse casting. The Savage X Fenty fashion show is known for its inclusive nature, and models of all sizes, races, and gender identities are featured.

Expert insight from Darren Black

Photographer Darren Black details some of his experiences in shooting fashion campaigns for over 20 years, and how the industry is changing to represent more minorities and marginalised groups. Black is also a Senior Lecturer at Istituto Maragoni and London College of Fashion.

A lot has changed since the BLM protests of 2020 and also just how much farther we need to go as image-makers – especially those of us who champion diversity in the fashion image, not the tokenism of just using models of a different race or religion; it's not about fetishising models with different colour skin.

It's about including models of different skin tones, different ages, ethnicities, body shapes, abilities, differently-abled people, and those who have a different gender expression than that of the binary. Human beings are not one thing or the other, we are not one-size-fits-all, cookie-cutter carbon copies of each other, we are multiplicitous. Diversity is intersectional – true diversity in fashion is fully inclusive and is about representation.

In January of 2020, I had the pleasure of photographing Ellie Goldstein from the pioneering northern agency Zebedee Model Management. Ellie lives with Down Syndrome and is one of the many new faces smashing down barriers and paving the way for a new generation of models that feels truly representative of our diasporic fashion industry. This fizzing ball of energy was shot before lockdown in a studio in Nottingham at a time that seems light years ago now; before we decided collectively in fashion that we need to do more – more about sustainability for the survival of the planet, more about ethical practices in the supply chain, and crucially more about inclusion in front of and behind the camera.

For all of its many faults, fast fashion has responded to the need we have for inclusion: go to any internet brand fashion house and you will discover models of different skin tones, proportions, ages, and gender expressions and, whilst it might be cynical to suggest that this is purely a marketing ploy, the fact of the matter is that the consumer feels included in this marketing regime and as such, wants to join the party and shop. For isn't that what fashion is all about? Inclusion? An invite to the party and an outfit to wear to it.

Societally, we've moved from trickle-down culture to bubble-up so where fast fashion leads, high fashion follows. These two unlikely bed-fellows are codependent: the fast fashion business model needs something to copy and the high fashion business model needs a popular portal to attract new customers. Evidence of this can be seen at the label Savage X Fenty; the manifesto of Rihanna – a true figurehead of 4th wave feminism was that everyone should feel confident, have the right to feel sexy and experience a sense of ownership and agency of their body – in essence, shifting society's paradigm of the "ideal woman."

So, what did she do? She included everyone in her catwalk presentations and ad campaigns, she created make-up formulas in many more shades than most other brands, and she gave permission for womxn to own their skin and take up space. As a result, not only is she providing an environment of creative expression for her customer, but she is also making paper! The umbrella-wielding powerhouse is now a billionaire – she knows that people will put money in her cash register if she includes a simulacrum of them in her imagery. It's not rocket science: include people of all categories in your marketing campaigns and see people of all categories spending money in your shop.

Many years ago, when I was shooting for a big brand (who shall remain anonymous), I was pulled into the office and told to stop asking for models of colour to be included in the packages I was requesting from agencies as they were never going to shoot them. I asked why and was told: "black girls don't sell." Their customer (at the time) didn't respond to images of models that weren't white. I pushed back by saying: as a big fashion brand, isn't it our job to educate our consumers and show them the way forward? I mean if Waris Dyrie, Mounia, Iman, Tyra, Naomi (Campbell and Sims), Vanessa Williams, Beverly Johnson, Donyale Luna, Alek Wek, Lena Horne, and Elizabeth Princess of Toro can break records for sales, surely we can use models of colour?

This is a lesson many in the fashion industry are now learning and not a moment too soon. It's never too late to be inclusive, but one would be wise to remember to give everyone a seat at the table when it comes to decision-making: don't just use a model of colour for a campaign but have people of colour, of self-expression, etc. making up the teams behind the camera, and, perhaps, a much more nuanced and interesting brand image will be created to encourage customers to walk across the threshold and buy your products. #ittakesanarmy.

FIGURE 8.4　BLM image. Credit Shutterstock / SJM Photos

INFLUENCER MARKETING

Influencer marketing is an area of social media marketing that uses co-created content, endorsements, and product mentions from people who have dedicated social media followings, and who are viewed as people of influence within a specific target demographic. The benefit and upside to influencer marketing is driven by the high amount of trust that influencers have built up with their community and followers, and recommendations from them are deemed as credible.

The greater the synergy and shared values between the brand and influencer, generally the larger community engagement with the activation or endorsement. Influencer marketing is underpinned by the authenticity of the activation, as audiences view and share activations that are honest and transparent, while they shun posts that feel forced and disingenuous. Successful campaigns can utilise the loyalty and engagement that an influencer has with its community to increase brand awareness, reinforce a marketing message, to grow a brand's own following, and to drive click-throughs to a brand's website or ecommerce platform.

Although influencer marketing is mostly used for brand and product promotion, there is an opportunity for brands to use influencers to help communicate their sustainable business practices and credentials. And when considering the enormous impact that some influencers have on their followings, influencers have the ability to successfully influence, teach, and guide audiences towards more sustainable choices.

Expert insight from Giorgia Pagliuca

Giorgia Paglucia is a green influencer who has devoted her personal, academic, and work life to sustainability. In April 2022, she published her first book, Let's fix the world: Diary of an environmentalist in the climate crisis. *Paglucia outlines her personal journey to becoming a green influencer and the importance of storytelling in driving sustainability forward.*

I personally started this journey four years ago, when I decided to create GGalaska, a platform revolving entirely on sustainability's issues and individual actions, to tackle climate change. The account can now count on circa 30K followers on Instagram and 13K on TikTok, while also being promoted on my personal blog. The aim of this platform is to educate, raise awareness, and activate social network users on sustainable development through social media contents and tools.

Storytelling and human connection are key to empower and inform people: creating an informative and participatory environment, something also in an eye-catching and entertaining way. Only relying on data is no longer effective: people need to be actively engaged in the sustainability dimension by being part of, and taking part in, the story. Understanding – on one hand – that our actions have social, economic, and environmental consequences, while – on the other hand – we all have to be participating in the global challenge of dealing with negative impactful human processes.

Moreover, the World Wide Web is crowded with green influencers and sustainability storytellers. Each and every one of us has their own unique way of explaining a piece of the complex puzzle, of cracking the code of broadcasting sustainable development. We need a variety of different spokespeople, coming from all over the world, in order to represent different cultures, social issues, and emergencies.

FIGURE 8.5.   Image of Giorgia Pagliuca. Credit Giorgia Pagliuca

BRAND ACTIVISM AND CAUSE MARKETING

Some fashion brands have started to provide opinions and focus their external communications on social causes that align to their core values. If done correctly this can be a powerful way for brands to further engage with their consumers, remain relevant, and emphasise their responsible practices.

Fashion brands weigh in on often controversial and political topics that are at the heart of the cultural conversation. However, getting brand activism right by supporting meaningful change and connecting with consumers is not easy, and requires a thoughtful, authentic approach and the belief should be embedded throughout the whole business.

FASHION INDUSTRY EXAMPLES

Lush Cosmetics is strongly aligned with a range of guiding policies on animal welfare, environmental responsibility, profit sharing, and charitable giving, with two of its founders having worked against animal testing prior to launching the British beauty brand. Through social media accounts, a dedicated content hub on its website, and formats like podcasts, the brand communicates and positions itself as a platform for "passionate people with an opinion."

In 2009, US fashion brand **Tory Burch** launched the Tory Burch Foundation, a foundation focused on providing women access to capital, education, and networking events. Since the Tory Burch Foundation launched it has given out over $75m in loans to female entrepreneurs, they have supported over 500,000 businesses, and they regularly host workshops and a day of panels for international women's day. These events bring together American feminist activists, while they also created a limited-edition Tory Burch Foundation collection, where 100% of the net-proceeds benefit the work they are doing to empower women.

Cause marketing often involves a collaboration between a company and a non-profit organisation for a common benefit. Cause marketing can also refer to social or charitable campaigns created and implemented by a business. Typically, a brand's association with a non-profit will boost their corporate social responsibility footprint. Fashion brands that show support of important and credible causes that their potential customer cares about will naturally resonate and connect well with that customer.

In line with their band DNA, New Zealand/American company **Allbirds** sends any lightly used shoes that are returned by their customers to the non-profit organisation Soles4Souls. Soles4Souls donates shoes to communities around the world who have been affected by disasters and poverty. Their broad mission is to provide footwear to the disadvantaged, while further protecting the planet by keeping unwanted shoes out of landfills.

US outdoor brand **REI** have an on-going marketing campaign called OptOutside. This campaign started for Black Friday in 2015 when the brand closed its stores and encouraged both staff and customers to enjoy the outdoors instead. This has been a very effective and successful long-term campaign that has further cemented the brand's sustainable credentials with their customers, who in turn now value and believe in the brands approach. In 2016, an additional 475 non-profit, government and corporate partners joined the movement, which also added an outdoor activity finder, to provide support and direction to those joining in. In 2021, The #OptOutside

movement attracted over six million participants. Founding brand REI/
retailer, again shut its 149 locations, processed no online sales, and paid its
12,000 employees to take the day off.

MINI CASE STUDY

In 2018, outdoor brand Patagonia launched the Action Works platform
which aims to connect users to local organisations working on important causes/issues in local areas.

   The Action Works platform allows users to find relevant organi-
zations by both the location and the issue. The system works the opposite way as well, with agencies able to find people who can help them
in specific ways. Ultimately the aim is to provide a platform to enable
the activist to connect with local environmental issues.

   Patagonia further explains the concept of the platform on their
website:

> For almost 40 years, Patagonia has supported grassroots
> activists working to find solutions to the environmental cri-
> sis. But in this time of unprecedented threats, it's often hard
> to know the best way to get involved. That's why we're con-
> necting individuals with our grantees, to take action on the
> most pressing issues facing the world today.
>
>   We built Patagonia Action Works to connect commit-
> ted individuals to organisations working on environmental
> issues in the same community. It's now possible for anyone
> to discover and connect with environmental action groups
> and get involved with the work they do.
>
>   1% for the Planet is our self-imposed tax. It's the percent
> of our sales that we donate to the preservation and restora-
> tion of natural environments.

Source: Patagonia

EVENTS, CAMPAIGNS, AND PROMOTIONAL MATERIAL CREATION

Sustainability should not just be focused on the messaging but should also be
applied to the actual creation and execution of events, marketing, and campaign materials. Fashion brands still need to promote and communicate their
offer to the customer, however the creation of these promotional events and
material should be designed and created while limiting their impact on the
environment and based on the principles and ethics of sustainability.

   Fashion brands are moving away from extravagant promotional look
books and opulent events and promoting their brand in more sustainable

ways. Flying models and production crews to different countries for fashion shows and shoots are now seen as unnecessary and harmful to the planet, and overly expensive. Fashion brands are moving to local events and production shoots, while sourcing production talent and models locally. In some instances, brands are using illustrations or even computer-generated images to illustrate their new collections.

FASHION INDUSTRY EXAMPLE

Aligned with their commitment to carbon neutrality, **Gucci** now certifies their fashion shows according to the international standard ISO 20121. The standard provides a framework and guidance for designing sustainable events from start to finish.

The brand measures and mitigates the environmental impact of their fashion shows to ensure they are environmentally efficient and aligned with the ISO 20121 standard by:

- sustainable sourcing, favouring materials that can be reused, recycled, or rented;
- prioritising local catering;
- avoiding single-use plastic;
- donating leftover food;
- using green electricity and LED lighting;
- choosing more eco-friendly transport;
- measuring the GHG (greenhouse emissions), resulting from the show and associated travel by guests and workers.

The brand then uses an accredited third party to verify and review the production and management of the show to ensure the environmental impact is in line with ISO standards.

Expert insight from Sara Vaughan

Innovator, Podcaster, Creator of Global Brands with Purpose, Global Chief Purpose & Sustainability Advisor to Marie Claire *and Fashion Avenger for Project Everyone. Vaughan outlines her tips on how fashion brands can take a more sustainable approach to the creation of marketing and promotional materials across:*

- *Creation of imagery.*
- *Working with models.*
- *Runway shows.*
- *Influencers and red-carpet events.*
- *Publicity.*
- *Sales promotion.*

The hard work is done, the ethically and sustainably sourced samples are ready, production at a trusted and transparent local manufacturer is about to start and it's all plain sailing from there. Right . . .? Well actually, that's where one would be wrong! The world of sustainable fashion promotion is full of potential pitfalls. Here are some tips on how one can avoid some of the most common mistakes.

Let's start at the beginning with marketing materials, the material you create to promote your brand, product or service

Imagery

Fashion shoots can be an environmental and human rights catastrophe if not managed very thoughtfully. One upside of shrinking marketing budgets and the COVID pandemic has been the reduction in the number of exotic destination shoots where small armies can descend on remote communities or islands, ill-equipped to accommodate them or the detritus of waste and plastic bottles they leave behind. In fact, it has forced this highly creative industry to do things differently and to think outside of the box. For example, at the height of the pandemic, Lisa Oxenham, Beauty & Style Director at Marie Claire UK, created one of the first virtual shoots with body positive model and activist, Charli Howard, back in February 2020. To find out more about how they did it check out the Marie Claire UK website or watch the CogX panel they did on YouTube back in June 2020.

Models

Which brings me to my next point. Models. Modelling is made out to be a glamorous and lucrative profession. The truth for a great many is not at all that. Traffickers pose as modelling agents, eating disorders abound and can even be encouraged, agency billing practices lead to models getting hopelessly indebted to them and that's just for starters.

Here's a selection of quotes from the Brighter Future Report 2020:

- "As a woman of colour, I am always the last to be styled and dressed."
- "I was pressured into shooting nude without notice."
- "You can wait at a casting for two hours. They will look at one picture of you and send you off. There is no respect for you as a human being."

The industry needs to do better than this. Fortunately, the remarkable force of nature that is Elizabeth Peyton-Jones CEO and Founder of Models Trust (the organisation behind the Brighter Future Report) has created a Models Trust Certification Mark based on anonymous, industry-wide, data-driven surveys. She has also advised LVMH and Kering on their own set of standards known as "We Care for Models." Do check out her interview with me on my Start Somewhere podcast and also consult their website www.modelstrust.com and also look for their Trust Mark when casting models.

Seasons and Runway Shows

Multiple seasons are just a marketing device for selling more stuff. Runway shows are not only expensive but also represent another potential environmental and human rights challenge. Below are some further quotes from the Brighter Future Report 2020; "I walked in a show in very high heels that were three sizes too small for me. At a show seven models fell because of the heels they had to wear."

Fashion Avenger, Burberry was one of the first to revise the traditional Runway Show; back in February 2016, they announced the merger of their men's and women's shows into two annual events. The pandemic temporarily hastened the demise of the season and the show but there does seem to be an uptick in both re-emerging. Resist the temptation! And if one can't, work with an environmental event consultant to ensure that one's show is as sustainable as possible. Also make sure the hair and make-up are sustainable and cruelty-free too.

Influencers and Red Carpets

The current system needs to change. Brand creates a new must-have item, pays influencer to wear it, images are picked up by social media followers and the press, publicity results in sales. And round and round we go, a perpetual cycle of promoting newness. Until now that is.

Led by the likes of Emma Watson and Susie Amis Cameron there is an increasing and much-needed movement of dressing sustainably on the red carpet. Susie conceived RCGD Global, a woman-led global change-making organisation during the press tour for her husband James Cameron's film Avatar. She and CEO Samata Pattinson work tirelessly to bring environmental and social sustainability to the forefront of conversation and action within the global apparel and design industry. One of their most high-profile initiatives is Red Carpet Green Dress™ in partnership with the annual Academy Awards (The Oscars) to bring sustainable fashion front and centre on the world's most famous red carpet.

Advertising and Publicity

Let me be crystal clear – one ethically produced range or product does not a sustainable fashion company make. And as of December 2021 (at least in the UK) misleading environmental claims can mean that one can fall foul of ASA standards. One company that really seems to get this is Baukjen a London-based womenswear brand and the highest scoring fashion B-Corp in the UK and winner at the 2021 UN Global Climate Action Award. Baukjen provides a sustainability index for each item in their collection. Of the seven current measurements, five are environmental, accounting for 70% of the overall score, while the final two are social, and count as 30% of the overall score. The brand is completely circular, carbon negative and zero-waste. And they are also growing! Why? Because their product is covetable and because, increasingly, people are demanding greater transparency of the brands they buy, calling out and eschewing greenwashing, choosing to wear clothes that represent their values.

Sales Promotions

In 2019, fashion brand Missguided, made headlines for advertising a £1 bikini on one of the UK's top rated television shows, *Love Island*. The backlash from the fast fashion critics was quick and swift. Now in 2022, the television show is partnering with Ebay, while the brand Missguided has gone into administration owing its suppliers millions of pounds with staff being made redundant by an emotionless auto-mated message. The problem? It just couldn't compete with the likes of Boohoo and fast-fashion behemoth, Shein. Competing on price and sales promotions to this extent is a risky business. Missguided rose and fell in just 13 years. The average lifespan of big companies now being just 18 years as opposed to 61 years in 1958, according to a recent study by McKinsey, 2021.

Conversely Patagonia was founded in 1978 by Yvon Chouinard (44 years ago) and is still going strong. Why? Well, that could be a whole book in itself, but one of the main reasons is because Patagonia has embedded its purpose deeply into its brand DNA and consequently every single thing it does. Its purpose being, "build the best product, cause no unnecessary harm. Use business to inspire and implement solutions to the environmental crisis." This purpose also informs the revolutionary way Patagonia does, or rather doesn't do sales. In 2011, Patagonia launched their "Don't Buy this Jacket" initiative for Black Friday. They were the only retailer asking people to buy less. And ever since then, they have been subverting the Black Friday and cyber-Monday sales and using them as an opportunity to draw attention to the environmental impact of the fashion industry and to promote more conscious buying habits. In 2021, they announced they would donate 100% of their global retail and online Black Friday sales to grassroots non-profits working on the frontlines to protect the air, water, and soil for future generations. It was coined a fundraiser for earth. They expected to reach $2 million in sales but they beat that expectation five times over and raised a record-breaking $10 million in sales. Along with many loyal customers, the initiative also attracted thousands who had never bought anything from Patagonia before.

Which brings me to my main point. A truly sustainable brand is one that not only understands its purpose and acts on it but inher-ently ties it to its commercial success. In this fast-changing VUCA world of ours, it is only purpose-led companies and brands that will survive.

This chapter has provided insight on the importance for fashion brands to develop honest and authentic marketing communication approaches. Key takeaways include:

- Sustainable marketing messages should also communicate the brand's longer-term commitment to a more responsible way of operating.
- Customers see through false sustainable messages and understand the term greenwashing.
- If a fashion brand makes a mistake, then it should communicate this, telling the customer how it aims to improve its practice.
- Credible sustainable influencers should be utilised in order to educate people to consume responsibly.
- Podcasts, live streaming, and other media activations can be utilised in order to have an authentic conversation with the customer.
- Fashion brands should develop manifestos and promote their CSR strategy in order to publicly declare their motivations, long-term intentions, and core values.
- Inclusive marketing should always be encouraged, the importance of this should never be overlooked.

REFERENCE

Ottman, J. (2012). *The New Rules of Green Marketing*, Berrett-Koehler.

FURTHER READING

Berners-Lee, M. (2019). *There Is No Planet B: A Handbook for the Make or Break Years*, Cambridge University Press.
Chevalier, M. and Mazzalovo, G. (2008). *Luxury Brand Management, A World of Privilege*, Wiley.
Doole, I. and Lowe, R. (2004). *International Marketing Strategy: Analysis, Development and Implementation*, 4th edition, London: Thomson.
Easey, M. (2009). *Fashion Marketing*, Chichester: John Wiley and Sons.
Ellen MacArthur Foundation (2021). Circular Design for Fashion, Ellen MacArthur Foundation.
Golizia, D. (2021). *The Fashion Business: Theory and Practice in Strategic Fashion Management*, Routledge.
Gwilt, A. (2014). *A Practical Guide to Sustainable Fashion*, Bloomsbury.
Grant, J. (2009). *The Green Marketing Manifesto*, Wiley.
Jones, R.M. (2006). *The Apparel Industry*, 2nd ed., Oxford: Blackwell Science.
Kapferer, J.N. (2012). *The New Strategic Brand Management*, Fifth Ed. London: Kogan Page.
McKinsey & Company Report on Agility 2018.
Posner, H. (2015). *Marketing Fashion*, London, Laurence King Publishing.
Thomas, D. (2019). *Fashionopolis: The Price of Fast Fashion and the Future of Clothes*, Apollo.
Tungate, M. (2012). *Fashion Brands – Branding Style from Armani to Zara*, 3rd edition, London & Philadelphia, Kogan Page.
Varley, R., Radclyffe-Thomas, N., and Webb, W. (2018). Patagonia: Creative Sustainable Strategy for a Reluctant Fashion Brand. Bloomsbury.

WEB MATERIAL

Amed I. et al. (2019). Fashion on Demand. McKinsey. Retrieved from: www.mckinsey.com/industries/retail/our-insights/fashion-on-demand.

Carufel, R. (2020). Consumers Expect Brands to Commit to Inclusivity in their Advertising. Retrieved from: www.agilitypr.com/pr-news/public-relations/consumers-expect-brands-to-commit-to-inclusivity-in-their-advertising.

Cho, R. (2021). Why Fashion Needs to Be More Sustainable. Columbia Climate School. Retrieved from: https://news.climate.columbia.edu/2021/06/10/why-fashion-needs-to-be-more-sustainable/.

Credit Suisse (2022). Research Institute: The Young Consumer and a Path to Sustainability. Retrieved from: www.credit-suisse.com/about-us-news/en/articles/media-releases/the-2022-path-to-sustainability-report—75—of-young-consumers-w-202107.html.

Eur-lex Europa Eu Legal Content (2022). Retrieved from: https://eur-lex.europa.eu/legal-content/EN/TXT/?uri=CELEX:32022R2346.

Fashion Revolution (2021). Take Back Black Friday: An End to Overproduction, Overconsumption, and Waste. Retrieved from: www.fashionrevolution.org/take-back-black-friday-a-end-to-overproduction-overconsumption-and-waste/.

Gordon-Smith, E and Devlin, K. (2021). The Lifestyle Boom: Active. Stylus. Retrieved from: https://app.stylus.com/fashion/the-lifestyle-boom.

Gordon-Smith, E. (2021). Nothing New a Revolution. Stylus. Retrieved from: https://app.stylus.com/fashion/nothing-new-a-revolution.

Gordon-Smith, E (2020). Sustainable Fashion: How to Market. Retrieved from: https://stylus.com/sustainable-fashion-how-to-market.

McKinsey (2017). Mapping the Benefits of a Circular Economy. Retrieved from: www.mckinsey.com/capabilities/sustainability/our-insights/mapping-the-benefits-of-a-circular-economy.

Ward, C. (2019). Communicating with Conscious Consumers. Stylus. Retrieved from: https://stylus.com/communicating-with-conscious-consumers.

(Please note all Stylus content is subscription only).

BRAND REFERENCES

www.lush.com.
eu.patagonia.com.
www.adidas.co.uk.
www.thenorthface.co.uk.
www.toryburch.com.
www.savagex.co.uk.
www.allbirds.co.uk.
www.rei.com.

CHAPTER 9

The Responsible 9 Framework

#9 = Storytelling Platforms

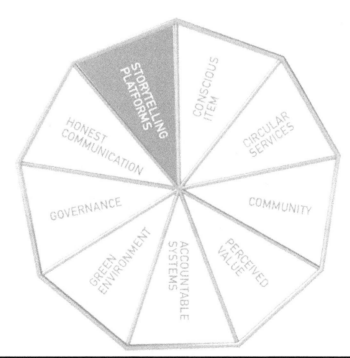

THE RESPONSIBLE 9 FRAMEWORK: #9 STORYTELLING PLATFORMS

DOI: 10.4324/9781003285915-10

INTRODUCTION TO THE CHAPTER

This chapter explores how different fashion brands are re-imagining their retail spaces by creating narrative, and using educational in-store experiences, as a vehicle to reinforce their brand values and positioning, and to further communicate their commitment to becoming a responsible brand or retailer.

Fashion brands are using in-store experiences and events to authentically immerse consumers. By creating activations and in-store experiences, or **STORYTELLING PLATFORMS**, fashion brands are finding new ways to better connect and educate contemporary consumers about their products and brand ethos, helping to demonstrate in a fully transparent manner, what they stand for and believe in. At the same time these retail spaces also provide opportunities for brands to provide insight into the roles individuals and communities alike have in helping to create a responsible and sustainable future.

The retail spaces of yesteryear provided a one-way dialogue between consumer and product. Today's retail spaces provide the opportunity to create a two-way meaningful dialogue between the consumer and brand, and through this dialogue and education of the consumer, brands have the ability (and some might argue the responsibility) to enlist and recruit individuals and communities to help ensure brands and consumers embrace responsible behaviours and practices moving forward.

Expert insight from Nick Pye
Co-Founder and Managing Partner of Mangrove Consulting, Pye shares his expert insights into his 3 Es of Sustainability: Educate, Experience, Enlist.

At Mangrove, we work on sustainability strategies across a range of clients and sectors, including luxury and apparel, and have come to believe in the positive role of brands and business in changing consumer behaviour and making sustainability commercially sustainable. There is an Anya Hindmarch quote, to which we refer often, she said that "any industry that can persuade someone to wear bell-bottom flares one day and drainpipes the next, offers an incredible platform to persuade people to behave differently . . ." In short, the industry has both the power and the duty to make a difference.

With its roots predominantly in physical stores, fashion has an advantage over many other consumables when it comes to engaging with a sometimes technical and complex, often ambiguous, and always challenging, topic like "sustainability." It is a simple truth that not all consumers are equally interested or have the same levels of understanding of sustainability or even are driven by the same motivations. There are some for whom sustainability is a key driver of choice based either on genuine moral concern, or a more superficial desire to tap into current codes of status and luxury. However, for most, it is a consideration at best. These consumers – let's call them "the considerers," have a gap between attitude (thinking it important) and behaviour (it impacts purchase decisions . . . or not). For them, the brand challenge is how to bridge this "say-do gap." Fashion brands could and should be leveraging physical stores to bridge the gap and this is why . . .

Sustainability is often intangible to consumers. We can't see our carbon footprints just as we can't see the impact of our choices as they happen in communities thousands of miles away. In fashion, in all but the highest end, consumers have been kept at arms' length around how, where, and by whom products are made, how they are shipped, raw material choices, and post-life impact. A radical change in transparency is key to building trust in an era of greenwashing, ever better-informed consumers (and investors), and increasing regulation. Stores provide a unique tool to make the intangible, tangible and "lift the curtain" to explain what is really going on. For consumers, the ability to experience sustainability "in the flesh," can be much more immediate and impactful than reading about it or seeing it on social media. We have seen that for those who value sustainability, physical spaces can help to *educate* consumers on key issues, to allow consumers (and staff and investors) to *experience* a vision of the future and to *enlist* consumers in brand-based activism. To do these things is to push beyond mere "storytelling". . . .

Educate: Consider Patagonia's in-store and in-garment communication of water usage, or Allbirds' push for carbon labelling across footwear, being explained and brought to life in stores. These are brands taking on bigger spending competitors, using their stores to highlight and explain complex issues and to share their evolving thinking on solutions. It is tough to leave a Patagonia store without being more aware of the impact of choices made.

Experience: Actions speak louder than words and consumers want to see both what brands are doing now *and* how they see the future. The principles here are clear – show stuff, accept it is not perfect, and let the consumer see and feel it. The power of doing and showing over saying is brilliantly brought to life by Adidas in their London flagship, with the focus on life beyond plastic reduction and recycling. The store feels part research/future lab and part retail, selling products which look and feel almost like prototypes. The likes of Stella McCartney and Balenciaga are starting to use stores to showcase new or experimental materials like Mycelium – allowing consumers to touch and feel the future with their own hands. Done well, this creates significant unpaid media benefits as consumers share their experiences with their peers.

Enlist: The final and most powerful step is to get consumers involved. The use of stores as hubs for content creation and community is expanding – this ranges from specific products or campaigns, such as Adidas' Run the Oceans, or shifts in the business model to repairs, recycling, or resale – even using space for experimentation and early-stage testing of new ideas before scaling.

Physical space is, therefore, much more than a place to purchase. For sustainability it provides a place to educate, to experience, and to enlist consumers on the changes required of us all. It can take consumers from the challenges to potential solutions and highlight the ways in which they can make a difference. Whilst all of this can then be amplified by social media, the best interactions on a topic of such complexity are physical.

FIGURE 9.1   3E's Model, Pye, 2022. Credit Nick Pye

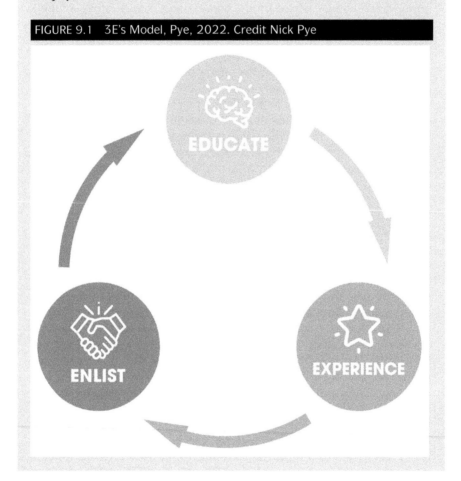

STORYTELLING RETAIL SPACES

Leading fashion brands are starting to understand that an effective way to engage with their consumers is to create in-store spaces that help their consumers to drive the sustainability conversation forward. Fashion brands are now promoting their stores as educational and sport and lifestyle spaces, supporting the customer in their drive to learn about, and maintain, healthy and sustainable lifestyles.

FASHION INDUSTRY EXAMPLES

Canadian brand **Lululemon** is a great example of a brand effectively connecting with their customers. Lululemon stores are heavily focused on interaction with local customers and community development. Almost all stores host weekly in-house events, with lessons ranging from beginner yoga to advanced yoga, self-defence, and goal-setting workshops.

Public Lands' store in Pennsylvania, USA, includes repairs and rental areas, targeting an emerging group of younger outdoors enthusiasts wanting to extend the life of their favourite garments and outdoor products. The store also includes a climbing wall where consumers can first try out equipment. As part of the brand, Public Lands is committed to helping protect public spaces, and in fact, 1% of all store sales go into supporting local and national outdoors organisations.

US brand **United by Blue i**s built on a platform of eco-activism, promising that for every purchase, it will remove 1lb of trash from the ocean and to, date, it has removed over 4.2 million pounds of trash from the ocean. Its headquarters and flagship store in Philadelphia, launched in September 2016, is built almost entirely from materials from a demolished local factory that had been converted into apartments. The store has a retail/café space which is used as a meeting point for ocean clean-up task forces, further acting on and highlighting their brand promise. Their purpose to create "great-fitting, long-lasting products with the exclusive use of materials that are environmentally and ethically sourced" is reinforced throughout their store through interactive and point-of-sale and marketing materials.

The brand further explains its mission on their website:

We are committed to making a tangible impact, so we confront ocean trash in the most direct way we know how: by getting our hands dirty and removing it from the waterways. By mobilising the community to join us, we aim to not only rid our shorelines of litter, but also to inspire individuals to live less wasteful lives.

Source: United by Blue

MINI CASE STUDY

The **Levi's** London "Haus," in the UK is used as an informative and educational platform for the brand to start the sustainable conversation with its audience, and as a by-product it showcases concepts and attitudes relating to the brand's sustainability credentials and future goals. The interactive and immersive store also provides services to their customers, when it comes to extending the life of their denim.

The store is merchandised as a hybrid exhibition and retail space, with different sections promoting and communicating different aspects of responsibility. Key brand strategies and product categories, like resale, upcycling, and waste management are placed in different sections at the forefront of the store, directing, engaging, and educating the consumers. The lower ground floor of the store is home to the repair section, an open plan and open to the public, multi-tailor workshop where consumers can see in real-time, repairs, alterations, and new bespoke creations being crafted.

The Levi's store further explains their vision for the store and products:

- **Repair:** Consumers are invited to bring their well-worn denim where tailors are on hand to stitch, patch repair, and customise their favourite Levi's®. They state that repurposing and repairing clothes requires minimal additional energy input, no water, no dyes, no global transportation, and no power needed to make more jeans.
- **Reimagine:** The brand is also partnering with Indigowares, a company dedicated to making well-crafted, low environmental impact designs using organic indigo dye. Founded by textile artist Lisa Reddings, Indigowares brings its unique dip-dying and shibori techniques to reimagine a range of Levi's® iconic products, from Trucker jackets to 501® jeans, ensuring that each piece is truly one-of-a-kind.
- **Recycle:** Levi's® by Levi's® also uses recycled products and materials to create accessories, including bucket hats, tote bags, and bum bags. Hand crafted by the Working Well Trust in Tower Hamlets, London, no two accessories are the same.

Source: Levi's

Within, **H&M's** Stockholm flagship store, there is a machine called the "Looop Machine" on display for consumers to use and watch. The machine can upcycle old knitwear into new pieces in just five hours. Looop was co-developed by the non-profit H&M Foundation, together with research partner HKRITA (The Hong Kong Research Institute of Textiles and Apparel) and Hong Kong–based yarn spinner Novetex Textiles. Garments, when placed in the machine, are shredded into fibres and then spun into a new yarn. Shoppers can then get involved with the interactive process by choosing what items their old knitwear should be made into. H&M are aiming to close the loop on all of its product's life cycles, while also instilling an appreciation for old textiles and garments with its customers. This is a smart and engaging way to educate the consumer on the importance of recycling, and it provides a platform to further solidify their green credentials.

Ethical jewellery brand **Vashi's**, Covent Garden, London, UK store is a cross between a retail store, workshop, and laboratory, which aims to make the jewellery retailer inclusive and transparent. The store provides visibility on every stage of jewellery production. The store enables visitors to look at, and engage with, the jewellery making process, and attempts to break down the exclusive barriers, which have often been associated with jewellery retail. The instore environment looks more like a creative workshop and lounge, while still managing to keep its premium and luxurious feel. In addition, a bespoke bar and lounge area in the store is open to everyone including those not making a purchase. Potential consumers can come to relax with a drink and watch and learn about the jewellery making process.

The **RÆBURN** store in Central London is a space which tells the story of the brand and has the RAEBURN ethos at its heart. The bright, clean, and modern aesthetic, which incorporates their iconic RÆMADE materials, provides an immersive experience for visitors and a clear vision of how the brand is progressing.

The store aims to take the customer on a journey through the brand's sustainability credentials, this includes detailed information on how the products are made, including materials and manufacturing process. At the forefront of the experience are the sales team that act more like storytellers rather than sales representatives, and are experts in the brand's sustainable and responsible initiatives. Fixtures within the store have been created to be fully modular, so it can be changed on a regular basis to accommodate functions and their sustainability workshops. Moreover, the materials used with the stores are either reused, recycled, or could be easily repurposed for future needs.

FIGURE 9.2 RÆBURN Design Store. Marshall Street. Credit Adam Duke

FIGURE 9.3   RAEBURN DESIGN store, Marshall Street, London Credit Chris Snook

FIGURE 9.4   RAEBURN DESIGN store, Marshall Street, Credit Chris Snook

In 2020, French footwear brand **Veja** opened an innovative concept store, event, and work space in Bordeaux, France called Darwin. The retail space unites 200 companies focused on reimagining the intersections of art, commerce, culture, work, and sport all with a view on sustainability.

One of the most popular areas of the store is a space dedicated to showcasing sneakers with minimal defects and pairs from previous collections. Complementing this section within the store is the shoemaker's workshop where visitors can have their shoes cleaned and repaired, and where old shoes can be recycled. The store is made from locally sourced wood and runs on 100% renewable electricity.

Nike has a 26,000 sq. ft. The House of Innovation flagship in Paris, supporting their commitment to take the brand into a zero-carbon, zero-waste, fully circular future. The store's design and display fixtures are created using sustainable materials, it also operates successfully on renewable energy.

Inside the Nike House of Innovation shoes from any brand can be donated and transformed into what they call Nike Grind, which is a material for making performance products, apparel, and sports surfaces.

Nike Fit ADV Weather Simulator, in the store shows how products last in weather conditions with a multisensory extended reality (XR) weather simulator. The experience is launched by scanning a QR code in one of three acrylic chambers, igniting dramatic nature-based visuals and soundscapes.

Expert insight from Vittorio Cosma and Mario Innocente
aaa/unbranded®.

Being true to oneself might seem difficult at first, but there's no easier thing than walking the walk, once you realise that sticking to your own values, your own identity, is what makes the journey worthwhile.

And it makes things easier as well: taking decisions following a first-principle approach means that any decision, from the strategic ones to the most trivial, is a direct consequence of the core values of your company.

aaa/unbranded® stands for an unorthodox approach to life, for a different approach to beauty, body care, and lifestyle through an unconventional take on perfumes and skincare. The three aaa/ stand for Assembled Around Aesthetics, and this means creating beauty and seeking harmony at every step along the way. Our core values are:

- Being Unconventional; we don't just choose the unbeaten path, we seek creating new ones.
- Being Natural; not just for our products, but as a lifestyle choice and throughout our processes.
- Striving for Excellence; seeking the best quality in all aspects of life.

Following these very few principles, we derived a number of best practices that we adopted across the company.

We chose the materials of our packaging based on their environmental impact. Recently, we've discontinued the production of our aluminium bottles, favouring plastic ones, as the former have a bigger footprint than the latter. In particular, the production of aluminium bottles pumps more CO_2 in the air, creates hazardous dust during its manufacturing and, for cosmetic products, needs an additional internal coating to avoid any contamination or chemical reaction.

At the same time, the quest to reduce paper consumption led us to create our iconic packaging. It doesn't just waste less paper, it's also new, fresh, and different. On top of it, we directly printed on the packaging all the information needed, leaving no need for an additional leaflet. The perfect synergy between functionality, sustainability, and beauty.

What about our production lines? Well, we are a small company, we create new recipes and outsource the production to our most trusted suppliers. This means that we should order a reasonable amount of product to stockpile in our warehouse and keep it ready for a fast and sweep delivery. Or so you might think. In reality, we do the opposite: after all we are here to challenge the *status quo* and we really don't care about cheap products of low quality that get delivered to your doorstep in 24 hours. On the contrary, we keep our inventory as lean as possible, and offer heavy discounts to the clients that are willing to wait longer to get their goods delivered. Quality takes time, and we are in no hurry. So, we engage in two different ways: with a traditional approach, where a client places an order that gets delivered in a few days and, where production allows for it, by offering a sizable discount for a more responsible process. In this case, we start production when a client places an order, and minimise waste and inventory while giving our customers a product explicitly made for them. This ticks all the boxes for us.

By being honest with ourselves, and always taking decisions based on our core principles, we not only take the right decisions at every step along the way, but we innovate and create new products and processes. It seems like another "P" is looming over our marketing practices: Principles.

Principles as moral rules and standards of good behaviour, but also as a first-principles approach, that enables a straightforward decision-making process based on the core values of the company.

Sustainability is not possible if we don't reduce the products we place on the market – products that oftentimes remain too long on the shelves and end up in the bin. And that's why we need to be responsible, in every aspect of our endeavour: towards our customers, as well as towards the products we create. Responsibility is crucial in maintaining the right equilibrium with our environment, and with ourselves. After all, we are a small buzzing part of nature itself.

FIGURE 9.5   aaa/unbranded®. Credit Vittorio Cosma & Mario Innocente

FIGURE 9.6   aaa/unbranded®. Credit Vittorio Cosma & Mario Innocente

LOCAL STORES

The travel restrictions brought about due the pandemic lockdown have altered working and living patterns for many people all over the world. A greater emphasis on supporting local, community stores has come out of this.

One of the key reasons it's worth shopping locally is that it reduces one's own environmental impact. Shopping locally means shopping at locally owned, independent small businesses in the area where you live, instead of always ordering from large corporations. These small businesses make up the backbone of the economy in many countries. Locally owned businesses also often invest in, and are further engaged within, the local community in which they operate, as highlighted by Rae Sims in the expert insight below.

Expert insight from Rae Sims
Co-Owner, WerkHaus Margate, UK. Sims is also a Lecturer at the University of Westminster.

With the ever-changing consumer landscape and saturation of online choice, quick deliveries, and effortless returns our increasing reliance on ecommerce has had a devastating effect on our High Streets. However, the traditional shop space is now more than ever so important. Running a physical shop is a real and tangible space, a place to browse, buy, and explore. Consumers want to feel part of something, they want to enter a world to take them away from everyday life, they want to touch clothes, soak in the atmosphere, and enjoy a multi-sensory buying experience. Only visiting an actual shop can you get face-to-face personal styling ideas and real, honest opinions about what suits your shape, style, and needs.

We sell modern utilitarian clothing, a mixture of hand-curated vintage pieces and new sustainable brands all mixed together in an eclectic space, the feeling and inspiration of which is instantly recognisable and customers understand this upon entering. This feeling creates a lasting impression that customers understand, returning time and again. This is in some ways visually portrayed using our social media platforms but cannot be replicated through an ecommerce platform and though we do sell online we do not rely on it and it in no way makes up a major percentage of our sales.

We utilise our immediate surroundings to shoot our stock both linking us further to the town and also making the landscape, and in our case breath-taking beachscape backdrops, part of our brand identity.

Independent shops like ours are a key member of the community in small towns, involved in events like the Margate First Fridays, where shops, galleries, and cafés open late once a month, POW Thanet, a festival championing equality, Margate Pride, and many youth and community connected charity events. We can directly support local CIC's and charities through offering a space to sell their merchandise for no profit and working with local artists to design and print small runs of T-shirts to raise money for a local refuge charity, Oasis.

Small businesses rejuvenate lost and vacant spaces and bring much needed revitalisation back to town centres. They also tend to sell more original items, support local makers, and can be much more involved in being sustainable in their business approach than bigger chains and multiples can afford or are willing to be.

FIGURE 9.7   WerkHaus Margate, UK Credit Rae Sims

RETAILERS SHOWING GENUINE INCLUSIVE BEHAVIOUR ON THE SHOP FLOOR

Fashion retailers need to continue to demonstrate a commitment to the inclusive consumer by evaluating and rethinking the brands they stock on their shelves, so that they are more representative of the population and local community. This spirit of genuine inclusivity really resonates with the modern consumer, who values respectful brands and retailers that wholly embrace inclusive practices.

A leading example of retailers rethinking their approach is the **Fifteen Percent Pledge**, a US-based non-profit organisation, that encourages retailers to pledge at least 15% of their shelf-space to black-owned businesses. The foundation conducts audits, shares its database of black-owned businesses, and offers business development strategies to participating companies. A number of brands, including **Gap**, **Macy's**, and **Sephora**, signed the Fifteen Percent Pledge's call.

It is becoming increasingly clear that since the pandemic, consumers are rewarding those more established fashion entities, (whether multi-brand retailers or larger fashion brands), that support and cultivate young and emerging, smaller brands (and brands that are not necessarily fashion related). A good example of this is American beauty brand **Glossier** who now provides $500,000 in grants to Black-owned beauty businesses, which come with advisory support and publicity across Glossier's many marketing platforms.

STORYTELLING IN DIGITAL AND ECOMMERCE SPACES

Fashion brands are now actively communicating with their consumers in a clear and concise manner. This has become key for the consumer who values full honesty, and in turn is more likely to forgive a fashion brand if it tells them honestly what it is doing, but also what it is not yet able to do. This is a far cry from traditional communication tactics that have mostly projected a polished product and an idealised brand image.

Many fashion brands now understand that to align themselves and engage with their consumers they need to be transparent and open about their brand. Many brands are now using their ecommerce platform as leading tool to communicate their green credentials to their consumers and have large sections on their ecommerce site dedicated to:

- Company Manifesto.
- CSR initiatives.
- Commitments to sustainable business practice.

MANIFESTOS

A Manifesto is a public statement developed by a business that helps to declare the company's motivations, long-term intentions, and core values. They have become very popular in the fashion industry. Manifestos tend to focus on goals that guide the fashion business' sustainability goals and general direction. These Manifestos act as a valuable marketing tool, they provide the consumer with a clear idea of the company's long-term intent and position it takes on different environmental issues. One of the main ways brands communicate their manifesto to their consumers is through their website/ecommerce platform. In many instances, a "sustainability" section is created on the site, where the manifesto and other CSR related activities are published and communicated.

FASHION INDUSTRY EXAMPLES

In 2020, Luxury British brand **Stella McCartney** launched a sustainability Manifesto in collaboration with artists including Jeff Koons, Peter Blake,

Olafur Eliasson, Alex Israel, Sam Taylor-Johnson, Joana Vasconcelos, Chantal Joffe, and Rashid Johnson. The Manifesto goes A–Z and drills down on terms as it progresses through the alphabet. A for accountable to Z for zero waste.

Source: Stella McCartney

UK brand **Mulberry** also has a sustainability manifesto centred around the "made to last" ethos. The company lays out their commitment to transform their business to a regenerative and circular model, which includes achieving net zero carbon emissions by 2035.

MINI CASE STUDY

Patagonia's Manifesto and core values are published on the brands website, it reads:

Build the best product

Our criteria for the best product rests on function, repairability, and, foremost, durability. Among the most direct ways we can limit ecological impacts is with goods that last for generations or can be recycled so the materials in them remain in use. Making the best product matters for saving the planet.

Cause no unnecessary harm

We know that our business activity—from lighting stores to dyeing shirts—is part of the problem. We work steadily to change our business practices and share what we've learned. But we recognize that this is not enough. We seek not only to do less harm, but more good.

Use business to protect nature

The challenges we face as a society require leadership. Once we identify a problem, we act. We embrace risk and act to protect and restore the stability, integrity and beauty of the web of life.

Not bound by convention

Our success—and much of the fun—lies in developing new ways to do things.

Source: Patagonia

COMMITMENTS TO SUSTAINABLE BUSINESS PRACTICE

Some brands communicate beyond their Manifesto and publish how they are currently implementing their objectives within their day-to-day business practice. They detail how data is used to measure the success of these practices. This all feeds into a brand's narrative about their journey to becoming a responsible fashion business.

FASHION INDUSTRY EXAMPLE

Fashion brands such as **Stella McCartney** and LA contemporary label **The Reformation** have space on their ecommerce sites to guide the customer in extensive detail through their sustainability commitments and practices throughout every part of their business.

MINI CASE STUDY

At the heart of **Stella McCartney**'s communication on their ecommerce platform is Stella's World, which outlines the brand's commitment to sustainability. It outlines three key areas:

- Measuring Impact.
- Social Sustainability.
- Circularity.

As detailed on their website under "Measuring Our Impact," the brand outlines their use of natural capital accounting methodology to measure and understand its impact on the environment, this goes far beyond traditional environmental reporting. The brand then uses the Environmental Profit & Loss (EP&L), a groundbreaking tool developed by Kering (which helps companies understand their environmental impact). Stella uses the EP&L to measure the impact of every part of their business activities, from the raw materials they use to the way they make their clothes and sell them in their stores.

Source: StellaMcCartney.com

MINI CASE STUDY

On its ecommerce platform **The Reformation** has a dedicated sustainability section that has three key sections:

- Impact of Fashion.
- We are Ref.
- Climate Positive.

Under "We are Ref," the brand outlines their methodology for measuring their environmental impact, called the RefScale. RefScale tracks the brand's environmental footprint by adding up all the pounds of carbon dioxide and waste emitted, and the gallons of water they use to make their products.

> The brand further explains the RefScale on their website:
>
> We calculate how the impact of producing Ref products compares with most clothes bought in the United States. We share RefScale results for each product we make on our website and publish the totals in our Sustainability Report.
>
> RefScale takes into consideration impacts from most processes in the product's life cycle. We publish our methodology so consumers can really dig in and understand what we include in our calculations.
>
> _____
>
> *Source: TheReformation.com*

LIVE STREAMING SHOPPING EXPERIENCE

Live stream shopping offers fashion brands the ability to demonstrate and ultimately advertise their products in real time, to a live online audience that has the ability to interact with, and engage in, the live shopping experience. Interaction with other live viewers can often generate debate about the brand, products, services, and other key attributes that a fashion brand may want their audience to engage around. Live streaming can also give brands immediate feedback and input on content such as product launches and exclusive sales offers, which can help the brand gauge the level of interest that a product may generate.

This live platform provides a brand with a very effective way to communicate information about a brand's green credentials and journey to become a more environmentally responsible brand or retailer. The long-form nature of live streaming and two-way relationship between brand and audience, provides the perfect vehicle for a brand to delve deep into specific sustainable practices and topics that would otherwise be impossible to communicate to the customer in the traditional sales experience.

FASHION INDUSTRY EXAMPLE

Beauty brand **Glossier** has the Glossier Live Edit service which connects up to 150 people with editors live for 15-minute appointments. This Live Edit service also discusses all other brands and not just Glossier, further cementing the brands authenticity, confidence, and authority in the marketplace. Audiences are consistently engaging and interacting with the brand, which in turn leads to more trust and overall brand satisfaction.

PODCASTING

Building a podcast arm into the retail experience, or building it as an extension of a brand's communication strategy isn't just about giving consumers another way to connect, it is also about giving fashion brands the opportunity, through long-form content and storytelling, to create deeper and longer-term relationships with their current and potential customer base on a broad array of topics from culture, lifestyle, politics through to opinions. The longer form format of a podcast gives a brand the opportunity to delve deep into these topics, to explore multiple perspectives and to share opinions that the time constraints of smaller forms of content don't allow. Podcasting has become very important in an era where the customer wants to know much more about the product they are buying and about the company they are purchasing it from. The development, planning, and preproduction phase of a podcast provides the brand this opportunity, as they or the producers of the podcast, are able to curate, guide, and to explore specific topics that are discussed, and therefore they have become a critical tool for brands to start and to lead the conversation around sustainable and responsible business practices.

Expert insight is provided by Samara Croci, who hosts **Sustainability@Work** and has 15 years of experience in advertising, media production, social media, corporate communications, and branding. She also worked for ten years in a multinational company, focused on circular economy, design for remanufacturing, and sustainable fashion, all while building partnerships with brands, NGOs, and institutions around the world. Currently, Croci works for a communication agency that specialises in sustainability and helps companies communicate their sustainability strategies.

Expert insight from Samara Croci: The value of podcasts

Samara Croci is a media expert and a leading podcaster on sustainability. Croci discusses the question: Systemic problems: podcasted conversation OR a podcast-based approach to systemic problems.

A bad reputation has caused the concept of promotion in sustainable fashion to change. A lot of brands and companies are moving away from the promotion of their products and services to a different kind of promotion. In sustainable fashion today, we are promoting values, a way of life, and a sense of community. In the case of sustainable fashion, it is particularly true as a certain view of promoting consumption, products, and trends had to be dismissed since it was completely at odds with the idea of sustainability.

Nowadays, promoting a brand, a service, or a company means being relevant in culture and not just to consumers. The simple yet challenging task of "promotion" means that businesses need to expand their efforts in order to create active communities, to foster dialogue, to encourage participation and to keep people, communities, public institutions, NGOs, and employees involved.

A professional in fashion today has a lot of options and content formats in their toolbox to promote sustainable fashion, but I think the great success of podcasting speaks to some characteristics that make it a very good choice.

The reason podcasts work so well as promotional tools in the new era is because the narrative structure is often built like a small galaxy with a central topic and many planets/episodes orbiting around it, each providing a unique point of view on the central topic.

Yet listening to all of the episodes opens up a journey into that topic, exposing you to different ideas, approaches, and solutions.

As far as sustainable fashion goes, we all know that no company can solve all industry problems on its own or be sustainable by itself. This is the definition of having a systemic problem. This is also where a medium like podcasts can be of great value to exchange best practices, ideas, approaches, trends, social movements, and invite everyone to the table.

My podcast Sustainability@Work was built in this way to provide a space for professionals and consumers to learn about sustainability in different industries, hear the challenges and discover solutions that can be applied to other industries, and also to understand the different approaches to sustainability and how we can collaborate to improve on a supply chain or society level.

In this new challenge, podcasts are an amazing tool for creating the kind of multi-voiced narrative that we need in both sustainability and in the world of today's brands trying to participate in cultural conversations.

I would even go so far as to say that podcasts are a narrative representation of how knowledge is formed today and how we can address complex problems. Since you can't be an expert on everything, you invite others to speak up, and you share solutions that, thanks to your podcast, come from a range of sources and connect and collide.

As a medium, a podcast can also contain a variety of formats (interviews, fiction, documentaries, only audio, video, live, articles…) and if connected properly, all of the different elements can contribute to the overall journey of discovery and also offer different entry points.

Podcasts can be a great tool for a variety of promotional challenges:

- For companies to share their sustainability efforts with their employees, establish a listening channel, and empower them to take action.
- For brands, public institutions, and nonprofits to express what are the important topics for them and how they can spark conversations and build communities with respect to those topics or problems.
- For consumers to show what matters to them and to create communities that share the same values and care about the same things or want to see the same changes.

In the long run, sustainability will not be a value in itself. The public will become more knowledgeable and demanding, and companies and brands will need to become more specific in their efforts. It is in this sense that podcasts are a great way to keep the conversation open, fresh, and evolving.

FIGURE 9.8   Image of Samara. Credit Samara Croci

This chapter has provided insight on how important it is for fashion brands to develop sustainable platforms. Key takeaways include:

- Stores should be educational hubs and community destinations.
- There is a growing importance in local stores that bring the community together.
- Fashion brands should wholly communicate their brand values inside their physical stores.
- The store is no longer all about selling product, it should now provide information about the brand and focus on increasing customer loyalty.
- Retailers serve as a strategic link between producers and consumers, and they are responsible for providing green products and encouraging green consumption.
- Services that help customers prolong product life, such as repair stations should present (as supported in Chapter 2, **CIRCULAR SERVICES**).
- Resale and rental areas should also be present inside the physical store (as suggested in Chapter 2, **CIRCULAR SERVICES**).
- The store should be a meeting place for activist groups such as clean up task forces.

- The store should be full of information that explains how the brand is being more sustainable through its whole practice (as highlighted in Chapter 8, **HONEST COMMUNICATION**).
- The store should be a platform, a place that also helps other brands and individuals grow.

FURTHER READING

Frings, G. (2013). *Fashion from Concept to Consumer*, Prentice Hall.

Gardetti, M. (2019). *The UN Sustainable Fashion Goals for the Textile and Fashion Industry*, Springer.

Golizia, D. (2021). *The Fashion Business: Theory and Practice in Strategic Fashion Management*, Routledge.

Posner, H. (2015). *Marketing Fashion*, London, Laurence King Publishing.

Tungate, M. (2012). *Fashion Brands – Branding Style from Armani to Zara*, 3rd edition, London & Philadelphia, Kogan Page.

Varley, R., Radclyffe-Thomas, N., and Webb, W. (2018). *Patagonia: Creative Sustainable Strategy for a Reluctant Fashion Brand*, Bloomsbury.

West, D., Ford, J., and Essam, I. (2010). *Strategic Marketing: Creating Competitive Advantage*. Second Ed., Oxford: Oxford University Press.

WEB MATERIAL

Amed I. et al. (2019). Fashion on Demand. McKinsey. Retrieved from: www.mckinsey.com/industries/retail/our-insights/fashion-on-demand.

Gordon-Smith, E. (2021). Nothing New a Revolution. Stylus. Retrieved from: https://app.stylus.com/fashion/nothing-new-a-revolution.

McGreavy, B. and Lindenfeld, L. (2014). Entertaining Our Way to Engagement?: Climate Change Films and Sustainable Development Values. International Journal of Sustainable Development. Retrieved from: www.researchgate.net/publication/261983833_Entertaining_our_way_to_engagement_Climate_change_films_and_sustainable_development_values.

Newbold, A. (2018). Why We Need To Talk About Transparency In Fashion. Vogue. Retrieved from: www.vogue.co.uk/article/sustainability-transparency-traceability-fashion.

Reuters; 2022 UK, Environment, Plastic, Aluminium Insight. Retrieved from: www.reuters.com/business/sustainable-business/plastics-clampdown-is-key-climate-change-fight-eu-environment-chief-says-2022–02–01/.

(Please note all Stylus content is subscription only).

BRAND REFERENCES

www.lululemon.co.uk.

www.publiclands.com.

https://unitedbyblue.com.

www.levi.com.

www.hm.com.

www.raeburndesign.co.uk.

www.stellamccartney.com.

www.mulberry.com.
www.thereformation.com.
https://eu.patagonia.com.
https://aaaunbranded.com.
www.nike.com.
www.werkhauslondon.com.
www.glossier.com.
www.gap.co.uk.
www.macys.com.
www.sephora.it.

Conclusion

The final expert insight is provided by Nicola Giuggioli. Giuggioli is the Founder and Director of Eco-Age, which was founded in 2008. Eco-Age is an end-to-end agency for sustainable business strategy. Over the past ten years Eco-Age have collaborated with NGOs, governments, and businesses across multiple industries to become a leader of transformation change in corporate responsibility. Today, through their ongoing advocacy work and high-profile events such as the Green Carpet Challenge and Green Carpet Fashion Awards, Eco-Age is widely recognised as the authority on sustainability in the industry and beyond.

Expert insight from Nicola Giuggioli

Giuggioli explains his perspective on how the fashion industry is evolving and what developments and changes the industry will likely see over the next decade.

OUR QUESTION: As **The Responsible 9 Framework** has highlighted, responsible fashion business management is critical. What do you see as the key themes that will push this forward over the next ten years?

At Eco-Age, we push for sustainable, responsible business management and we have seen a lot of movement towards sustainable practises over the last 15 years, from simple legal compliance to businesses transforming to a value-based strategy. Though still more needs to be done! The challenge is still here and sustainability is a complex issue.

Sustainability and responsibility should be the focus

The first point is that sustainability and responsibility must become the main strategy of any business, this includes every aspect from how one manages their business to how one creates or designs products, and finally how one manages the life of their products. Every aspect (division or people) of one's business should have a say and feed into

DOI: 10.4324/9781003285915-11

a master strategy. One of the most important factors that we must acknowledge is that credible, accountable, and responsible business management is critical to the future success of our company.

The importance of transparency and traceability

Transparency and traceability are the next key factors. Transparency refers to being open and honest about how brands conduct business without hiding their flaws. Companies must be clear and upfront with their stakeholders and customers about the difficulties that they might be facing and how they plan to address them.

Traceability is part of this; before they buy, customers want to know where their items come from and what materials they are made of. Throughout the supply chain, social and environmental standards must be adhered to. New tools and technologies, such as blockchain technology, are already paving the way and adding significant value to the fashion industry by increasing the transparency and traceability of products.

The roll of circularity

Another component that will have a significant impact on the fashion business landscape is circularity. This means that brands should consider circularity even at the beginning of a product's life not its end. The focus should be on how one can manage waste and what one should do when a product reaches the end of its useful life.

Additionally, circularity is an important driving factor because of resource scarcity. The price of many resources has been increasing dramatically over the last few years, further accelerated by COVID-19 and the war in Ukraine. Sadly, we do not live in a stable world, we are moving into multipolar Power World where some of the most powerful countries retain many of the key resources, limiting their supply, while driving prices higher.

Circularity today is seen as a cost, but it should be seen as a way for brands to save money. Brands should consider that they don't need to continually buy new resources but instead look at new ways to reuse what they already have. The more technology develops, the more the regenerative process will become cheaper and appealing to brands, this will in turn enable businesses to save money across the whole of their commercial model.

Regulation will be another key driver of promoting circularity strategies within businesses and helping to drive positive environmental change in both the Western World and in less developed nations. Two key regulations are Path and the European Taxonomy. These two regulations will drive change because ultimately, they will put more costs and more taxes onto companies that don't comply.

Shifts in technology and resources

Dematerialisation is going to be another big driver of change in the upcoming years. Today many companies have started creating NFT's (Non-Fungible Tokens) in place of, or in conjunction with, their physical products. We are seeing companies doing NFT's of shoes and companies putting products in the Metaverse, this could be a very interesting way for fashion businesses to develop new revenue streams that are not connected to physical resources. As a dematerialised product does not deplete physical resources, fashion brands can design that product and then replicate it many times, uploading it into spaces such as the Metaverse and virtual stores. However, it should also be noted that this is not necessarily a 100% sustainable business practice because one needs to understand how the NFT is developed and operated (because blockchain is still going through a lot of changes too). There needs to be a focus on the social side of dematerialisation because these technologies could ultimately replace jobs. One needs to understand how to manage this, educating younger individuals in that process, to deal with these new innovations appropriately.

Changing consumer behaviour and user experience of products

Another crucial factor to consider is the shift towards the user experience of products. Disposable income is decreasing for many, and with this, topped with sustainability concerns, comes a change in the way people, and in particular younger generations, want to use products. New business models such as rental and swapping will continue to develop, and with that, the durability, quality, logistics, and insurance of a product will continue to improve.

Another immediate concern is water scarcity, it is a critical topic that we do not talk about enough. Unfortunately, we have already crossed the planetary boundary of fresh water. If we do not find a way, water resources will continue to deplete. This will affect us all personally and of course will have a huge impact on the fashion industry which traditionally uses a lot of water.

Through these valuable insights, Giuggioli has highlighted the vital importance of responsible fashion business management, further demonstrating the need for new frameworks such as **The Responsible 9 Framework**.

The Responsible 9 Framework offers a precise criteria for students to utilise when exploring a fashion brand's sustainable practice across the whole of a fashion business. The structure of the book has taken the reader logically, by chapter, through each part of the framework, providing a clear perspective for each component. For each of the nine aspects of

The Responsible 9 Framework a series of specific contemporary case studies and perspectives have been provided by current, leading experts within the fashion world.

The theme of the book and framework thoroughly explains the move away from a singular product commercial focus, to a **CONSCIOUS ITEM** approach and **CIRCULAR SERVICES** business mindset. A businesses' people are at the heart of the new framework, and have been rebranded as **COMMUNITY**. Next addressed is the **PERCEIVED VALUE** of an item or brand, and how sustainable pricing initiatives actively influence consumer purchase. Insights into **ACCOUNTABLE SYSTEMS** are reviewed in order to examine the importance of responsible processes when considering and integrating a successful, sustainable supply chain into a business. The section on **GOVERNANCE** looks at the different global organisations available to fashion brands and customers alike, that support their transition into a responsible and sustainable future existence. The last two sections of the framework are labelled **HONEST COMMUNICATION** and **STORYTELLING PLATFORMS**, here transparent and honest strategies are highlighted and discussed from a viewpoint of how modern brands are engaging and connecting to the new modern, conscious consumer.

Through studying this book and its associated content readers will gain a greater insight and have a clearer perspective on responsible fashion business in practice.

THE RESPONSIBLE 9 FRAMEWORK

1. CONSCIOUS ITEM
2. CIRCULAR SERVICES
3. COMMUNITY
4. PERCEIVED VALUE
5. ACCOUNTABLE SYSTEMS
6. GREEN ENVIRONMENT
7. GOVERNANCE
8. HONEST COMMUNICATION
9. STORYTELLING PLATFORMS

Ghebreab and Heale 2023

RESPONSIBLE 9 FRAMEWORK. Authors own

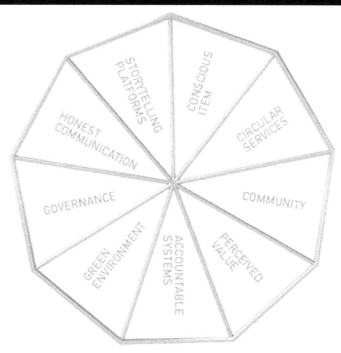

INDEX

Page numbers in italics refer to figures.

For Product Safety Concerns and Information please contact our EU
representative GPSR@taylorandfrancis.com
Taylor & Francis Verlag GmbH, Kaufingerstraße 24, 80331 München, Germany